Library of
Davidson College

Origins
of the
Crisis
in the
USSR

Origins
of the
Crisis
in the
USSR
Essays
on the
Political
Economy
of a
Disintegrating
System

— Hillel Ticktin —

M.E. Sharpe, Inc.
Armonk, New York
London, England

Copyright © 1992 by M. E. Sharpe, Inc.
80 Business Park Drive, Armonk, New York 10504

All rights reserved. No part of this book may be reproduced in any
form without written permission from the publisher.

Available in the United Kingdom and Europe from M. E. Sharpe, Publishers,
3 Henrietta Street, London WC2E 8LU.

Library of Congress Cataloging-in-Publication Data

Ticktin, H. (Hillel)
Origins of the crisis in the USSR: essays on the political economy
of a disintegrating system / by Hillel Ticktin.
p. cm.
Includes index.
ISBN 0-87332-861-2 (cloth).
—ISBN 0-87332-888-4 (paper).
1. Soviet Union—Economic conditions—1985–
2. Soviet Union—Economic policy—1986–
3. Perestroika.
I. Title.
HC336.26.T53 1992
338.947—dc20
91-4282
CIP

Printed in the United States of America

The paper used in this publication meets the minimum requirements of
American National Standard for Information Sciences—
Permanence of Paper for Printed Library Materials, ANSI Z 39.48-1984.

MV 10 9 8 7 6 5 4 3 2 1

Dedicated to the memory of my father,
who taught me Marxism and the meaning of Stalinism

Contents

Preface		ix
1.	Introduction: The Aims and Achievements of Gorbachev	3
2.	Theory and Concepts	6
	Western Sovietology	6
	The Concepts Used in This Work	10
3.	The Nature of Social Control in the USSR	16
	The Question of Ideology	17
	Stalinism and Its Disintegration	23
	Atomization	24
4.	The Nonpolitical Politics of the Soviet Elite	48
	Factions and the Emergence of Opposing Currents and Parties	50
	The Ligachev–Yeltsin Rivalry	52
	The Nature of the Soviet Elite and Its Factions	55
	The Nature of the Party and Political Differences	57
	The Secret Police	58
	The Soviet Ruling Group	60
	Characteristics of the Soviet Elite	64
	The Soviet Elite in the Context of History	67
5.	The Intelligentsia	73
	The Political Economy of the Intelligentsia	74
	The Debate on History and Rehabilitations	76
	Legality and the Rule of Law	78

6. **The Working Class**

   The Sale of Labor Power
   The Labor Process and the Changes Demanded
   The Question of Class
   Reforms and the Process of Establishing Control over
      the Working Class
   The Position of the Workers and *Perestroika*
   The Nature of Actual and Potential Divisions of the Workers
   The Necessity for Control Measures
   New Measures Introduced to Control Workers
   Economic Reforms and Their Effect on the Worker
   The Necessary Failure of the Economic Reforms

7. **The Nature of the Soviet Political Economy**

   Control over Labor in the Brezhnev Period
   The Laws and Contradictions of the System
   Growth and Disintegration

8. **The Present Economic Crisis in the USSR**

   The Law of Value and Its Absence in the USSR
   The Nature of the Contradiction within the Product
   Consequences of the Defective Product
   The Underlying Reasons for the Crisis
   The Problem of Technology in Historical Perspective
   The Contradictions between Departments One and Two
   The Increasing Power of Labor and Its Effects

9. ***Perestroika* and the Disintegration of the USSR**

   The Policy of Reorganization
   The Pseudo-market Reforms
   The Market, Prices, and Social Relations
   The Ruble, Real Money, and a Genuine Market
   Social Solutions
   The Redirection of Foreign Policy
   The Disintegration of the USSR
   The Inevitable Failure of the Market Solution
   Why the Market Solution Cannot Work
   The Market Socialism Argument

10. **Where Are We Going? The Nature of the Transitional Epoch**

Index

Preface

This book was long in gestation. By the time many of the fundamental ideas had been presented in lectures and seminars or published in the journal *Critique*, events had "proved" the thesis: the USSR was disintegrating. I had been working to produce a kind of general theory of the USSR, but the system had now become history. So I have instead discussed the political economy of the USSR in the context of Gorbachev's attempt to restructure the system.

I have refrained from discussing certain important aspects of the political economy of the USSR in depth due to the constraints of space and time. In particular, the national question, the peasantry, and the position of women are all discussed, but not in the form of separate chapters. I have also not discussed other theories of the USSR, except in passing.

This book was made possible in part by a grant that Stephen White and I received for the topic of policy making under Gorbachev. Another kind of debt is owed to the editorial board of *Critique* and to the many students who criticized and argued with me over the last twenty-five years. Michael Cox, Sandy Smith, Suzi Weissman, Bob Arnot, and Bohdan Krawchenko have all discussed different ideas with me over the years. On a different note, Scott Meikle and David-Hillel Ruben taught me the importance of philosophy and of language. To the Soviet citizens who showed me the reality of the USSR, I can only express my gratitude. Finally I have to thank my companion, Lindy Barbour, for her patience (and her insistence on correct grammar).

Origins of the Crisis in the USSR

1

Introduction: The Aims and Achievements of Gorbachev

We can summarize Gorbachev's *perestroika* years as a period in which the Soviet elite factionalized; a political alliance was established with the intelligentsia; the economy was given a jolt; the regime, for the first time, admitted the need for democracy; and then an intention to institute a form of market economy was announced. During this same period, the country seemed headed pell-mell toward disintegration. One might say that for a while the process of disintegration was covered over with demands for change. But in reality the disintegration continued, as manifested in the more or less open warfare between elite factions, the exacerbation of social tensions, the escalation of republican demands for autonomy or independence, and an accelerating economic decline.

During the Twelfth Five-Year Plan (1985–89), both wages and investment rose faster than the planners had intended. Although the economy seemed to pick up in 1988, the plan results showed wages outstripping productivity by a wide margin (for the first time in decades). Until that time, investment in department one (producer goods) exceeded investment in department two (consumer goods), as was the usual pattern. In 1988, consumer goods production grew faster than that of the producer goods sector. The plan results for 1989 continued the reversal in the relative growth rates of consumer goods and producer goods production, but this in part reflected a very low (1.4 percent) growth of industrial production in general, which thereafter dipped to negative growth. The trend for wages to outstrip productivity continued in 1989, and there was a massive increase in money supply; inflation reached increasingly higher levels. The result was shortages. Rationing became general. It was a watershed year.

The constant harping on the extraordinary economic situation in the summer of 1989 raised suspicions that it had been engineered by either pro- or antireform interests. Much was made of the budget deficit, although the USSR has not functioned on the basis of money or the budget since at least 1929. Nonvalue economic plans had been the centerpiece of the economy. That the state used direct emissions of rubles to balance its budget was quite clear, but hardly significant, given the trivial role of the ruble in the economy. The stress on the urgency of economic crisis, coming as it did from sections of the ruling elite, could only be a reflection of their need to effect a rapid change in economic policy.

Meanwhile, the demands of workers for a higher standard of living and control over their own lives were in no way being met. The more concessions were made to the intelligentsia in terms of material benefits and freedom of speech, the more blatant was the declining position of workers. In this light, the most important event of the period was the miners' strike of July 1989. The miners' economic demands were not difficult to concede, at least in verbal terms. Consumer goods could be imported, but that was only a one-time solution. Genuine workers' committees were another matter. So too was the miners' demand, echoed by the trade unions, that private enterprise be limited. The underlying egalitarian ethos of the workers opposed the whole of Gorbachev's economic platform in all its many guises. These demands struck at the heart of the system and could not be conceded.

While the handling of the miners' strike showed that the regime remained master of the situation, nonetheless the workers had given warning that elements of the reform program were unacceptable. Higher prices, cooperatives (often a euphemism for the private provisioning of the well-off), unemployment, and attacks on labor were barred unless the regime wanted a strike wave on its hands.

Could the market be introduced against popular resistance? Promarket economist Gavriil Popov quite bluntly acknowledged that dictatorial action would be required to institute a market economy in the USSR (*New York Review of Books*, 16 August 1990). Gorbachev could only move toward the market at the price of enormous internal instability, and most certainly a radicalization of the working class. By the end of 1990 even Soviet enterprise directors—who had long demanded more control over their enterprises and who, it might seem, had the most to gain from a transition to the market—had seen the light and were calling for a return to old-style "planning" (*Financial Times*, 7 December 1990). Who, indeed, could picture the Soviet Union following Poland's path?

The logic of reform dictated that the transition to the market and the march toward genuine democracy and freedom of speech and organization should both proceed—ultimately sweeping away the elite itself. This was Gorbachev's dilemma. He either had to permit events to dictate his course or he had to draw in the reins at some point. Either way he would lose: in the first case, the elite and so Gorbachev would lose power; in the second, he is left with no policy other than the one he so deplored—stagnation—and the fate of a defeated and ultimately discarded leader.

The controllers of the USSR realized, at the very abyss, that it would be better to pause and consolidate than to advance—and to lose all power.

What, in fact, were Gorbachev's aims? He spoke frequently of the need to reinvigorate the economy, ultimately, perhaps only implicitly, through the full introduction of the market. He never ceased to speak of the need for order and discipline, meaning by this the introduction of a nonarbitrary legal system under which the worker worked hard and the manager had the right to manage. In short, his aim was the achievement of a stable oligarchy buttressed by the rule of law and the market. Along the tortuous road toward that goal, reforms had to be introduced that might stabilize a regime under severe threat.

If the population accepted as genuine Gorbachev's declared intentions, to raise the standard of living of all and improve their position, he would have achieved a propaganda victory. This, however, could only be accomplished through real concessions. If these could be kept minimal, in the sense that the position of the elite was only marginally affected, but the population accepted them as real concessions, he would have bought more time for the regime. But Gorbachev's immediate problem was one of reestablishing order in the elite itself. He had to find a workable political and economic program that was acceptable to the different factions in the elite, so that it could be implemented. Thus, Gorbachev was walking a tightrope.

The solution that the regime adopted at the end of 1990 had the characteristics of classical Stalinism as much as Brezhnevism. Gorbachev ordered the KGB and other police agencies into action to ensure that goods were delivered and central power was locally in evidence. Thus, he had taken the regime full circle, from anti-Stalinism to anti-Leninism and moves toward marketization, democratization, and decentralization, back to an attempt to reimpose control by the center. The new period was one of continued and even accelerating disintegration, punctuated by attempts at reintegration, such as the planned Union Treaty. And then the tightrope broke.

The coup that occurred in August 1991 had long been predicted. Both the coup and the counter-coup displayed in concentrated form the conflicts and tensions in the country. The coup failed because of divisions within the elite which were reflected in the army and, crucially, in the KGB, and which will be described in this book. But what was not sufficiently noted during this period was the "benign neutrality" of the workers. The coup plotters appealed to the workers by promising to bring down prices, while the liberal forces offer the hope of freeing their labor from bureaucratic controls. Yet the workers remain the chief obstacle to a transition to the market entailing rising prices, high levels of unemployment, increased work demands, and expanded wage differentials.

The disintegration of the Soviet political economy promises a long and continuing period of instability both in the society and internationally.

At this point it is not possible to exclude any possibility.

2

Theory and Concepts

The purpose of this book is to provide an outline of a political economy of the USSR. It is my intention to grapple with that system's real—as opposed to imagined, imposed, or believed—contradictions. The advent of *glasnost'* has shifted the study of the USSR away from a process of detection. There are more facts and statistics available, and truer histories as well. What remains urgently needed is a theoretical analysis that is neither apologetic nor ideologically opposed. The regime is still producing its own apologetics, even if they are of a more sophisticated kind, while much of the Western literature can only analyze the USSR in terms of orthodox economics, ideologically committed, as it is, to the market.

The task of this book is, therefore, to take part in the discovery of the nature of the laws governing the USSR. In this endeavor it tries to describe the changing social relations in the country. At this point the reader may object that there are numerous such books available, both inside and outside the USSR. While the objection is valid, the fact is that Soviet writings have hitherto been of the purest apologetics, based neither on fact nor on theory. On the other hand, much of the work of the same kind in the West has been vitiated by a parallel attempt to impose a preexisting idea or concept on reality.[1] While there are interesting insights to be found in much of this work, it is less than useful for purposes of understanding.

Western Sovietology

The field of Soviet studies in the West has swung from the totalitarian to the interest-group model.[2] Both models have had their uses. The totalitarian view argued that no independent organizational form could exist in the USSR, and hence the population was atomized. The essential dichotomy was one of elite and masses, and the Communist party played the crucial role in the society insofar as it was coterminous with the elite. All instructions came from above and no dissent was tolerated. This attitude was correct in pointing out the atomization of the population and the concentration of decision making in the elite. The problem with the totalitarian model, however, was that it looked at society in purely political terms, where politics was defined as the act of making decisions.

The totalitarians failed to understand the USSR because their concepts were incorrectly grounded. The term "Communist party," for example, might suggest that this entity is the same in the USSR as it is in the United States or the United Kingdom. That is dubious. If the CPSU were abolished as a party, it would have to be reinvented as an integrating agency, which might simply be called the Civil Service Inspectorate. To say that the Communist party is in power in the USSR means as much as saying that the elite rules. The totalitarians knew that the CPSU was not Marxist; but if it is not Marxist, and if today it is pragmatic and little else, then it is not very enlightening to discuss the USSR primarily in terms of one-party rule rather than no-party rule.

This school of thought was succeeded by a more empirical view among scholars who see the USSR evolving under the influence of different interest groups. These scholars were found equally wanting, although for different reasons. At least the totalitarians pointed to a real relationship, however superficially. The empiricists could only repeat the Soviet literature in Westernized form. While pointing to the existence of interest groups in the USSR, they left unexplored the crucial question: How does the elite rule?

The term "totalitarian" is now enjoying a renaissance in Eastern Europe, used to express the opposition of the new regimes and the ruling intelligentsia to the old forms of rule. Their use of the word is not very different, in that they counterpose multiparty formal democracy to the complete absence of real politics. The problem, however, is that Eastern Europe is different from the USSR. Nobody in Eastern Europe saw the Communist party as a real ruling party. Its chief instrument was the secret police, an agency that was immediately attacked throughout Eastern Europe. The Communist party itself very quickly dissolved with a mass desertion of members, most of whom had belonged only out of economic or political necessity, and with a rapid change of structure and title. These regimes only existed through the domination of the USSR, expressed through occupying troops and the control of the secret police.

In fact, to make the same point in more detail, it was really Khrushchev who created the Stalinist party as an instrument of rule, with regular congresses, committee meetings, and an invulnerable party apparatus. Accordingly, there is an argument to be made that the CPSU has only existed for a short time.[3] But it has never existed as a party in the usual sense of the term, for the simple reason that a single party cannot be a political party. A one-party system is a no-party system, a fact easily demonstrated by looking at the internal life of the CPSU. It does not exist, in any real sense. Local parties simply have accepted instructions and decisions from above. In other words, there has been no real discussion, election from below, criticism from below, or indeed any real function for the local party, other than the reception of documents, which no one reads or heeds.

On the other hand, the party had no necessity to contest elections, campaign to change minds, or perform in the manner that communist parties did before 1917 or in the rest of the world. The party congresses and Central Committee meetings were a forum for the elite, where the great bodies of state—the army, the secret police, and the bureaucratic apparatus, in their factionalized form—could display themselves.

From this point of view, the introduction of an elected Congress of People's Deputies has created the potentiality of an actual party of the elite. That few would vote for the Communist party if given genuinely free elections became quite clear. This did shake up the party and compel internal discussion. Yet, factions within the party are still banned, even if they do exist, and open platforms cannot be presented. There are no real elections to the relevant party bodies, only forms of representation of different sections of the party. Even where there are elections, they are carefully controlled to ensure the acceptance of the candidates.

The Plenum of the Central Committee that met on 6–8 February 1990 marked a turning point, celebrated by the Western press. Article 6 of the Constitution enshrining the special role of the Communist party was slated for removal, the party was to become more democratic, and multiparty elections were to be permitted. What this really meant was that the Soviet elite would prefer to rule using formal elections, assuming that their own party would obtain sufficient consent to maintain the system.

For the interest-groupers, the different sectional divisions provide an understanding of the elections to the Central Committee and the in-fighting over policy. Their picture of the Soviet elite is also more realistic than that of the totalitarians. Nonetheless, the peculiarity of a regime that relies on a special form of atomization as a means of control needs to be understood and discussed. The totalitarians at least stressed this aspect of the society. It led them to conclude that the society was stable, and without pressures at the top of the kind discussed by the new Soviet scholars. On that point they may have been wrong, but they did at least attempt to explain the nature of control in these societies.

The advisory group around Ronald Reagan in his first term were the successors of the totalitarians (Richard Pipes, in particular, was a theorist of this type). But they went a step further and found that the USSR was dangerous as it was both expansionary and disintegrating. Logically, the correct policy was "the squeeze." The economic inefficiency of the regime conflicted with the harsh forms of control it maintained. The introduction of the element of economic inefficiency provided a dynamic for a view that until then had had none.

The problem with this view is that it sees the market as both eternal and necessary. It assumes that only the market can provide the efficiency and elements of democracy needed for a stable and modern society. Adherents of this view fail to see that the majority of society will actually lose through the introduction of the market. Marketeers usually point out that this is temporary, and that in the long run everyone will gain. Even were this true, a political question is posed that is, at the very least, formidable. Allowing prices to rise, requiring people to work harder, and mandating a greater differentiation of incomes immediately benefit sections of the elite and the intelligentsia. The ordinary worker would actually be worse off, bad as his present position is. It is this dynamic that the supporters of the market, of whatever ilk, neglect to face.

The modern-day totalitarian theorists see only that a group of the Soviet elite have to be vanquished so that the market may be introduced. This assumption is extremely dubious. There is in fact no real evidence that the Soviet elite would not have preferred a market from the beginning. The logical founder of Stalinism is Bukharin, the inventor of the Stalinist doctrine of the possibility of building socialism in one country, who supported the continuation of the market-type economy of the 1920s.

The obstacle to the introduction of the market, and hence a real change in the system, lies in the social structure. This is where the totalitarians failed, since they were unable to find a social structure at all. Had they done so, they could no longer have maintained that the USSR was strong, stable, or a world menace. Their explanation of atomization itself is political and hence insufficient. After all, how was it that the secret police were actually more powerful in the USSR than in Nazi Germany? Hitler destroyed mainly his political enemies and the Jews; under Stalin whole layers of the population were decimated. Trotsky, who still regarded the USSR as a workers' state, was nonetheless moved to remark in 1937 that the USSR under Stalin was politically worse than Germany under Hitler.[4] In other words, the absence of a market and the strong internal controls reflect extreme instability, not stability. The elite would accept any solution that kept their power intact. The market would indeed do so, even if not for every member.

Put differently, the reason for the proscription of politics in the USSR lay in the danger of a rapid shift to the left and the overthrow of the Soviet elite. Even if the initial stages of democratization were favorable to the elite, this would rapidly cease. It is this problem that lies at the root of the enigma of Soviet politics.

From this point of view, the failure of the different schools of establishment Soviet studies lies in their characterization of the USSR as an absurd deviant from the natural market economy. Both viewpoints fail to see that the USSR constitutes a conservative social formation that has taken on a monstrous and *sui generis* social form precisely in order to *prevent* social revolution. That is why many of its forms so resemble fascism, which was similarly concerned with avoiding social revolution.

The interest-group school has moreover failed to understand the real nature of the groups that they discovered. It is always possible in any economy to find a whole range of different interests. What is really the important is the dynamic involved. Are there any social groups that are crucial? Are they exerting pressure? Is there a social group that is in control of the economy and is allocating privileges to itself? What is the nature of the challenges that it faces?

The real question is not who supports what interest, but rather what is the social dynamic of the regime, which ultimately provides its politics. Here the interest-group approach can actually detract from a more profound investigation of the nature of Soviet politics. If politics is concerned with the nature and forms of control over power in society, then the crucial issue is the nature of the social group in power and its relations with subordinate groups. Its own divisions and factions will then reflect this fundamental relation.

The Concepts Used in This Work

The key concepts used here are those of the surplus product, atomization, disintegration, contradiction, and class. The term "surplus product" needs some explanation, especially in view of its checkered history. Marx used "surplus value" to apply to capitalism, "surplus product" to apply to much or all of human history. Clearly, one cannot use a term applying to capitalism for the USSR unless one assumes that the USSR is itself capitalist. As investigators, we therefore have to begin with the more general term.

The category of surplus product applies to that portion of the social product that a whole or part of the society has decided to allocate for uses other than the immediate satisfaction of the needs of those engaged in productive work: in other words, those who produce the surplus product itself. The consumption of those not engaged in productive work is therefore part of the surplus product. The privileges of the Soviet elite, hidden as they are from view, are part of the surplus product. The state apparatus is paid out of the surplus product: hence the campaigns of both Gorbachev and Western countries to cut it back. In the case of the USSR, the unproductive consumption of the surplus product by the repressive apparatus is enormous. The army, the secret police, and the consumption of the elite all absorb a considerable proportion of that surplus product. Yet it is the thesis of this book that it is not these forms of absorption that determine its direction, although they are crucial to our understanding of the USSR, but rather the enormous levels of useless productive consumption or waste that result from the instability of the system.

The category of waste as used in my work in *Critique* has been criticized by various writers and interlocutors. Baran and Sweezy in their work employed the term "potential surplus" to denote the difference between what could be produced and what was actually the end product.[5] They therefore invented the categories of actual and potential surplus. This had the great merit of reintroducing the concept of the surplus product in a period when it had fallen out of favor; it had the problem that it insufficiently theorized the difference between surplus value and the concepts that they had fashioned. No one else, however, has taken up the challenge of dealing with the differences between what could be produced with full utilization of the productive forces, and what is produced. The effects of unemployment, undercapacity utilization of plant, arms production, and duplication of effort and resources as a result of competition are all examples of waste under capitalism. The USSR has its own forms of waste, and it is part of the aim of this book to show the nature of that waste and its causes. Above all, it is our task here to discuss the form of the surplus product and so to show the nature of the different kinds of utilization of the surplus product. The point, of course, is that the wasteful nature of Soviet production is a peculiarly Soviet form of the absorption of the surplus product.

It is now possible to discuss the concept of waste more precisely. The simple use of the term "waste" is too broad to constitute a category. More precisely defined, however, it refers to the use or lack of use of the surplus product in a manner that fails to lead to a product; in other words, labor is expended without any result. In principle, either necessary or surplus labor could be expended in a way that would lead to no product or even to a decline in production. The failure to use surplus labor also falls under the same rubric. The utilization of surplus labor in a way that leads to little or no increase in use values constitutes waste.

In capitalism there is a dual possibility of waste. If surplus value does not lead to further surplus value and so capital, we can speak of waste. If capital is employed but the commodity produced cannot be used and so produce further exchange value or be consumed, then we can speak of waste. The latter case is that of arms production. Under capitalism the question of wasteful production is essentially a question of use values; but since capital is concerned with exchange values, the issue of waste appears secondary. Indeed, in terms of the contradictions within the system, it is secondary. The fact that there is potential for producing more use value is interesting and important, but not the immediate cause of difficulty for the system. It is proof that the system is in decline, because it shows that an alternative system could utilize the productive forces more fully. It is also true, as various writers have argued, that the absorption of surplus value by the unproductive sector is important in reducing the rate of accumulation of capital, but this is quite another argument. There is no reason to equate the unproductive sector with waste.

In the case of the USSR, however, use value is all important. Hence the same problem that may appear as one of many difficulties in capitalism is of crucial moment under the Soviet system. The production of poor-quality housing under capitalism is a fact of life that may increase the profits of the construction companies. In the USSR it leads to enormous costs of repair, problems of replacement, and so to an absorption of resources that the system cannot afford.[6] It can also lead, coincidentally, to the collapse of that housing under stress, as in the Armenian earthquake of December 1988, at which point it can then become of political importance. At all times the poor quality of the Soviet product constitutes a contradiction of the system.

Indeed, it is now possible to go beyond the category of waste to the essential dynamic of the USSR. This will be discussed in a separate chapter, but it is useful to go through the fundamental thesis as well as basic terms. The quality of Soviet goods, the very long periods of time taken to construct anything, and the low level of Soviet technology are symptoms not just of a wasteful use of the surplus product but of the nature of the contradiction in the USSR. Whereas under capitalism the contradiction is between use value and exchange value, in the USSR it is *within* the product itself. It is not, therefore, a question of waste being a fundamental category; waste is a symptom and a result of more profound forces at work.

The argument is that the contradiction within use value itself leads to the production of goods with defective use value. In turn, that contradiction is seen as lying between a real use value and a potential use value. In other words, a jacket will serve as a jacket even if one arm is shorter than the other, so it has a real use value; but the use value is less than that of a jacket with two arms of the same length. A machine tool with a defective part might turn out products that can be used in the production of an automobile, but it makes the car closer to a heap of nonperforming metal than it need be. The effect is to drive consumption and production apart, and throughout the system the contradiction between what is produced and what is needed tends to be aggravated. The history of the Soviet Union is the history of the measures taken to ameliorate that tension. Market surrogates, terror, and administrative measures have all been used in attempts to establish the viability of the system.

The contradiction between the two forms of use value is in its turn a consequence and a cause of the nature of labor in the USSR. Since commodities are not produced in the USSR, labor power cannot be a commodity, but it can be alienated. In other words, the nature of labor power as a product is also defective. It cannot be bought and sold as a commodity, and so the worker retains a degree of control over his labor power. On the other hand, he has to alienate his product to the management. He cannot choose not to work, but he can choose not to work as management would prefer he work. His actual work differs, in other words, from his potential work. His product, therefore, is of the same kind.

The labor process is therefore driven apart from the product. On the one hand, the product is alienated to the management and so to the elite or bureaucratic system, while on the other hand the labor process remains in the control of the laborers themselves. The contradiction derives from the defective nature of the product and so of labor power as a product, and leads to a sundering of the process of production itself. Such control over the work process, however, has acted as a means of stabilizing the system by atomizing the worker. The worker relates to his own work process rather than to other workers, so that his control is an individual control rather than a collective control as it might be in the West.

A chapter of this book is devoted to this process of atomization. The atomization of the population stabilized the system. At the same time it provided the basis for the production of defective use values, and so created an insuperable barrier to production itself. The atomization of the population was established in the 1930s in the course of a long struggle with the workers in the USSR. It has moved from a simple individual form to one that is less individualized, and we can expect it to become collective, at which point the system will have little life left in it.

The worker today controls his work process by individually working at his own rate. The norms are spontaneously set at low levels to conform to this situation. When the norms are set by agreement with the work force, through a general meeting or by some form of election of delegates, there will be a limited collective form of control over the labor process. But it is still an atomized form to the degree that it is performed by each unit rather than by the economy or society as a whole. This latter point, however, has not been reached even under Gorbachev.

All the controls over the individual remain in place through the instrument of the secret police: controls over movement, severe limitations on organization, and the absence of genuine trade unions. The degree of criticism of the previous regimes has been vastly expanded, and criticism of the present government is permitted within limits. The atomization of the individual in the USSR, then, has been through a number of stages. Beginning with the ban on all nonstate organizations, it was extended to a total atomization, which has been gradually dissolving since the death of Stalin. It is in the analysis of the stages and levels of atomization, which is so crucial to the system, that an understanding of the process of the disintegration of the system can evolve. The period of Gorbachev can then be understood as the elite's last-ditch attempt to maintain itself in power by making minimal concessions before its controls disappear altogether.

The argument, to sum up, begins with the symptom of waste, and shows that underlying waste is a contradiction in the nature of the product, which in turn is based on the contradiction within labor and labor power. The contradiction leads to an antagonism or an absolute contradiction between consumption and production, labor and the labor process, production and circulation, and indeed in all aspects of the economy. The question is not why it is breaking down but why it functioned for so long and why it is breaking down now.

The word "contradiction" is used extensively in this book. It is used in its Hegelian and Marxist sense of a necessary relation between opposites that interpenetrate and change each other. The opposites are part of an entity. In the case of capitalism, the entity is the commodity and the opposites are use value and exchange value; in the USSR, the entity is the product and the opposites are the actual (real) use value and the potential (formal) use value. The change wrought by the interpenetration of the opposites ultimately leads to the supersession of the entity. Until the new entity is formed, the poles of the contradiction may stand opposed to one another in direct conflict. In such a case the system will be in a crisis. The crisis can be resolved either through supersession or through a return to the interrelation between the two opposite poles. If it is not resolved, then the system itself must disintegrate; this, we will argue, is what is occurring in the USSR.

In this respect, the category of "disintegration" is employed and needs to be explained. What I am arguing here is that the USSR is not a viable social formation, that it is not a mode of production, comparable to capitalism or feudalism, as indeed follows from the above discussion; but this does not imply that the USSR will break down tomorrow. On the contrary, the USSR has its own form of limited stability as well as its own form of decay. The USSR is a regime that cannot permit opposition to exist, and hence its decline can only take the form of disintegration of the system. The pulling apart of the poles of the system, so that the social groups, factions, and economic categories each stand in opposing and noncooperating forms, is the form of disintegration. In the end, the disintegration must reach a point where the workers will constitute their own collectivity and so become a class and make their own bid for power.

"Class" here is defined as a social group that has constituted itself a collectivity around a specific relation to the surplus product. In the context of the USSR, those who alienate their labor power in order to produce the surplus product are the workers. They are at present atomized, but when the disintegration proceeds to the point where that atomization is overcome, they can become a collectivity. At that point the system will have to change. It is, of course, in the nature of the system that it has done and will do its utmost to prevent the formation of such a collectivity. It does so by atomizing the population, but it is increasingly inefficient to maintain the atomization and consequently its limits are rapidly being reached.

The system is today in process of rapid change. This book tries to illustrate its thesis with an analysis of the present situation. The situation under Gorbachev is certainly different from that under Stalin, but the essential problems are the same. The USSR is a society, neither socialist nor capitalist, that has the incentives of neither but is driven to expand production in order to maintain the ruling group in power, while it lacks means of calculation, control over labor, or the stimuli needed for action and decision making. It is neither planned nor based on the market, and yet there is no third way. In philosophical terms, there are only capitalism and its essence, the law of value, and socialism with its essence, the law of planning; anything in between can only fail precisely because it has no essence, no nature. It can have no laws except ones of formation and decay. The Soviet elite desperately want to introduce the market or the law of value and so secure their own position.

There is no mature form of the USSR. It is a historical accident, an accident brought about through the defeat of the October revolution in the form of the seizure of power by a bureaucratic ruling group. Just as Neanderthal man could never become man, so the USSR can never reform to become socialism or capitalism. It is an unfortunate deviation of history, which is now, under Gorbachev, coming to an end.

Notes

1. I include in this category such work as that of the state capitalist and workers' state writers. See Tony Cliff, *Russia: A Marxist Analysis* (London: Pluto, 1970); and Ernest Mandel, *Marxist Economics* (London: Merlin Books, 1968), pp. 548–604, and *Beyond Perestroika: The Future of Gorbachev's USSR* (London: Verso, 1989).

2. For the totalitarian view, see Carl J. Friederich and Zbigniew K. Brzezinski, *Totalitarian Dictatorship and Autocracy* (New York: Praeger, 1969); and Leonard Schapiro, *The Communist Party of the Soviet Union* (London: Eyre and Spotiswoode, 1970). In their view, the party is coterminous with the elite and almighty as against the masses. There is no social analysis at all. On the other hand, H. Gordon Skilling and Franklyn Griffiths, in their edited volume *Interest Groups in Soviet Politics* (Princeton, NJ: Princeton University Press, 1971), show the existence of different interest groups on the Central Committee, but in failing to see that the groups lie exclusively within the elite itself, they fail to see the real dynamic in the USSR.

3. Roy Medvedev, in *Let History Judge* (New York: Knopf, 1972), stressed the radical discontinuity after the death of Stalin.

4. L. Trotsky, *The Death Agony of Capitalism and the Tasks of the Fourth International: "The Transitional Program"* (New York: Pioneer Publishers, 1964), pp. 50–51.

5. Paul Baran and Paul M. Sweezy, *Monopoly Capital* (New York: Monthly Review Press, 1966); and Paul Baran, *The Political Economy of Growth* (New York: Monthly Review Press, 1956).

6. In an article devoted to Soviet housing, one author points out that new Soviet housing becomes dilapidated so quickly that around 20 percent of it is unusable. See M. Krushinskii, "Khvatit' li resursov?" *Izvestiia*, 14 July 1988, p. 4.

3
The Nature of Social Control in the USSR

There are only a limited number of ways in which a ruling group can exercise control over other social groups. Direct force or repression is omnipresent, even if only in the background, wherever one social group rules over another, but this is never sufficient to ensure the consent of the governed. There has to be a political–economic form of compulsion to establish the subjection of the subordinate group or groups. The serf obtained his livelihood through the manor, and escape was only meaningful under very specific conditions. In capitalism the worker is controlled through his need to sell his labor power. Only when workers actually threaten the system, or a particular employer, is force used.

The justification of subordination is normally called an *ideology*. Under feudalism the ideology was religion. In capitalism, uniquely, the ideology is provided by the political economy itself, through what Marx termed commodity fetishism. The acceptance of the ideology is connected with, though not necessarily provided by, the political economy of the society. In the case of precapitalist societies, the ideology is conditioned by the precariousness of life, the lack of an alternative form of organization, and the nature of the community provided by the purveyors of the ideology. In other words, the political economy of the society is crucial in understanding the form of control.

In the case of the USSR, the crucial aspect of control is that established through the atomization of the society. That atomization, however, is a close intermeshing of repression with the political economy of the society. The ideology, or more correctly the official doctrine, contrary to Orwell or much of what has been written in the West, plays little or no role in ensuring consent. To do so it must be believed, and few people can actually accept the truth of the official line.

Ideology in the USSR is not an easy topic, not because it is inherently difficult but rather because of all the misconceptions that have been developed around that theme. It is not necessary to get involved in a detailed argument on the definition of ideology. There is no doubt that the regime has used forms of conscious indoctrination and censorship to propagate a particular outlook. The misconceptions concern the effect of that propaganda. The right-wing (if not far-right) views of recent Soviet émigrés have made it clear that the official doctrine has not been conspicuously successful in indoctrinating the population. Indeed, paradoxically, Ligachev made that quite clear when he referred to the need to counter alien ideas with a view "closer to reality." This will be discussed below.

The Question of Ideology

The picture of a country so subject to ideological control that everyone is compelled to think along similar lines, even though they might struggle against it, itself has little in common with reality. In fact, one might question whether there actually is a dominant ideology at all in the Soviet Union. The definition does not alter this point: both in the case of the Marxist use of the category, false consciousness, and in an understanding of ideology as a world outlook, certain requirements have to be met. In order to constitute some level of consciousness, there has to be some correspondence with the recognizable world. There also has to be a degree of coherence and compatibility of its internal elements such that it can be believed, adhered to, and used over time. The fact that it is not true—that is, that it has only a limited correspondence with the real world—must be gainsaid then by internal coherence and some reflection of the world. The Soviet doctrine, as produced in the schools and the media, cannot be used to understand the everyday world of the citizen and, still worse, may be so completely riddled with incompatibilities that no one could possibly believe it.

We may then question whether there is an ideology in the USSR. Of course, the word ideology could simply be used to denote any form of belief pattern. Even so, it is not easy to argue that the official doctrine constitutes a series of statements sufficient to constitute a belief pattern. This point is worth exploring.

The problem is that the doctrines expounded by the newspapers, journals, and the educational system under the names of Marxism and Marxism–Leninism, as argued above, are both internally conflictual and unpredictably changeable. For instance, anti-Semitism is undoubtedly condemned by Marxism and is hence officially regarded as reprehensible, and there has been no official doctrine of anti-Semitism, yet the regime has promoted anti-Semitism since the time of Stalin. Similarly, the regime condemns chauvinism, but it clearly promotes Russian control. The regime claims to be socialist and in favor of equality, but it has declared from Stalin to Gorbachev that inequality is essential to the regime. Under Stalin, egalitarianism was declared a petit bourgeois deviation. Gorbachev has to juggle with words by saying that Marxism is in favor of equality but against what is translated as "leveling." The regime is officially in favor of the abolition of privilege, but it promotes the privilege of its own elite. The source of this contradiction obviously lies in the difference between Marxism, which is opposed to anti-Semitism, national oppression, privilege, and inequality, and the actually existing form of exploitation in the USSR.

There is a further conflict between what exists and what is justified. The regime has proclaimed the supremacy of the building of producer goods and turned this into a principle; on the other hand, it also declares that the satisfaction of the population is the fundamental law of socialism. In reality, one or the other must be true, not both. No one can be satisfied with an enormous pile of producer goods, which is what the regime has manufactured. The source of this contradiction lies in the transparency of the system. As a result, the half-truths of the ruling class in the West cannot be replicated in the East. When it is said, in the West, that wages cannot be raised because the country cannot afford it, this is partially or wholly believable because the statement is true within the context of a particular capitalist system. In the USSR it is not believable, because it is quite clear that the elite live much better than everybody else, although they claim otherwise and so allocate resources to themselves as they see fit. More important, it is also quite clear that they organize the economy from the top down, leaving the pay of the majority to be squeezed as far as is possible. In other words, because the elite are in conscious charge of an administered system, an alternative always seems possible. As a result, the elite have to resort to direct falsification.[1]

Systematic, conscious untruthfulness is a symptom of a system that is inherently unstable. The elite find it difficult to tell the truth lest they be toppled. Such lies do not convince the population, both because the system is transparent and because the lies are inevitably shown as untruths over time, precisely because of the constant and continual failure of the system to perform.

The reason for the failure of Soviet ideology lies in the inability of a failed regime to establish a believable justification. The system has to thrash around materially, and so in terms of ideas, in order to find a means of existence. It cannot find it, and hence must continually find new forms of justification. The new forms in turn undermine the old forms. In a short historical period the new forms themselves become old forms and are refuted by yet another justification. All previous leaders turn out to be either wrong-headed or monsters or both. While Lenin is nominally revered, his teachings are in fact ascribed to the left opposition, who are regarded as both wrong and monstrous. No human being under these circumstances can believe much of what the regime teaches.

In short, there is no ideology, but rather a complex relation of doctrines and belief patterns.

Upon further exploration, it becomes obvious that there are four different levels of so-called ideology or, more properly, belief patterns. At the most obvious and apparently basic level there is an appeal to Marxism as derived from Marx and Lenin. In the second place there is the official doctrine of Marxism–Leninism, which has been discussed above in terms of its inner incoherence. (The empirical discussion hitherto makes it clear that neither Gorbachev nor the

Soviet elite has much use for Marxism, yet the term is widely used, even today.) In the third place, there is an elitist viewpoint, which the state apparatus uses to govern; even the ordinary worker must use an official form of discourse. In the fourth place, there is a more conscious understanding of reality, which is held by the individuals who actually govern. At this level there is a parallel and (even if partially) critical view of the system held by the different social groups in their own ways.

At the first level, the regime espouses Marxism. In fact it rejects the essence of Marxism. It could hardly be expected that a social group dedicated to its own self-preservation would maintain the doctrine of a thinker opposed to the existence of separate social groups in control of the surplus product. Pragmatism has always ruled in the elite in fact. Stalin was clearly not guided by either Marx or Lenin. Since both were in favor of direct forms of democratic control and were vehemently opposed both to a privileged group in control of the society and to a strong state, their doctrines in fact stand as an indictment of the regime. But because the regime officially espouses Marxism, citizens are taught Marxist terminology and provided with the works of Marx and Lenin. A screen is thereby created that deceives both the local population and the rest of the world.

In the second place, the elite supports the doctrine called Marxism–Leninism, first codified by Stalin in his *Short Course*. The crucial pillars of this doctrine involve (1) the concept of the construction of socialism in one country and thus the use of Russian and Soviet nationalism; (2) control over literature and the arts with socialist realism; (3) the primacy of department one (producer goods) over department two (consumer goods); (4) centralized control over society, provided by the elite in the guise of the apparatus of the Communist party. These four doctrines are then delivered in a package of emasculated Marxism. Crucial Marxist concepts, such as abstract labor, surplus product, finance capital, the long wave, and atomization, are dropped, if not directly, then in fact. Others are changed in their content. Still others are added, such as the law of increasing misery (held until very recently to apply to the West), state monopoly capitalism, and the view that socialism is a lower phase of communist society where the reward is based either on the market or on input.

Since the elite would not dare let loose a genuine Marxism on the society, an emasculated Marxism is ideal in "embezzling concepts," as Adam Przeworski put it. In other words, the very revolutionary critique that could provide an analysis and theorization of the regime is rendered impotent through reinterpretation. It is, however, not enough to embezzle the concepts, the categories have to be thoroughly reworked and so confused that they cannot be understood at all. That is the real problem for the population of the USSR, in theoretical terms. They cannot arrive at a critique of the system because the Marxist words appear wrong and inappropriate. Everyone in the USSR eventually understands the misuse of Marxism, but very few understand the nature of that misuse. Even someone like Solzhenitsyn, brought up in the doctrines of the regime, remains within its orbit in a negative sense.

Once concepts have been destroyed, only empiricism remains, and empiricist is what all Soviet analysts, of whatever hue, become. It might be asked why they do not use non-Marxist concepts. They would if they could. The problem is that they are not familiar enough with the literature, but above all they have not had the opportunity to discuss and evolve the concepts. Because the USSR is a novel form of society, new concepts have to be invented, whatever theoretical system is employed, and in the absence of the opportunity for discussion, only primitive solutions can be produced. The official doctrine then intervenes and provides concepts that have to be overcome in order to proceed further in theorization. In fact, however, as Hannah Arendt pointed out, the bourgeoisie has had no theory since the beginning of the nineteenth century. A promarket doctrine can certainly evolve and has evolved in the USSR, first in Aesopian, mathematical form, and now more openly. Yet it says nothing new, and is, if anything, a more primitive version of Western views. That, however, is not the same as a theory; it is simply a statement of belief in the superiority of the market over an organized economy.

Marxism can provide the alternative theory. This already exists in the West, although largely in undeveloped form. Much of the Western left has excluded itself from this discussion by its dogmatism and lack of knowledge of the empirical details of Soviet society. In large measure the failure in the West is a reflection of the success of the propaganda from the East. The muddle so produced has led to such wrongly conceived works as that of Marcuse, who saw the USSR as raising productivity at the expense of the humanity of that society. As the problem is now seen—in terms of the low productivity of the economy—Marcuse has little to contribute.[2]

We can see how successful Soviet central doctrine has been. It effectively stopped internal thought, and so prevented the emergence of a critical revolutionary theory. On the other hand, it has not prevented empirical opposition to specific measures or to the system. But neither the regime nor its opponents can mobilize the population or gain their support for any changes. The doctrine, as explained above, is a form of apologetics for the existing regime, and it has sufficient plausibility to muddle the intelligentsia. It has also acted as a form of recognition and a basis for discussion among the elite, but such discussion is necessarily limited, for the elite does not actually believe in any form of socialism, which would imply its own abolition. Thus, it is a language of rule. At the same time, individual members of the society, the elite included, have their own view of how to exist and what to believe. As a result, there are effectively four competing levels of belief in the society.

We may conclude as follows. There is Marxism, which is not understood at all in the USSR. Then there is the official doctrine of Marxism–Leninism, which has served the purposes outlined above. Third, there is the language of rule for the elite and of intercourse for the other social groups. Fourth, private discussion, in the family group, is more open and intimate and is a muddled mixture. It can be seen that none of these belief patterns falls under the description of ideology.

Preferring to see itself as science, Marxism rejects the view that it is an ideology, which it regards as false consciousness. The anti-Marxist has no need to object, since Marxism is not used in the USSR.

Marxism–Leninism is false, and in any case is not believed (no serious person can actually make sense of the textbooks on the political economy of socialism). There is no logic to it. It is so internally contradictory that only learning by rote permits students to pass an examination in that subject. Marxism–Leninism functions as an antitheory, muddling ideas and preventing the emergence of concepts and theory.

The elite, however, have to converse and have their own view of how to rule. Their discourse pattern, however, is limited by its secrecy and necessary conflict with what they profess to believe. As a result, their private outlook is very different: it is fundamentally cynical and highly elitist, even Victorian, in its contempt for ordinary people.

What is the ultimate theoretical reason for the absence of ideology in the USSR? The answer is derived from the theory of the USSR itself. The USSR is not a mode of production; it is not a viable historical social formation. As a result, it is impossible for the elite to formulate a set of doctrines that would at least partially conform to reality.

By contrast, the false consciousness of the bourgeoisie assists it to govern because it corresponds to the needs of the capitalist class. It cannot admit to itself that it is a group of exploiters, bound to be overthrown as all previous exploiting classes have been; but it can understand that the workers are opposed to the capitalist class and that they must be made to work, using the reserve army of labor and force when necessary. The falsity of the doctrine ensures that they perceive of themselves as eternal. While such a view might prevent the capitalist from seeing the form of his overthrow, nonetheless he maintains a useful optimism. In the USSR, the elite have no such faith in their own future, or in the system. They cannot find a method of making workers work except to pretend that socialism exists and that it is in the interests of workers to work, when every worker knows that socialism does not exist and that it is not in his interest to work. There is no objective means of control over the workers, and the elite doctrine must reflect this. As a result, as with everything else, the elite can only produce a muddle. Their doctrine is little more than an accurate reflection of the confusion of the economic system itself. Every attempt at introducing order only produces more chaos.

The problem for Gorbachev can now be made clear. Real discussions require, if not theories, at least concepts and some reality. Gorbachev needs to jettison Marxism–Leninism and use words descriptive of a real society. Reforms cannot take place on the basis of a false understanding of the society. However elitist the ruling group, it needs to know the extent of opposition and the genuine feelings of the populace. In effect, the elite cannot even discuss within itself its own separate needs. On the other hand, its executive arm, the secret police, was able to discuss the real situation. That was their license and hence it is not surprising that they became the organ most demanding of change. Not only did they know the extent of crisis in the society, unlike even the Central Committee, they could discuss it. Indeed, they *had* to discuss it with the political prisoners they were incarcerating.

The extent of the ideological problem was illustrated by Ligachev when he was the secretary of the CPSU in charge of ideology. He said that the task was to help young people "see life in its real contradictory multilayers." It was necessary, he said, to teach the youth how to analyze reality, which existing textbooks on society could not do. He also mentioned the need to counteract other views, given the uselessness of the existing books and teachings.[3] In other words, the old muddle was no longer working.

The regime needs an ideology that serves two functions. First, the elite need to speak among themselves in a manner that permits open-ended discussion. This postulates terminology that assists the formation of workable solutions. Second, they need an ideology based on a recognizable world and that can be believed by subordinates, as opposed to an incoherent series of apologetic statements. Of course, if the USSR were to move over to the market, the problem would be solved, since the market produces its own powerful apologetics. The domination of the commodity is both actual and apparently eternal. However, until they arrive at such a desirable state of affairs, an alternative is vital to the survival of the regime.

The present criticism of all aspects of the economy and the society serves just this function. Of course, the criticism is actually very limited. Nonetheless an impression is created that the elite are doing their utmost to improve the society and that they are listening to the lower orders. At the same time some real discussion can take place at higher levels. The problem, however, is that this breakthrough is limited in time, since a real solution to the alienation of the majority, as opposed to discussion of such a solution, is imperative.

For Gorbachev the sweeping away of the old shibboleths of Stalinism has the not inconsiderable danger that real critical thought might ensue. Such thought might attack the elite itself as the prime obstacle to change. It might turn to the authentic voices of Marx and of Lenin. Hence, Gorbachev must proceed slowly in his jettisoning of even the carcass of Marxism–Leninism. Yet, until both the aspirations of Marxism and the muddle of Marxism–Leninism have been removed, the other two layers of belief cannot be rendered meaningful. The elite must be able to speak to itself, but if it does so, it runs the risk of opening the door to its own abolition. The discontent of the population is still confused. When it is clear about its goals, there will be no place for the elite.

Gorbachev thus had to move to the market or nowhere, even in the sphere of ideology.

Stalinism and Its Disintegration

The doctrine of Stalinism is "socialism in one country." As the society disintegrates, so groupings have arisen that espouse different aspects of the contradictory doctrines contained in the doctrine of socialism in one country. These are nationalism (both Soviet and Russian), anti-Semitism, belief in the superiority of mother Russia, populism, liberalism, support for the market, and antagonism to the market. Obviously, until the period of Gorbachev, these different attitudes conflicted with one another.

It is of considerable interest to observe how the belief patterns of the new groups that have emerged derive from the original Stalinism. Pamiat' and the various Russian nationalist groups are only taking the essential core of Stalinism, its nationalism, while eliminating the Marxist verbiage. On the other hand, the liberals' move to the market harks back to the early period of Stalin, when he allied with Bukharin. It was Stalin who, in his *Economic Problems of Socialism*, began the move back to the market.

Nationalism was always a dangerous doctrine to use and it is naturally disentangling itself into its component parts. The problem with the use of nationalism under Stalin was that Soviet nationalism really made no sense. What, after all, had the Estonians in common with the Uzbeks? While the regime spoke of a common socialist fatherland, few people considered the USSR socialist and even fewer really wanted to defend such an entity. The whole point of a nationalist doctrine is that it is interclass or intergroup, and while a common language or culture might be made to appeal to the exploited workers and peasants, Soviet nationalism could only have appeal against a common invader like the Nazis. For that reason Hitler actually did the regime a considerable favor in supplying it with a doctrine, common defense against Germany, that provided a level of unity. But such a doctrine has only a limited use and in any case was even insufficient during the period of the war, when Russian nationalism and Russian orthodoxy were extensively employed to secure support for the regime.

The use of Russian nationalism reached its apogee in the period immediately after the Second World War, when the regime proclaimed the superiority of Russian civilization in practically all respects. At this time, anti-Semitism and the imposition of Russian language and culture on all the different national groupings of the USSR, with the concomitant suppression of the local languages and cultures, reached its height. It is no wonder that the disintegration of controls under Gorbachev should have led to the formation of openly Russian nationalist and anti-Semitic organizations.

In this respect, the meeting of the Sixth Plenum of the Union of Writers of the RSFSR in November 1989 was instructive. Writers denied that they were anti-Semitic at the same time as they called for a separate organization of Russian writers in Leningrad on the ground that they were a national minority there. The clearly anti-Semitic session led by well-known Russian writers even contained a plea for writers to stand up for holy Russian martyrs such as the last tsar and his family. The fact that an important section of the Russian intelligentsia could express this component of Stalinism, without the language of Marxism, showed clearly the doctrinal influence of the ruling group of the USSR.

Atomization

The USSR has changed somewhat under Gorbachev in that there are numerous political clubs, meetings, and even multicandidate elections. Yet workers remain under the old regime: there are no independent trade unions able to function as such, nor in fact any real trade unions at all. The KGB remains as powerful as ever; even it adapted somewhat to *glasnost'*. There is no public attack on the elite as an elite, calling for their abolition and the introduction of an egalitarian society, which is what socialism would be. There are attacks on the bureaucracy, seen as the controllers of the society, but not on the elite as such. The atomization of the society continues, but in a disintegrating form. The paragraphs that follow describe the atomization of the society and the dissolution of that atomization.

The Totalitarian School of Atomization

The term "atomization" has been used in a number of different senses. One use has been that of the totalitarian school of Sovietologists. They see atomization as the absence of organization of the masses. Between elite and society there is no form of combination of individuals possible, and hence every individual is atomized from his fellow human beings. Friedrich and Brzezinski in their classic work on totalitarianism specifically discuss atomization. They go through the various aspects of control that separate the individual human beings in the totalitarian societies. They discuss the terror, unanimity, ideology, the party monopoly over communications, and argue that the party and ideology are crucial. Nonetheless, they find "islands of separateness" in the family, the church, etc., and forms of resistance. This is how they describe the atomization:

> The totalitarian regimes seek to divide and rule in the most radical and extreme way: each human being should, for best effect, have to face the monolith of totalitarian rule as an isolated "atom." By being thus atomized, the people with its many natural subdivisions becomes the "mass," and the citizen is transformed into the mass man. This mass man, this isolated and anxiety-ridden shadow, is the complete antithesis to the "common man" of the working free society.[4]

Friedrich and Brzezinski's work performed the singular service of providing a general theory to embrace modern antidemocratic formations; moreover, it dealt with them comparatively. The comparisons made between Stalinism and fascism, or indeed Marxism–Leninism and fascism, were violently rejected by both liberal and left-wing scholars. Today, however, it has become commonplace, in the USSR and elsewhere, to point out the common features of the two social systems, and the Friedrich and Brzezinski book appears as a pioneering work. In fact, of course, the word "totalitarian" was used in the 1930s by Trotsky and Hilferding, among others. Franz Neumann, the author of *Behemoth*, the classic semi-Marxist socioeconomic account of Nazi Germany, is given credit in the preface to the Friedrich and Brzezinski work. That the theory of totalitarianism was used to buttress the Cold War does not mean that it did not seize on important elements of truth.

The general theory provided by the totalitarian school is wrong, but not because their facts are not correct or because there is no comparison to be made between Hitler and Stalin. They are wrong because their method is one of generalizing over the whole historical period of the USSR and then finding similarities with fascism. An alternative is to find the sources of the changes in totalitarianism in both societies and then look at their interrelations. The Friedrich and Brzezinski framework is static, with no beginning and no end to totalitarianism: it appears as a system that has unfortunately arisen in the twentieth century for reasons that are really unknown. Their method is also one of abstracted empiricism because they simply compare empirical details over all the relevant societies over the whole time period they have chosen, instead of looking at the socioeconomic systems at different periods and discovering the essence of the movement to totalitarianism, which can then be compared over time periods and over different countries. The effect, in relation to the question under discussion, is to reduce the particularity of Soviet-style atomization. In fact, atomization in the USSR is actually far deeper and more significant than it ever was in Nazi Germany. Friedrich and Brzezinski appear to be aware of this but unable to explain it or describe it as a phenomenon. Obviously, anyone who regards Nazi Germany as noncapitalist will see the latter and the USSR as closer than they were.

Friedrich and Brzezinski reject the view that Hitler's Germany was capitalist, because of the absence of competition and the interference with the free market. They part company here with Neumann, who considered that the German worker sold his labor power since his free time was his own. Instead, Friedrich and Brzezinski argue that his free time was not his own, since it could be called on for a number of purposes and was also under intense investigation.

This leads to a third objection to their work. It is confused. On the one hand, they find that fascism is not capitalist because there is interference with the free market, but on the other hand they are constrained to argue over labor time, really to consider Neumann's Marxist argument. From a Marxist perspective, however, the question of whether a society is capitalist is not one of markets, although that is an indication of the nature of the society, but whether surplus value exists. Did firms work on the basis of profit? Did they accumulate their profits? Did they fix prices or were prices centrally controlled? Did workers sell their labor power? The answer in all cases is definitely positive in the case of Nazi Germany, whatever qualifications may be made. However controlled the workers were, they were paid for their labor power and an incentive system did exist. It is not a question of whether they were exploited, in the sense that a surplus product was extracted from them by those in control, but of the form in which they were exploited. Either they alienated their labor power or they sold it. Those are the only two choices. If they sold it, then the society was capitalist. In fact, descriptions of the German working class in this period make it clear that although they could not have forms of collective action, they could and did act individually to raise the price of labor power. In contrast, in the USSR, movement from one job to another, from one firm to another, does not guarantee anything, as money itself does not exist in the way that it did in Nazi Germany.

In relation to the USSR, it is quite clear that until very recently there were no organizations independent of the state. That is simply empirically true. Commodity production is not a feature of the USSR. If, therefore, any honest theorist looked at the USSR, he or she might feel bound to take the totalitarian view, implicitly or explicitly. The usual form was one that stressed the absence of democracy and the considerable controls over the individual.

Neumann, however, in 1942 rejected the elite/masses dichotomy of Emil Lederer, later adopted by the postwar totalitarians:

> The essence of National Socialism consists in the acceptance and strengthening of the prevailing class character of German society, in the attempted consolidation of its ruling class, in the atomization of the subordinate strata through the destruction of every autonomous group mediating between them and the state, in the creation of a system of autocratic bureaucracies interfering in all human relations. The process of atomization extends even to the ruling class in part. It goes hand in hand with a process of differentiation within the mass party and within society that creates reliable elites in every sector. Through these elites, the regime plays off one group against the other and enables a minority to terrorize a majority.[5]

Neumann argues further that "National Socialism did not create the mass-men; it has completed the process, however, and destroyed every institution that might interfere."[6] For Neumann, then, the elite/masses dichotomy is wrong because the class structure is maintained. The society is totalitarian because there are no autonomous organizations and there is no competition between bureaucratic institutions. He was, of course, speaking only of Nazi Germany, but he provides a deeper understanding of the nature of atomization in modern society. He sees atomization existing through the suppression of independent organizations, which has the result that the citizen cannot choose which bureaucracy to address; he becomes dependent on a particular institution and particular bureaucrats.

To assert that there are no independent organizations, although correct, is superficial and possibly misleading. In order to have no independent organizations, there has to be a powerful group suppressing such organizations: that is, an organization that is part of the state is bent on preventing others from establishing an independent existence. The usual answer is that such an organization does exist in the USSR and it is called the Communist party. But only the hierarchy of the Communist party is able to issue instructions and have independent meetings. There are meetings of area and building residents, meetings of various kinds in the factories, meetings of the different levels of soviets, and so forth. There are organizations in existence and there is not always a Communist party viewpoint for each of these organizations. There is no necessary view on residents' quarrels. Nor is it immediately apparent why members of these organizations should follow the line that they are given. No extra compulsion is applied. Hence, it is clear that some extraparty force must be operating: that, of course, is the KGB, in a bureaucratic structure where no independence can exist for any citizen.

It is never enough to specify the party as the instrument of rule: the vast majority of the party's millions of members have no influence whatsoever. It is always necessary to speak of the party apparatus and then discover the way in which they maintain power. They clearly do not do so through elections or through money; but the apparatus cannot rule without a means of rule. In economic terms, if they control the surplus product, they must have a means of ensuring at least some compliance on the part of the population. It could, of course, be a question of ideology, but we have every reason to rule this out as a means of control. While the system functions to befuddle the population and rule out an alternative, it cannot prevent the population being both discontented and opposed to what exists. Hence, the real means of control consists of the use of force in a system of dependency, all buttressed by the historic despair of a population that has suffered so deeply for so long.

The totalitarian theory can be seen to have been correct in the statement that there are no independent social or political organizations, but it ignores the bureaucratic dependency to which Neumann referred. The stress on the single party and the pulverized mass meant that the totalitarians were not able to grasp the real mechanisms of control or the reasons for the existence of the atomization in the first place.

A New Theory of Atomization

Whereas the totalitarians see atomization largely politically, Marx adds a social dimension. He saw human beings atomized under capitalism by the nature of commodity production. As a worker who sold his labor power, a person was reduced to the level of a commodity competing with other commodities on the labor market. Alienated both from his product and from his labor process, the worker was alienated from society. He was alienated from himself insofar as his nature required creative social labor, and from others insofar as his social labor was not truly social. The concept of alienation was then contained in Marx's view of commodity fetishism. Instead of controlling the commodity, the worker was controlled by it and consequently dominated by his own labor. By being dominated, his natural social integration was mediated through the commodity, and hence his integration in the division of labor was indirect and so individualized. Although part of society, he was an atomized part of it. This is a very sketchy preliminary outline of Marx's viewpoint.

The word "atomization" immediately conjures up a picture of individualization imposed on mankind by some external agency. It therefore stands counterposed to community, or forms of communal organization. Forced individualization as opposed to forms of democratic or spontaneous cooperation is the concept that underlies the term, but that does not provide a sufficient understanding in itself of the nature of atomization. In contrast, forced cooperation or forced communal organization as under feudalism or slavery is compounded of the two elements, force and community, which stand opposed to one another. Where cooperation is forced, it is not truly cooperation. Thus, it is possible to imagine the slave being part of a household community in terms of a division of labor and supply of necessities of life, yet belonging to a slave organization in revolt. This might imply that in the household itself he was isolated from others, so that his cooperation was only in work and only extracted by force. On the other hand, he might also be part of a wider slave community in revolt and so could not be said to be individualized or isolated. If such organization was impossible he might appear then to be individualized. Yet there would remain a problem, for he would be part of the household and would naturally tend to be part of a slave community when allowed. Unless he were alone in the house, he would be bound to be part of such a community in which the master had paternalistic responsibility. The essential point is that, hitherto, there has not been a society in which the community is not a forced community.

This illustrates the difference between an enforced community such as the slave in the household and the absence of such community in modern society. The enforced community was still a community in some sense. It was and was not a community. In modern society the worker steps out of the community of the factory when he leaves the workplace. Inside of work he is competitive with his fellow workers and subordinated to his employers by the need to work in order to survive out of work. To establish a community with his fellow workers is extremely difficult, although to establish a common organization is not. Neither employer nor fellow employees have a responsibility for the worker. In contrast, in feudalism there was such responsibility, if only to ensure that the labor was present. And yet it is possible to speak of a real interdependence inside the factory and outside. This is based on the division of labor alone. The contrast is thus between a greater degree of independence possessed by the worker outside of production and the lesser isolation of the slave and feudal serf.

Atomization thus is a modern category. The precapitalist slave or serf could not be individualized in the manner of modern man since he did not possess the requisite independence. The community was an enforced community in precapitalist times and hence one in which the state, whether local or central, always had to play a crucial role. It is the specific contribution of capitalism to have introduced equality and hence a right not to work, and so to starve, hitherto unknown to mankind. In capitalism the earlier role of the state is replaced by the competition among work seekers. It is both more subtle and more effective as a means of control. The individual becomes truly an individual cut off from society, or so it seems to the individual. The contradiction is that the individual is not cut off from society since he has to work in order to live, and hence the person is subjected to the division of labor of society; but on the other hand, he is only related through money and hence he has an independence that is real. The real dependence is thus masked by a real independence, which is only partial since the individual is powerless to affect most of his or her own life. The term "individualization" is thus seen to express the real contradiction of modern society: the existence of aspects and the possibility of independence, but a reality that makes the term "individual" a mockery of its apparent meaning.

Mankind is necessarily social and it is only through and in society that the individual can exist. The ant is social in this sense, but there are no individuals in ant society; all ants must conform to a preset pattern that can never be changed. The development of mankind has been an evolution away from such patterns toward a greater degree of control over human society. In principle, however, it can only be at the point when everyone has an input into planning and so deciding the present and future of the society that the individual can be said to be truly an individual. No one can stand outside the society, so that it is in the degree to which all can participate in controlling the society, and hence themselves, that the progress of freedom of the individual has to be judged. In being able to control the society, the individual can then express his or her own peculiarly individual nature separate from others. The term individualization then expresses the antithesis of this process. It states that the individual stands powerless in the face of modern society, accepting it as it stands and fighting with other individuals for a place in the social order. Since societies do not exist without those who do indeed control the wealth of that society, this only means that those who are subordinated to those who do control are prevented from developing beyond their isolated existential form because they believe in the illusion of independence provided by antagonistic or competitive individualism. The social order is maintained at the expense of the individual through his or her individualization.

This individualization expresses the atomization of modern society. The worker exists as an isolated atom reacting and competing with other atoms to obtain a job with a good wage and prospects for better wages. It is a highly successful mode of control.

This brief introduction expresses the nature of the problem and provides an orientation to the concepts of organization, individualization, and dependence, all of which will later be explored in greater depth. The purpose has been to show that atomization is a general concept, not to be confined only to a society that does not permit freedom of speech and assembly, such as the USSR or Nazi Germany. Furthermore, it will soon be clear that these aspects are not sufficient to explain the nature of Soviet atomization. The impossibility of spontaneous organization or organization independent of the state is an important aspect of Soviet society, but it is a result of the atomization of the society, rather than its cause.

There can be no doubt that the existence of a permanent secret police that has enormous power in the society is of the utmost significance for understanding Soviet society and its political economy. But this power is not self-derived; it derives from the close integration of the secret police into a society whose political economy permits them to control the life of an individual in a way that is unique both in modern history and probably in all of human history. Furthermore, there is some doubt whether the society could exist at all without the secret police. The close integration of the secret police with the political economy, both in directing that political economy and in using it to maintain the society, is what characterizes the peculiar power of the secret police. In modern society it is the market that serves as a safeguard for the individual against victimization. He may lose his job but he does not necessarily lose his house. He may be jailed but that does not entail loss of all else when he is freed. In the USSR the individual who runs foul of the secret police may lose his job, his educational degrees, diplomas, and titles, his home, his right to live in a particular town, all the money that he possessed, and perhaps as a result even his family, not to speak of his reason. Whatever the secret police did under Stalin, today the sanction of imprisonment or exile is less important than the aspects mentioned above, which affect everybody at some time and some people frequently. It is not that everyone loses some aspect of his or her existence to the secret police but that everyone has to decide whether to inform the secret police when requested, whether to leave the USSR or stay, whether to change jobs or towns, whether to support those victimized by an official, whether to report the wrong-doing of officials, whether to join a protest over food shortages or to participate in a strike. Such decisions inevitably invite police scrutiny and as often as not their active hostility.

Thus, in capitalist society the individual is individualized, yet he is not fully an individual because he is not in control of his own life, although he may have that illusion. In contrast, in the USSR he is individualized, yet feels that he is not an individual but a dependent of his peers or those immediately around him in position. It is not that he feels he is dependent only on his superiors, since he can be dealt with by anyone with whom he comes in contact. He is part of an organization and cannot establish any space between his identity and that organization. He has no illusion that he is in charge of himself, and hence he stands in permanent antagonism to the organization to which he belongs. In contrast, in capitalism the individual may stand in antagonism to his fellows but not to the organization for which he works until the system begins to malfunction. Then the worker stands in antagonism to the organization controlling him by merging his identity with his fellows in order to eliminate the organization. At the moment of liquidation of the organization, he stands as an individual merged into the new movement. If the new movement does not take steps to establish control from below, then the worker exchanges an illusory independence for a perceived dependence. At that point, the worker must ask whether he has not lost something, even if it was an illusion. That illusion of independence from the division of labor and control by the capitalist class is only sustained through the existence of forms that provide an independence from peers, though not from an immediate superior.

Other members of the ruling class may have no relation to the individual involved. In contrast, in the USSR the individual is dependent on all superiors, and to enforce that dependence he becomes dependent on his peers as well. In other words, his dependence is total: he is totally dependent and hence totally individualized. Dependence and individualization are two poles of the contradiction of the atomized individual in the USSR. It is in fact only the particular expression of the more general contradiction between the organization of the society and the self-interest of the unit, brought down to the level of the individual.

On the one hand, the Soviet worker exists within a factory, inside a building and its social organizations, within other formal organizations such as trade unions, work units, and possibly the Communist party, receiving particular instructions and acting accordingly. On the other hand, the worker has no social organizations, no informal groupings that permit him to advance his knowledge, interests, or existence as a class. The bureaucratic incorporation of everyone produces its opposite—their atomization into discrete units. At the same time, atomization of the individual leads to undemocratic organizations controlled from above, and so to bureaucratic organizations. The natural solution or supersession of the contradiction is one in which the atomized individual comes to control the organization and so loses his or her atomization at the same time as the organization loses its bureaucratic nature.

Atomization is thus a feature of both capitalism and the Soviet system. Its extreme under capitalism is reached in so-called totalitarian regimes such as Nazi Germany. These are nonetheless different from the USSR insofar as the market is retained. In a certain sense they are not as atomized. The Friedrich and Brzezinski definition relies heavily on the view that atomization is a result of political powerlessness. Since individuals cannot organize, they are atomized and become "anxiety-ridden shadows" who are preyed on by the organs of the state. The problem with this view of the USSR is that it fails to take account of the real organizations to which individuals belong. Nor do they necessarily have a gun at their backs when they support the "democratic centralist candidate"—they know what is good for them without being told. The atomization is actually deeper than has been described. It is not the lack of organization that produces the atomization but the atomization that produces the lack of opposition-type organizations. In the examples of fascist countries, it is true that absence of organization is a significantly different feature of the atomization of the individual, but in the USSR it is only a symptom.

Comparison with Nazi Germany

In view of the totalitarian thesis, propounded before the 1940s by Hilferding and Trotsky, among others, and later by various American and British scholars and Cold Warriors, it is important to note how Nazi Germany and the USSR are similar and how they are not similar. Here the crucial features are the role of the secret police, the bureaucracy, and the party, and control over the economy.

That the secret police were powerful in Nazi Germany is not to be denied, but their power was in two respects limited compared to that of their counterparts in Stalin's Russia. The German haute bourgeoisie was relatively inviolate, whereas the Soviet elite was decimated. There is no comparison between the numbers of social democrats, communists, and various oppositionists arrested in Nazi Germany and the number of members of the capitalist class proper who were victimized. By contrast, in the USSR, the old revolutionaries, the newly powerful bureaucrats, and the potentially powerful elite all went to the camps and death.

The second difference lies in the totally bureaucratized nature of the Soviet economy as opposed to the partially bureaucratized fascist form. The market economy, which continued to function in Nazi Germany, even with bureaucratic deformations, allowed a degree of independence that was impossible in the USSR. When housing, jobs, and transport were allocated not by fiat but by money, people could continue to exist, however harshly, in the interstices of the system. The range of controls held by the secret police is always less in any market-type system. In the USSR, by contrast, the center had control over labor power in a manner that would be impossible for a partially functioning market economy. Hitler remained afraid of his workers throughout his period of office, while the Stalinist regime actually achieved the result of removing the collectivity of the workers. This was in part a function of the backwardness of the USSR and in part a result of the abolition of the market.

The third difference lies in the nature of the party. Stalin virtually destroyed the Communist party as even a nominally functioning organization. In Nazi Germany the National Socialist party actually did function as a means of control over the population. Its ideology was crucial in maintaining some level of support, not to speak of the mobilizing campaigns led by Goebbels (whose activities cannot be compared to the descriptions provided by Machiavelli, since they insult even the cynical Italians of the Renaissance). It is a popular myth in the

West, propagated by the totalitarian school, that the party in the USSR plays a crucial role in maintaining the system. To do so, a party must, among other conditions, have an ideology that is believed. We have already treated this question, but here we may briefly point out that Hitler at least was a consistent anti-Semite. His propaganda was nonsense, but it was consistent: the Jews were capitalists, Bolsheviks, and cheats, and clearly the one thing Bolsheviks and capitalists had in common was that they cheated the shopkeepers, the peasants, and the upwardly mobile of their just reward. In the USSR, Stalin and his successors (who may have been anti-Semitic, but only while claiming otherwise) have stood for equality for the common man while also declaring that the idea of equality is a petit bourgeois delusion. They have railed against nationalism while supporting Russian nationalism as well as a Soviet nationalism. They have said that they were democratic while abolishing any vestiges of democracy. What is their ideology? Hitler, by contrast, had a message and his propaganda minister succeeded in conveying that gruesome message in part by using the Nazi party. The CPSU, on the other hand, which had no congress for thirteen years, and whose Central Committee and Politburo hardly operated except as a frightened audience, had no role as a party and played no such role.

Finally, the fourth point of difference lies in the nature of the economy. Clearly, this is crucial and explains the other three arguments in the final analysis. The Nazi economy, for all Hitler's railings, remained an economy controlled by a capitalist class. It operated through a real market with real money. By contrast, the USSR claimed to have abolished value in this period and did in fact largely abolish even the form of money in the early 1930s, in order to deal with the massive shortages operative throughout the economy. This effectively meant that the atomization of the workers in Nazi Germany was based on the existence of the commodity and the necessity to sell one's labor power rather than on the particular relation of the worker to production, described below, and the dependence relation.

The term "atomization" is employed by Detlev J.K. Peukert in his very useful work on Nazi Germany. Peukert quotes Robert Leys saying that only those asleep have a private life. "Either way, the end result was still an individual stripped of social relationships, fighting for himself alone, 'scraping by.' " And he continues, "The 'fellow traveller' and the non-participant, then, were equally threatened by the atomization of everyday life, the dissolution of social bonds, the isolation of modes of perception, the shrinking of prospects and hence the loss of the capacity for social action."[7] Clearly, this description of Nazi Germany does not rely on commodity fetishism. It is fundamentally arguing that the individual in Nazi society is separated from his fellows and so bereft of social action. This is done politically through the system of political controls. At the same time, the ordinary worker would also be atomized in the ordinary manner of a capitalist society. Capitalist society, however, also engenders, in its decline, a socialization of production such that labor breaks through its atomization in order to realize its full potential as a working class. It is this formation of a collectivity that Nazi society dealt with so effectively. In other words, it repaired the break in the pattern of commodity fetishism by political means. No organization of any kind was possible. The individual was entirely shorn of his social context. The essential point is that commodity fetishism cannot be repaired without a thoroughgoing political–economic penetration of the society. Hence, the Nazi party had indeed to individualize the society to the point where the social context vanished. Hence, Peukert could remark: "Private spheres of behavior were impoverished and isolated, relapsing into a self-serving individualism devoid of all potentially dangerous connections and meanings. The *Volksgemeinschaft* that had been so noisily trumpeted and so harshly enforced became, in the end, an atomized society."[8]

In contrast, the USSR abolished commodity production. Money, commodities, and the sale of labor power all ceased to exist. Commodity fetishism is not there to repair. The individualization described above would not be enough to contain the society. The problem with Peukert's description is that he has left out production and the commodity, which do indeed provide an integrating mechanism for Nazi society. In the USSR, if there were simply an absence of potentiality for organization and nothing else, the society would not last one day.

This does not mean that the USSR is a variety of fascist state, or that it is worse, or for that matter the same. It only indicates that the atomization of the population in the USSR has been necessarily greater than was the case even in fascist Germany. The atomization of the USSR relies first and foremost on the total dependence consequent on a bureaucratized economy. The concept of dependence is absolutely crucial in understanding the USSR.

Dependence

The theory of dependence is derived in particular from Marx's perception of dependence in relation to money and the evolution of human history. Marx argues that there are three states of mankind. The first is one of direct dependence of an isolated producer. In this instance, the direct producer is a serf who is dependent on the lord and the apparatus of the manor. His dependence is direct and unmediated but, fortunately for him, a considerable geographic and social distance is established between himself and the hierarchy. This gives him some independence since supervision then becomes intermittent and is more attuned to results than to the process itself. The isolation is a result of the undeveloped nature of the division of labor. This also, however, implies that the producer is largely working for himself and not for a market. The integration with the society is thus limited and hence his dependence on others is similarly limited.

We may next consider the society of so-called primitive communism. Here Marx speaks of a comparison with the society of the ant, where members of the society find that their life is largely determined for them. Dependence here is total, personal, and direct, although in the final analysis it is a dependence on nature. The individual is compelled to perform certain functions and engage in particular tasks day in and day out. Clearly, the individual in one sense hardly exists. The individual can only exist as an individual when there is a certain command over nature such that scarcity is less dominating. From this point of view, the movement of society is one in which there is a progressive overcoming of scarcity. The social surplus product gradually increases to the point where the individuals in society can have a large measure of control over their own lives.

In contrast with these two previous states of society, capitalism is one in which dependence is indirect and integrated. The massive development in the division of labor leads to a tight interlocking of the different aspects of production and so of society. The isolation that permitted some independence for the direct producer through history has come to an end, and the potential for total societal or centralized control is established for the first time. However, the individual is saved through the nature of capitalism itself. The development of exchange value is such that it becomes the very nature of the society itself; hence, money, the epitome of exchange value, mediates between the individual and society. The indirectness of this dependence on the division of labor provides a measure of independence for the individual. Money provides the individual with the possibility of an impersonal choice that otherwise would be absent. The impersonal nature of social relations is crucial to this level of independence from the society. While the worker is compelled to work, the compulsion is neither personal nor direct. He is forced to work because he needs money in order to survive. He can then, in principle, choose his employer. If he saves money he can choose not to work for a while. He could leave the region or even the country. For most workers the choice is actually very limited. Nonetheless, for the first time in history the individual has a kind of independence.

In contrast, a socialist society removes exchange value and so money. As a result, dependence becomes direct and personal. Worse, it also becomes total, as in primitive society. In the latter case, however, the dependence was externally determined. Now dependence is internal and increasing as the society becomes ever more interconnected. That difference is the crucial point. Society now permits the individual to take control over itself and himself in two ways. In the first place, the individual now has direct and indirect forms of control over the different units of the society. In the second place, his position is determined by himself alone. He can change his position in the division of labor both hierarchically and horizontally as he sees fit. His consumption, in a society where scarcity is largely or completely abolished, is his own affair. Choice, therefore, is at the highest possible level. Labor becomes man's prime want, as opposed to his curse. His working day becomes a day of creativity. The individual, therefore, has only one interest in relation to other individuals, one of cooperation to ensure the common individual interest. Humanity through its social forms becomes truly human.

Now consider what happens if the abolition of money is not accompanied by the forms that permit the individual to take control over the society in cooperation with other members of the society. He is then at the mercy of the society. He is personally and directly dependent on others. He can be completely controlled from the center. The development of the division of labor and so of industry is such that he becomes a small, tightly integrated cog in the larger whole. What is more, the lubrication of money is absent, so that there is constant friction with peers, superiors, and inferiors. At all levels dependence is personal, unmediated by either isolation or money.

In the USSR money exists formally, but it is largely absent in its content. The individual, as Gorbachev has pointed out and as sociologists bemoan, simply receives a nominal wage for turning up at his place of work. With that money he cannot acquire an apartment, a car, or most consumer durables without being placed on a waiting list, and often he needs to belong to a particular institution with a particular status. Even food often falls in this category. At home, he is normally part of a housing collective that regulates his neighborly relations. At work, after work, and at sleep, the individual is regulated consciously and obviously by others. His conditions of existence at work are dependent on the goodwill of others around him. It does not matter whether he is a manual or white-collar worker, a worker or an executive, an executive or the factory director, for in all cases the individual reports to others. Since a fine means little, the worker has to have a reward system that is more direct, such as being praised or denigrated by name on a poster. Not only his hierarchic but his geographic movement is controlled, and he has to have series of documents to permit this personal relation.

Integrated personal dependence transforms itself into bureaucratic relations for all in the society. Personal dependence of this kind is by its nature undemocratic. Atomization, then, is the condition of separation of every individual into a separate unit with apparent independence. Paradoxically, the conditions for such individualization can only exist when its contradictory nature is being torn apart. In order for atomization to exist at all, there has be such a development of society that the individual is no longer immediately dependent on others. The result, however, is that the division of labor has itself become so complex that the real dependence of all members of society is total. The independence thus granted to the individual is illusory and worse than illusory, in that it is his very illusory independence that compels him to conform to the wishes of those who control the society.

Atomization and the Social Group

The difference in social group between those in the elite and those in lower social positions is crucial in understanding the nature of atomization in the USSR. At one level, as Sergei Khrushchev's account of his father's downfall shows, every member of the elite including the most powerful is subject to the secret police, either on its own or in the interests of a particular faction. So great is the atomization that Nikita Khrushchev clearly was unable to confide in his own son, although the latter was acting in his father's interest. Anastas Mikoyan took pains to mention in his notes on the meeting to plan the overthrow of Khrushchev that he considered the plotters honest, and good party men. He knew that they would search his wardrobe, where he placed the document.

On the other hand, the elite are in charge of the administration of the country. Under Stalin they were subject to the leader and his entourage, but today the secret police cannot arrest a member of the party without the consent of the party. This provides some protection for the elite. The dependence of the members of the elite on each other is different from the dependence of members of the intelligentsia and the working class. In the end, the reason for the dependence of the elite is their inability to control the surplus product more than partially. Their constant failure to ensure that their will is carried out leads to continual changes and so ensures their insecurity. Under Stalin the purges performed the function of maintaining control and acted as an alternative to real change in the social system. Stalin was attempting to have his will obeyed by destroying those apparently incapable of fulfilling orders. His successors have had to find alternatives to the purges. They reform the society and the system, and shift members of the elite and the intelligentsia around or dismiss them from their positions, without murdering them. The failure of the system therefore makes for the insecurity of the elite. In economic terms their partial control over the surplus product means that they are less than a class and consequently have less security than a class in their social positions. Nonetheless, since they do possess command over others, they have a limited degree of independence, at least in relation to their inferiors.

The failure of the elite to establish themselves on a viable basis means that they are eternally atomized in a more competitive environment than under capitalism. At least in the market the individual capitalist does not risk jail and loss of life (or at least, way of life). Of course, he may go to jail for fraud, embezzlement, or other crimes, but jail is not an everyday penalty for failure. In the USSR under Stalin, the penalty for members of the elite who failed was death. Since Stalin the penalties have been loss of job, disgrace, demotion to a lower social group, and jail (in the case of corruption). All this was masked for a time by the immobilism under Brezhnev. Individuals in the elite are therefore competitive, individualized, and worried about their position.

Members of the intelligentsia are in a different position. Although they may have a degree of control over others, they are not in control of the administration. As a result, they are the subject of the changes and the purges without ever knowing why the changes themselves take place. They are completely insecure. This is what Gorbachev has attempted to change. It might appear as if concessions on freedom of speech, or *glasnost'*, are changes of an essential kind that affect all equally. This is not true in the context of the USSR for two reasons. In the first place, the USSR has proved that it is possible to give freedom of speech to the intelligentsia but not to the workers, since the latter cannot organize genuinely independent trade unions. In the second place, the security of the intelligentsia is dependent on the extent to which they can speak their mind. It is obvious that a poet or writer who is able to write as he wants without penalty will be more secure than he was in the pre-Gorbachev period. It is not quite so obvious that the same is true of the engineer or doctor. Yet, the doctor who wants to undertake new forms of treatment of a patient would find that he could not speak out easily in favor of change. *Mutatis mutandis,* the same is true of the engineer.

The worker's situation is quite different in that his free speech would involve the overthrow of the system. He wants genuine elections of the management of enterprises, from the planners down to the individual directors of plants. He wants independent trade unions and the realization of Lenin's view that the salary of the skilled worker should be the maximum paid to anyone. Today these demands are being expressed in terms of greater democracy at the shop level, opposition to the antileveling campaign, and attacks on privilege, but not in any direct venting of worker's demands. The result is that the worker remains atomized under Gorbachev in much the same manner as before.

The most important aspect, however, of the worker's atomization is that his dependence is turned into a dependence on the labor process itself. The worker under capitalism is alienated from both his product and his work process and, as a result, is dominated by both. The worker under the Soviet-type system is also alienated from both, but the domination of the worker by the machine under capitalism is driven by the need for profit, whereas in the USSR there is no special drive or screen. The effect of the transparency of the system at this level is that it permits the worker to control his own work process or, in other words, to determine his own level of productivity with a given technique. As a result, his focus of struggle is around the technology and his conditions of production. Historically, this has tended to be an individualized struggle with management. Because the worker was unable to unite in a genuine trade union or any real collectivity, his struggle had to be an individual one. The problem, however, is that the worker then tended to seek salvation in an individual bargain with the management over the labor process. The fact that the bargain is largely tacit does not alter the fact that the worker related to management in this atomized way and consequently became dependent on a new social relationship.

Management has colluded with workers in maintaining a low level of productivity, largely because that was the only way they could ensure some steady level of production. The system accepted it, however unconsciously, because this provided a stability that would not otherwise be there. The stability is based then on the worker accepting his individual and particular relation to his labor process and so to management. As the individual worker is also controlled through a series of bureaucratic police forms, he becomes dependent on those to whom he relates in his labor process. In this case, however, the dependence is mutual. It is this very power that the worker possesses to limit production that has been used by the system to control him and atomize him, since the worker appears to have achieved his own personal bargain.

The Institutional Forms of Atomization

Atomization in the USSR may then be described as the process whereby the politically individualized person interacts with his bureaucratic dependence. The institutions that maintain the political individualization are the KGB, the police system of passport controls, the apparatus of labor management (which includes the labor books and personal files), the militarization of the economy, and the control over the means of communication in all its forms. The bureaucratic dependence is a consequence of an organized system using nationalization without any form of social control. In other words, it results from a particular system of exploitation in which the elite extract a surplus product from the workers but in a form over which they—the elite—have only limited control. In a sense, this book is really about this whole question of bureaucratic dependence placed in a political–economic context. We will return to this question below. We now turn to the institutions of political individualization.

In the first instance, it is necessary to return to the discussion of the Soviet secret police, now called the Committee for State Security or KGB, as opposed to its earlier incarnations as the People's Commissariat for Internal Affairs (NKVD), the Unified State Political Administration (OGPU), and the Extraordinary Commission for the Suppression of Counterrevolution (Cheka).[9] The division that deals with espionage is another matter and does not concern us here. As far as can be ascertained, the numbers of people employed in the KGB amount to hundreds of thousands, as opposed to the few thousand that are usual in most police states. Until Gorbachev, the tasks of the KGB included prevention of any demonstrations, deterring the formation of any groups, surveillance of all kinds, and information gathering on the state of public opinion. In principle, everyone was watched. Nor was the KGB unsuccessful in its tasks. There were few if any public demonstrations, groups were quickly broken up, strikes and mass stay-at-homes were relatively rare, and when they did occur they were dealt with quickly. Censorship was effective at all levels. For the above purposes the secret police has maintained a presence in all enterprises and institutions. It needed to know of and deal with any individual who was dissident. Dissidence includes differences with the local administration of the enterprise, institution, or region of the USSR and hence may not imply any real political disagreement. The effect, of course, is that the KGB has penetrated to the heart of the society.

We can distinguish four broad periods of the KGB's activity since Stalin became the Soviet leader. During the early transitional period, until the Seventeenth Party Congress and Stalin's murder of Kirov in 1934, the KGB was

largely a Stalinist political police, with considerable though limited powers. While it incarcerated and killed people, the numbers were small compared to the next phase (the deaths of millions as a result of the forced collectivization were not their direct responsibility). During the next period, to 1953, the secret police became the prime instrument of rule, administering vast labor camps essential to the economy. It was responsible for the death of millions through direct execution and the imposition of intolerable conditions in the labor camps. In this period it penetrated to all levels in the society, becoming a political police, economic controller, and pulverizer of the society itself.

Under Khrushchev it was radically reformed. The leading personnel were executed and its powers limited, particularly in relation to the elite. New cadres were drawn from the Komsomol. Its role became more subtle. The camps were largely, though not entirely, dissolved. Its role became one of maintaining order in an inherently unstable society. While imprisonment and killing were still employed, its prime penalties were bureaucratic. It could arrange for an individual to be deported from one town to another, to lose his job or his housing, and even for academics to lose their titles and degrees. What the state has conferred, it can remove. Physicians who objected to the political use of mental hospitals were themselves declared insane. The power of the KGB was (and still remains) affirmative as well as negative. It could and did arrange for people to be promoted, obtain jobs, get scarce goods, and even get degrees and academic posts. While the power of the KGB was much less than under Stalin, it remained crucial to the stability of the society. It accomplished its tasks through an enormous network of collaborators and part-timers. While many would not actually collaborate, few could withstand its pressure. The difference between the KGB and the political police in terrorist-type states like the former regimes in Argentina, Portugal, and Nazi Germany is that the political police in those dictatorial market regimes were actually operating on the margin of the society, a margin that might have been bigger or smaller in size. Contrast the words of one of the USSR's major writers, Bulat Okudzhava: "the secret police became a way of life among us."[10]

In addition to its own members the KGB has thousands if not millions of informers (KGB head Vladimir Kriuchkov prefers to call them "helpers"). Boris Yeltsin, at a meeting of the Supreme Soviet in July 1989, said of the KGB: "In my ten years as a regional party secretary they did not catch a single spy. This is an army of thousands that informs on what is going on at the workplace. It is unacceptable in this period of democratization."[11] The exact numbers are unknown, but one author cites a number of sources putting the numbers (apart from the KGB troops) at 150,000 technical and clerical workers and 1.5 million officers, plain clothes agents, and informers.[12] Around them, in turn, there is the whole population to be informed on and leaned on to the point that they do what is required.

An interview with Semichastnyi (*Ogonek,* 10–17 June 1989), the head of the

SOCIAL CONTROL 41

KGB in the period 1961–67, is instructive. After Brezhnev removed him as head of the KGB in 1967, Semichastnyi was given a series of minor posts. His bitterness allowed him to reveal more than he might have otherwise done. The interviewer skillfully drew out the enormous power the KGB possessed under both Khrushchev and Brezhnev. Semichastnyi tells how the Central Committee would demand information on the reactions of the population to its decisions (information gathering and reporting has been the function of Russian security services for centuries). The central role of the KGB in displacing Khrushchev is also made clear. So too is its function in enforcing decisions on censorship, as in the cases of Pasternak, Daniel, Siniavsky, Solzhenitsyn, and others. Semichastnyi expresses the view that the role of the KGB ought to be prophylactic rather than punitive.

Semichastnyi's bitterness at being replaced by Andropov led him to criticize the latter for not doing something about the corruption in Uzbekistan and other areas, as well as in other spheres such as the Ministry of Internal Affairs (MVD). The point, however, is that Andropov, according to Semichastnyi, had to know all about the corruption. Implicitly, he is arguing that Andropov did nothing about it because he did not want to risk the consequences of decisive action. In fact, however, it was knowledge of the corruption at the highest levels that permitted Gorbachev to purge his opponents very rapidly. No doubt Andropov would have done the same thing, had he been well enough.

The KGB, then, is the prime institution of the state. It gathers information on the nature of public opinion and on the views of crucial individuals, and as a result necessarily gathers information on the real state of the economy. It alone knows the fine details on the standard of living, levels of employment, and economic problems of Soviet society. It needs the information not only to report to the Politburo but, more importantly, to understand and predict the troubles that will arise in Soviet society. If the KGB is to be prophylactic, to use Semichastnyi's word, it needs to have a full and complete understanding of the pressure points of Soviet society. In that way it can avoid riots, demonstrations, and strikes. It prevents the latter, in the best case, by targeting the dissident individuals in the weak spots of Soviet society.

Of course, the contradiction within the function of the KGB is that its very omnipotence stands against its role in the state. Knowing the problems of Soviet society, its functionaries come to understand that only a change in social relations will deal with the problems that they are suppressing. From being a tool of the elite, they become the controllers of the elite, since they alone possess both the information on the state of society and the means of blocking or promoting change. From being the zombie-like creatures of an elite in formation, they become its Platonic Guardians. At that point, when it is apparently in charge of the society, it becomes the society and so falls apart.

In plain English, the members of the KGB are in a position to perceive the developing tendencies in the economy and society and to estimate the likelihood of their success or failure. Different sections and individuals take up different political positions, depending on their intellectual viewpoint and their social position. Such differentiation automatically follows once the society is seen to be falling apart. Either the KGB increases repression or it attempts to find a solution to the problems of the society. If repression, however, has not yet succeeded in maintaining the stability of a society that has passed through an era of concentration camps and continues to be under firm control, then it can never work. The KGB, in other words, knows that it cannot put a disintegrating society back together again. Semichastnyi himself appears to have taken a hands-off approach. The modern task of the KGB has become one of assisting the orderly transition to a market economy. It is the only institution in the society capable of overseeing such a transition, as it possesses both the knowledge of the failures of the economy and the apparatus to prevent disorder. If its function hitherto had been to infiltrate and break up groups, its new duty becomes one of entering and directing new groups.

The functions of the KGB have become more subtle over time. First it arrested and killed, then it intimidated and controlled, while today it watches, guides, and controls as required. Arrests, intimidation, and killings are still used, but discriminately (or because some section of the secret police is too stupid or untrained to use the alternatives). The regime is playing cat and mouse with the Popular Front organizations. On the one hand, their members have been elected to the Congress of People's Deputies, while on the other, they are kept under control. Formerly, of course, such organizations would not have been permitted to exist and their members would have received long sentences. Even a leader of the opposition such as Yeltsin was delayed in receiving an external passport, and then received it only an hour before his plane left for New York in September 1989.

This is the situation under Gorbachev.

Linked with the KGB, but organizationally separate, is the apparatus of censorship. This was officially abolished under Gorbachev in 1985, but now functions through editorial control and the relations of the editors to the relevant party committee. The censor formerly occupied an office in every publication and other relevant means of communication. While the horizons of what can be published have been widened, the control has remained and, it is now clear, can be reimposed.

It is useful to look at cases of victimization under Brezhnev to illustrate the argument. Consider the case of a worker at a combine harvester factory, E. Kuleshov. Kuleshov tape-recorded from Western radio broadcasts a reading of Solzhenitsyn's *Gulag Archipelago,* and the KGB came to discover this infraction. In the course of 1977–78 Kuleshov was interrogated by the KGB, as was his foreman, Slinkov, who had kept the tapes. "Slinkov," according to an Amnesty International account, was asked about Kuleshov's acquaintances and sphere of interests, whether Kuleshov was thinking of writing a book, whether he intended to campaign against the existing system, and even what Kuleshov's view of Brezhnev was."[13] Although threatened, Slinkov refused to give evidence against Kuleshov. On the other hand, a student, Chernopiatov, through whom Kuleshov was discovered (although he was not the original informer), denounced Kuleshov and gave the names of other individuals who had helped him photograph another of Solzhenitsyn's works. Chernopiatov graduated successfully from the university. Kuleshov and Slinkov were cautioned after interrogation. This case illustrates the control over all literature, whether published inside or outside the USSR, and the apparently amazing ability of the KGB to discover tape recordings of such literature. The process of punishment and reward is also delineated. The student did not hold out, whereas the ordinary workers did. Finally, no one was imprisoned. Cautions were handed out. In contrast, during the Gorbachev period jamming of Western radio broadcasts has ceased, some of Solzhenitsyn's work has appeared in print, and more is promised. The KGB searches for literature no longer have the same point.

Connected with censorship in its function, though not in its operation, is the surveillance of the population through internal means of communication. When letters can be opened, phones tapped, and all public forms of communication are controlled, the citizen is at the mercy of the state for information and contact with other members of the society.[14] The difference between the USSR and other societies has been the global nature of the control. Thus, one writer speaks of 70,000 censors under Brezhnev. This form of surveillance of the population operates on a far larger scale than in any other state. There is a whole department that deals with the opening of letters on a mass scale, largely mail received from abroad or being sent to foreign countries. Internal mail surveillance is also standard, but not blanket.[15]

A third form of control has been geographical. The internal passport has meant that peasants, until they were enfranchised in 1977, had no right to leave the village without permission. Of course, no one else had the right to leave their place of residence either, but at least with a passport temporary visits were possible and ways of evasion could be found. Gorbachev has not changed these controls at all. They amount to a form of control over movement such that individuals cannot migrate to more desirable towns (although movement to less desirable locations is possible). The effect has been, in part, to reduce mobility and so knowledge of events in the country and the world. Such restriction has prevented organization across towns and villages. It has provided the organs of power with a method of dividing the populace between the better-off and the less privileged (this is be discussed below in connection with the divisions within the work force). The KGB has the function of deporting from one town to another the unfortunates who fall foul of the regime.

Yet another aspect of state domination over the lives of individuals is that over the place of residence. Not only can people only reside in the town where they were born or are permitted to move, but their flat is normally allocated by the local council and watched over by a committee of residents. It is easy for the KGB to insert itself into this situation, if it requires.

The final form of control has been that over the workplace, as Yeltsin remarked above, where the KGB normally has its representative. In addition to the labor book, where details of the nature of the work and employment are recorded, there is the personal file, which records misdemeanors and more serious offenses. Since both the labor book and the personal file follow the worker throughout his career, he is effectively deterred from forms of action that would affect his position in a negative manner. Technically, the worker has had the right to strike throughout the Soviet period, but in practice workers were prevented from exercising that right through forms of repression, including incarceration and even shooting of strikers. The Gorbachev decree legalizing the right to strike under certain conditions has not given workers any more rights than they had before, but it can be argued that workers cannot be repressed if they follow the rules. The new question is the nature of those rules.

There are additional forces at work that tighten the dependence and so the power of the state. The enormous size of Soviet enterprises and their subunits, the centralized nature of industry, and indeed of the economy, and the communal or at minimum close-knit nature of life in Soviet apartments and apartment blocks makes the dependence of the individual unique in its directness. It is not necessary for the state to enumerate the population since everyone is contained within the economic system. That is why those who do not work are declared parasites. By so doing they are opting out of the system. They are not controllable in the same way through the same pressures, and so must be dealt with through the judicial system. In fact, a moment's reflection will show that the centralization and large size permit easier control from the center. It is obviously easier to deal with a small number of units that can be policed internally very easily because of the close relation of everyone within the unit. But it is one thing to police and it is another to ensure that the unit functions efficiently. In fact, under these circumstances the two stand opposed. The atomized worker has no interest in performing efficiently. The efficient worker finds the dependence and police control a hindrance to his activity. The instability of the Soviet elite led them to choose their own survival above efficiency. Today the slogan of the Gorbachev regime is one of decentralization, while maintaining some level of centralization. In other words, it wants efficiency without losing control. It is trying to square the circle.

The control over communication, whether of the mass media or over individual relations, combined with the control over horizontal movement, has given the state unprecedented power. When this is added to the control within the workplace and over the place of residence, there is ample scope for the KGB to exert its influence.

The form of bureaucratic dependence both at work and at home thus permits the state to exert almost total control. This can be relaxed or tightened as circumstances permit. The point, however, is that the KGB and the associated state forms derive their power from this bureaucratic dependence, which, in turn, signifies that Gorbachev will only remove the power of the KGB when he either democratizes himself out of power or goes over to private enterprise.

The Contradictions of Atomization

The atomization of the Soviet population has its own limits. The worker will necessarily work at his own pace, and far less efficiently than if he related in a more socially integrated manner. Inefficiency cannot be sustained forever. Unreliable and poor-quality goods can be produced for some time, under definite conditions. (This is discussed below in the section on political economy, where the reasons for decreasing tolerance of inefficiency are adduced.)

The individualization of the population has its counterpart in the individualization of the units of the economic system. Organizational dependence is the other side of the individualized activity of each part of the system. In other words, each enterprise and its structural units strives to establish its own autonomy, even autarky, within the system. It has to do so in order to survive under conditions where its suppliers are unreliable and the demands for its products are unpredictable. From this point of view every unit's necessary tendency to autarky is an understandable and essential means of survival. The atomization of the worker creates a situation of uncertainty and uncontrollability within the system. Every enterprise develops its own system of relations with its work force, which has to be protected to ensure the optimum output under unpredictable conditions. The paradox is that maximum output is attained through minimal dependence on a system that tries to hold all units directly in a centralized mechanism. Complete dependence on the organizational structure leads to maximum autarky.

The effect, for example, of hoarding labor and raw materials is to compel the center to establish stronger centralized control. The dishoarding of raw materials puts the enterprise in the unenviable position of complete dependence on unreliable suppliers, which creates greater pressure on the center to control the suppliers. They, in turn, demand more investment or supplies from the center, which is compelled to seek methods of maintaining stability at a central level. This requires the establishment of autarkic units at a ministerial or trust level. The center, therefore, retreats when faced with potential disruption by creating further autarkic units.

The costs of such atomized units are obvious but the price is paid in order to maintain stability. The ultimate cost of such stability is low to negative growth. As with the increased inefficiency brought about by individual atomization, the autarky of the unit can only be tolerated as long as the economy can supply the units. In principle, here too there is a limit.

The economic limits of atomization are supplemented by social limits. The relative independence of units creates friction between the units and the center. Hence, anti-Moscow antagonism becomes endemic in the system at all levels. Because their independence is based on a real dependence, the units necessarily attempt to establish not just an economically autarkic regime but a social cocoon as well. Patronage, nepotism, and so-called corruption, all of which have been revealed and condemned by Gorbachev, become endemic. Most obvious in the peripheral republics such as Uzbekistan, where a clanlike network was running the republic, it is in fact a feature of the society at all levels. In an unpredictable and brutal society, personal dependents or relatives are more reliable than those who are unknown.

Every unit, therefore, opposes the center, fearful that its working relations will be disrupted. This natural tendency to disintegration is then countered by the center deliberately reorganizing its relations with its units from time to time. At a certain point this reorganization becomes counterproductive. That point was reached under Khrushchev and formed the basis of the so-called stagnation under Brezhnev. Under Brezhnev, paradoxically, the different units remained quiescent because they were mindful of the alternative, which operated under the previous rulers. Once such an alternative was ruled out, however, and moreover decentralization was embraced, under Gorbachev, the only result could be direct disintegration.

As an alternative to commodity fetishism, atomization is most particularly inferior in that the system is transparently unequal and exploitative. It is quite obvious to all that an elite both rules and has privileges. As a result, the elite has to hide both. No one is deceived, but it is hard to prove privilege when someone like Ligachev will state (as he did at the Nineteenth Party Conference) that party officials are not better off than anyone else. The transparency of the system makes for a vast inchoate demand for equality, to which the elite today keeps responding. Time after time, Gorbachev and his minions rail against so-called leveling and those who support it. At the June 1989 Congress of People's Deputies session Gorbachev defended the right of the apparatus to have dachas. He was accused himself of having one and he replied that some people had such a right, but not very many.

It is to be noted that the demand is not for the abolition of a class or the overthrow of a group, it is for an egalitarian society.

Notes

1. In an article that discusses deception and refusal to acknowledge reality in the presence of workers, Agranovskii attacks what passes for a necessary secrecy. He begins with a quote from a letter reproving him for writing a satirical article that could be used by workers. See A. Agranovksii, "Sovershenno sekretno," *EKO*, 1988, no. 4, pp. 132–41.

2. Herbert Marcuse, *Soviet Marxism* (New York: Vintage, 1961).

3. Speech by E.K. Ligachev at the February 1988 Plenum of the CPSU (*Pravda*, 18 February 1988, p. 3). Throughout the speech Ligachev talks of the need to criticize, speak the truth, and uncover what really happened in the USSR.

4. Carl J. Friedrich and Zbigniew K. Brzezinski, *Totalitarian Dictatorship and Autocracy* (New York: Praeger, 1969), p. 279.
5. Franz Neumann, *Behemoth* (London: Victor Gollancz, 1942), pp. 298–99.
6. Ibid.
7. Detlev J.K. Peukert, *Inside Nazi Germany: Conformity, Opposition and Racism in Everyday Life* (Harmondsworth, UK: Penguin, 1989), p. 239.
8. Ibid.
9. See Amy Knight, *The KGB: Police and Politics in the Soviet Union* (Boston: Unwin Hyman, 1988), pp. 183–220. Knight argues that the KGB is sophisticated, well educated, intelligent, and well behaved. It is familiar with the literature, goals, and methods of the dissidents (p. 194). Descriptions of the nature of the KGB's internal operations are limited. Chapter 5 of John Barron, *KGB: The Secret Work of Soviet Secret Agents* (London: Hodder and Stoughton, 1974), provides a semidescriptive, semi-anecdotal account. See also Nicholas Garland, "Emerging from Stalin's Shadow" (*The Independent*, 15 July 1989).
10. Bulat Okudzhava, "Puteshestvie diletantov" (*Druzhba narodov*, no. 8, 1976, p. 123): "Spying among us is not a service but a form of existence, instilled in childhood and not by people but by the air of the empire." The author is discussing the Russian empire, but the reference to the contemporary USSR is unmistakable.
11. *Financial Times*, 15 July 1989, p. 3. The occasion was the confirmation of Kriuchkov as head of the KGB. Yeltsin refers to the occasion in his autobiography as being based on his personal experience as party secretary in the Sverdlovsk region. See Boris Yeltsin, *Against the Grain* (New York: Summit, 1990), p. 61.
12. Alexander J. Motyl, "Policing Perestroika: The Indispensable KGB," in *The Harriman Institute Forum*, vol. 2, no. 8 (August 1989), p. 4. Motyl argues in terms of a close relationship between the KGB and *perestroika*.
13. *Chronicle of Current Events*, no. 51 (London: Amnesty International, 1979), p. 42.
14. This was graphically illustrated in the trial of one Buzinnikov for criticizing the system in the USSR, in 1978; a letter, which he wrote to Sakharov, was cited against him, although the letter never reached Sakharov. The first department of the Physics Institute of the Academy of Sciences handed it over to the KGB (the first department of all institutions is the local representative of the KGB). See ibid., pp. 12–13.
15. Knight, *The KGB*, pp. 183–220.

4

The Nonpolitical Politics of the Soviet Elite

Politics in the Soviet elite exists on two planes. On one plane, there are the three major political institutions that hold power in the USSR: the army, the KGB, and the party apparatus. On the other plane, there are the representatives of the social groups: the elite, the intelligentsia, the workers, and the peasants. Each of these groups finds sections of the elite that either control or ally with it and so come to express in a distorted way their interests at the level of the elite.

Within the elite, decisions have to be made as to the mode of control and forms of alliance with the other social groups. Clearly, divisions are bound to arise on the advisability of different forms of control and the nature of alliances. Here, the division in the elite between the "controllers" and the "organizers" is crucial. This is discussed in some detail below. It should be noted that this division has nothing to do with the so-called "technocrats." If we start from the definition that *the elite in the USSR consists of those people who have some limited control over the surplus product,* then we can see that there is a division between those who prefer to apply maximum force to extract the surplus product and those who prefer to cajole. For the first group, order and discipline is the slogan, while for the second it is so-called economic accountability. We must also note that the elite have been divided over their attitude toward the intelligentsia and hence the workers. The traditional policy has been to play one off against the other. The fundamental issue has always been one of stability, or, put differently, ensuring the continuity of the Soviet elite. The problem for the Soviet elite is precisely that their control over the surplus product is less than complete, and hence they cannot achieve either their personal goals or those of the group as a whole.

Under these circumstances politics in the USSR consists of interactions between the holders of political power and the factional divisions. In turn, the factions run through various shades of opinion, depending also on their relation to the other social groups in the society.

Khrushchev, for example, cleverly used the army to ally with the party apparatus against the secret police to oust Beria, and then used the reformed secret police with the party apparatus to oust the army.[1] In this process, he turned to the higher intelligentsia and incorporated them in the elite. He made concessions to the peasantry and to the workers. Their standard of living rose. On the other hand, his agricultural policies failed. Once he lost social support, a coalition of opposition interests found it easy to turn on him. Finally, the party apparatus opposed him, and, with the support of both the army and secret police, ousted him.

Thus, the immediate post-Stalin period saw the introduction of a particular political process. It could only proceed through the formation of amorphous factions. Since factions were banned, no informal or formal factions could exist; but in fact discussions clearly took place and a common platform was established. There can be no detailed description of what was an extraconstitutional process, but no other explanation would fit the shifts over the past thirty years in which groups gained and lost power. In the last period the Brezhnev group lost power under Andropov, regained it on his death, and then found themselves beleaguered.

In the end, the factional differences have hinged on the speed of the introduction of the market, the question of civil rights for the intelligentsia, and the extension of democracy. All factions agreed on the need to maintain control over the workers. Discipline was the watchword of even the most liberal faction. What was not agreed on was the means of maintaining that discipline—whether through command or through the market.

The party faction that is out of power has always had difficulty formulating its program, since it could not formally constitute itself and retain the necessary apparatus. Yet, in the Brezhnev period, powerful individuals were able to set up institutes that became think tanks for alternative economic and political strategies. Thus, Germen Gvishiani, Aleksei Kosygin's son-in-law, set up the Institute of Systems Analysis, which included on its staff the mathematical economist Leonid Kantorovich; and Abel Aganbegian established his fiefdom in Novosibirsk with his own journal, *EKO*. Leonid Abalkin is the head of the Institute of Economics of the Academy of Sciences. Tat'iana Zaslavskaia became head of the new Institute of Public Opinion. All were early, prominent advisers of the current regime. Thus, the institutes provided the basis for Gorbachev's *perestroika,* in terms of both personnel and program. They were able to develop ideas on the introduction of the market and to conduct surveys of public opinion on important questions. In turn, each round of debate that took place permitted the recruitment of new individuals.

Under Stalin and later, when any dissent was regarded as dangerous, even if it was intended to preserve the position of the elite itself, the elite itself was atomized. The newer forms of consultation have permitted the elite to establish itself as a more collective body. The more collectively it is able to exist, the better able it is to establish its needs and ensure that the system moves in the direction of meeting those needs. In the end, that is what Gorbachev has been trying to achieve. The Congress of People's Deputies and the Supreme Soviet have permitted a limited amount of discussion of this kind. The members of these bodies are either from the elite itself or are subject to its demands.[2] The applause in the Congress of People's Deputies that greeted the decision to eliminate elections of enterprise managers showed quite clearly where the deputies stood.

The problem is that the ultimate objective may be agreed upon, but not the means of attainment. The political division over the direction and speed of reform coincides with the division between those who control and those who administer. The first group, in the secret police and the party apparatus, can more easily observe and predict the chaos if the regime were to move too quickly. They also have more to lose themselves, since a genuinely democratic society would dispense with their services and might even punish them for crimes committed. On the other hand, the economists and economic functionaries know that a move toward the market has to be made rapidly if at all. Inevitably, there must be a third grouping of those who expect no move to the market but see a continued deterioration internally. For them the solution can only be authoritarian, and hence there has emerged a Russian nationalist variant.

**Factions and the Emergence of Opposing
Currents and Parties**

Paradoxically, the fact that Brezhnev was weak was the secret of his survival. For a time it appeared that there was every reason to support a leader who basically allowed the individual factions and institutions to go their own way. Such an approach led the Sovietologists and state-capitalist theorists to conclude that the position of anyone in the elite was stable—a view that has had to be radically revised. Gorbachev within a few months dismissed fifty persons from the Central Committee apparatus, and promoted more members of the Andropov–Gorbachev faction to the Politburo. He put men of the same faction into important jobs, shifted the man who had nominated him as general-secretary to the presidency, removed Romanov and Grishin from the Politburo, and promoted Shevardnadze to foreign minister. Half of the eighty ministers, including the prime minister, were replaced, while 46 out of 157 regional party secretaries lost their jobs. Over time, this initial burst of bloodletting was repeated until the new men in charge, while of different factions, had entirely ousted the old Brezhnevite/Stalin group.

References to different views became legitimate in the USSR. The word "pluralism" was accepted by Gorbachev. By 1990 the differences had become sufficiently wide to be openly canvassed. Not only were there national parties in the various republics but there appeared to be four tolerated factions, or protoparties. These were the social patriots (or as one article called them, the national statists), the liberal democrats of various kinds, the supporters of the center (i.e., Gorbachev and his supporters), and finally the extreme right, who supported Pamiat' and so Russian chauvinism and possibly a semifascist program. This evolution took place over five years.[3]

The shift toward open factions and so to parties speeded up from 1988 onward. At first the debate was around Stalin. The newspaper *Sovetskaia Belorussiia* was chided by an author in *Izvestiia* (10 March 1988) for its denigration of those who had been rehabilitated. The author explicitly attacked Stalin and those who continued to support him, even though their support might be hedged around with expedient qualifications.

The most startling evidence of early open factional dispute was in the series of attacks on the newspaper *Sovetskaia Rossiia*, which printed a fairly standard, almost Khrushchevite defense of Stalin by the now notorious Nine Andreeva (13 March 1988). *Pravda* then attacked *Sovetskaia Rossiia* for printing Andreeva's letter and went further in attacking Stalin than had ever been done in the pages of the official party newspaper: Stalin not only knew of the crimes committed in his name, *Pravda* declared (5 April 1988), but actually organized them personally.[4] The message was clear: supporters of Stalin were responsible for the present misery and had to atone for their sins.

But the chief weapon of the other side was never countered or mentioned by *Pravda*.[5] The Andreeva letter had spent one whole page column arguing that the Jews were a reactionary nation and that Russians ought not to be ashamed of being nationalist. Trotsky had declared to a delegation of merchants that he was not a Jew but an internationalist, the letter thundered. Cosmopolitanism was not acceptable.

The target was clearly the other faction, which has Jews among its prominent supporters. At the same time, the letter represented an attempt to court popularity among the anti-Semitic intelligentsia and delegates to the party conference of June 1988. Articles in support of *Pravda* then appeared in various places, but the other side found an outlet in *Molodaia gvardiia*.

The disintegration of the elements of Stalinism has proceeded apace. It is these component parts that are now warring.[6]

The elements of the faction fight were fivefold. In the first place there was the role of Stalin; second was the question of Russian nationalism, and linked to it the matter of anti-Semitism; third was the issue of democracy and legality, and so the role of the Communist party in the political process; fourth was the nature of the economic reforms to be introduced; and finally, the question of privilege appeared as a crucial question at the Nineteenth Party Conference and at the first session of the Congress of People's Deputies.[7]

Logically, the demands for democracy, the elimination of privilege, and the full rehabilitation of all of Stalin's victims would lead to the abolition of the elite itself. They therefore cannot be conceded. Instead the elite has attacked corruption, rehabilitated all except Trotsky, and introduced a very limited form of elections. Thus far it has retained censorship while nominally suspending it. It has all but ensured that elected bodies will be dominated by the Communist party, although in many republics the popular fronts have won majorities. But whatever their complexion, the renovated soviets have an elitist, antiworker majority.[8]

The differences over democracy are, at root, almost certainly over the extent to which concessions can be made to the workers. Hence the importance of the abolition of privilege. If bureaucratic privilege did not exist, the demand for democracy would lose some of its force and the elite would be somewhat more stable—but then they would not be an elite. The point is that the elite would prefer to obtain their privileges openly on the market using money, as in the West, where privilege is called wealth.

The fundamental question, then, is whether the USSR can be reformed without letting loose the revolutionary forces of the working class. Civil rights have not been extended to the workers. The strike laws are more restrictive than they were before. Genuine trade unions and workers' organizations have had to struggle to exist alongside the official unions. Labor books, controls over movement, and bureaucratic and police control over the worker have not changed at all.

The divisions in the elite, then, are really over the possibility of reform without letting the working-class genie out of the bottle. On the one hand, the relatively more Stalinist sections worry that the workers would act immediately once they were able, while on the other hand, the reformers think that they can contain the workers (if not, the game is not worth the candle). The Russian nationalists, who ally with the old-line Stalinists, effectively supply an alternative method of integration of the workers. They may be permitted to take power if the elite finds that they have no other solution.[9]

The terminology of the Soviet intelligentsia is confused. They prefer to call the conservatives right-wing and themselves, or the supporters of reform, left-wing. It has been an article of faith of many in the East that the political divisions there were different from the traditional right–left differences. This has never been true. On the contrary, the real reason that such a view could be put forward was that the reform movement in the East could not admit its right-wing credentials. Today the left is much more identifiable in Western terms.[10]

Nonetheless, the reform movement, many of whose best-known representatives would find themselves on the right of most Christian Democratic parties or even the American Republican party, persists in seeing itself as being on the left. It has to be said that the result has been a great deal of confusion on the left in Western countries, not to speak of the traditional constituency of the left in the USSR.[11]

The Ligachev–Yeltsin Rivalry

In November 1987 Boris Yeltsin was removed as the Moscow party secretary and replaced by Lev Zaikov, who himself lost out in September 1989. Yeltsin was obviously not just representative of himself, or else he would not have had the power to speak out and the ability to enforce rules, as he did with his staff at the Moscow party. Indeed, that Gorbachev attacked Yeltsin so strongly and that the whole Central Committee session devoted to the attack on Yeltsin took on a 1930s style demonstrated both that Yeltsin represented a more general threat and also that little had fundamentally changed within the party. That Yeltsin should have been declared bureaucratic, a supporter of the Black Hundreds, an ultraleftist, a bonapartist, an adventurist, vain, and personally ambitious may be ludicrous in itself, but it is an indication of the weakness of the dominant grouping that it had to eject someone who pointed to their failure, and yet retained his services in a subordinate post. The end result, however, was a pyrrhic victory, for it was Ligachev who was demoted and Yeltsin who became the leader of the main opposition, which secured the majority of seats in the elections in the RSFSR, so indicating that Yeltsin and his faction, unlike Ligachev or Gorbachev, had a popular mandate.

Yeltsin remained a member of the Central Committee and was elected to the Congress of People's Deputies with an 89 percent vote in his favor. Meanwhile, a Central Committee commission was set up specifically to investigate his views. The opposing factions tried to control him after November 1987, but failed to halt his progress, ironically, because their very attack on him created support for him.[12]

Yeltsin quickly became the standard bearer of the new liberal platform. But the differences with Gorbachev appeared more and more to be ones of tactics and speed rather than of final aim, inasmuch as Yeltsin by 1989–90 represented a particular group within the Soviet elite that wanted a radical market reform. The one issue on which he clearly differed from the leadership was the question of privilege, which was extensively discussed at the Nineteenth Party Conference. In an interview during the election campaign of March 1989, he declared again that he was against privilege but in favor of differentiation of incomes. He also stated that the standard of living ought to be the first priority of the regime; to that end, the arms and space programs ought to be slashed. He also favored devolution of power to the republics, which would be sovereign except in specific areas. He stood for cooperatives. In other words, he wanted private enterprise to be extended, but he could not put it in those words at that time, since he remained subject to the normal controls over individuals in the USSR. In 1989, during his trip to the United States, he praised Wall Street and visited Ronald Reagan, making his orientation clearer. By 1990 he was the main opposition leader, with a right-wing and populist program that included attacks on both the KGB and privilege.

On the other hand, Ligachev, who sustained a series of demotions over the years, led a more traditional Stalinist grouping. When Yeltsin himself, and others such as Gavriil Popov and Nikolai Shmelev, openly declared themselves to be in favor of a full market (i.e., capitalism), Ligachev called for brakes to be applied and talked of the gains of socialism. In real language, he was calling for the maintenance of the status quo, with limited change.

That the two opposing factions should have shown themselves through two personalities is not accidental, under conditions where both factions and parties were banned. The whole tendency over five years has been one of a systematic shift toward the market and so toward capitalism, with Stalinist reformers such as Ligachev gradually shifting toward a more reformist orientation while the liberals become increasingly liberal.

As the veneer of Marxism is discarded, the real nature of Soviet politics is being revealed. Under Stalin, it was possible to use Marxist vocabulary to mask a policy that was fundamentally chauvinist. Since in the different republics local nationalism cannot be used except in a corrupt form, anti-Semitism was employed. Indeed, the only link among all the far right-wing groups throughout the USSR is anti-Semitism. Just as Yeltsin appealed to antielitist and egalitarian sentiments among the workers, so the old-line Stalinists could use nationalism and anti-Semitism, which they supposed to be popular.

It can therefore be seen that the move from total repression to less repression required that the elite acquire a measure of popular support. A shift to the market, with unemployment and higher prices, had no popular appeal. The majority of the workers opposed privilege and expressed strongly egalitarian sentiments, while on the other hand nationalism had a strong appeal across the USSR, even if in a fragmented way. Hence the two popular forces were the nationalist successors to Stalinism and the direct demands of the workers, which a number of groups not represented in the Supreme Soviet attempted to express. These latter forces were either repressed or marginalized as far as possible, using the force of the state.

The struggle had taken on a three-cornered form by 1990. On one side stood the old bureaucratic elite who used chauvinism and anti-Semitism to secure popular support when possible, while on the other side the liberals tried to achieve some support through their anti-Stalin, rule-of-law, and pro-intelligentsia measures. Thus, it is not surprising that Gorbachev was forced to take on the role of an executive president. There was no real popular support for the market, although various opinion polls in the West purported to show a declining opposition. Gorbachev was really left with only two polarized alternatives by the end of 1989. Either he had to use force to introduce the market or he had to adopt a directly repressive approach, combined with an element of nationalism and anti-Semitism and cosmetic egalitarianism. Thus, he was faced with the need to use force whichever solution he adopted.

The third possibility, that of turning to a radical left alternative, was of course ruled out, since that would mean the abolition of the elite itself; yet, it is the ghost haunting the regime. The demands of the working class for self-management and the abolition of the elite were constantly refracted through the programs of the different political groups. The liberals had a populist leader,

Yeltsin, who opposed privilege without stressing that he did not oppose market privilege. The Ligachev "social patriot" bloc opposed the market and its emotive demands for a rise in prices and unemployment.

The only real question was whether enough workers could be persuaded to support either of the two elite poles, permitting a shift to a parliamentary-style democracy. That question remained open until 1990. Workers did vote for the two blocs in the elections in the Russian Federation, but they continued to strike and put forward economic and political demands that ran counter to the premises of a parliamentary system.

It is now possible to discuss the nature of the factions and parties that are supporting Gorbachev in more detail. Gorbachev himself would not be there if he did not head a coalition.

The Nature of the Soviet Elite and Its Factions

During the period of the Stalin purges a new Soviet elite replaced the former revolutionaries, bourgeois specialists, tsarist officials, and the majority of the officials recruited between 1917 and 1935; the new elite sought stability in socialism in one country. The specific feature of the new elite was that it had the function of control through discipline and repression. In principle the bureaucratic apparatus and its controlling group, here called the elite, administer and so organize the economy and the state. This new group saw its function somewhat differently: it was to administer the economy through the state apparatus. The purges had the function of installing this group in power, although they could not in fact fulfill the function of controlling the economy through command alone. As a result an elite came into being that was a mixture of those whose nature was one of command and discipline and those who saw campaigning, cajoling, bargaining, and deception as the means of control.

The problem for the elite is that while discipline and persuasion have had their purposes, both have clearly failed to ensure stability. Although both views may be held by one person at different times, in fact the two attitudes have been represented by different individuals and institutions. What appears to have happened under Gorbachev is that wings of both groupings coalesced in the face of a common danger. The secret police and the army are seldom advocates of democracy or simple persuasion, but a part of them recognized that the Brezhnev approach of stability through commands from on high had failed. On the other hand, part of the secret police and the party apparatus, supporting the previous status quo, preferred apparent stability, until the deluge came on them. Some leader like Gorbachev was bound to emerge, if not in 1985, then a few years later and with even more furor.

Socially, the factions have to be described as deriving from the purges as outlined above. In other words, the elite is driven to control through discipline today as much as during the purge years, but it no longer has effective instruments simply because the economy is no longer what it was. (This aspect is described below.) Ideally, in an administered, controlled, or command economy the center wants to control everything in a manner that ensures perfect knowledge and perfect implementation. Stalin tried, but failed, to achieve this. His apparatus, however, lives on with its utopian object of centralized control. It is not simply a goal, it is built into the Stalinized party. Since its commands are not obeyed, the logic of the system is to increase the degree of centralization, discipline, and control. On the other hand, the bureaucrats on the spot—the managers, the engineers, the local party secretaries—perceive the meaninglessness of the centralized commands and hence demand greater decentralization, bargaining, and aspects of democracy. In principle, it has always been in the interests of the elite to introduce the market to ensure their own stability as a social group; but at the same time it has always been against their interests to introduce the market in fact, since that would destabilize the whole system. This contradiction of the system has been ever-present and impossible to resolve. Hence there have always existed those whose function has been to repress, discipline, and control from above, and those whose function has been to cajole and persuade. The latter have become more important as the former have become progressively more counterproductive, but the controllers are still needed and will continue to be needed until there is either a market economy or a socialist economy. The economy cannot simply run on persuasion; discipline and control are also required from time to time.

It may be seen that the nature of the repressive or controlling faction changes over time. At one time it was Stalin, then Molotov and the "antiparty group," then the Shelepin group, whose successors exercised some influence under Brezhnev, then Ligachev. Since Ligachev fell, the mantle has passed to leaders who no longer bother to affect a Marxist vocabulary. Their attitude is a concomitant of their occupational position of control, which clearly has been changing over time. As the advocates of the market have become more and more strident over the years, the controllers have become continually more market-oriented. They realize that although their exact function may be removed, their position in the elite need not be disturbed. But they are more aware—precisely because of their position, whether it is in the secret police or the MVD, or in a major ministry—that any change could be dangerous to the system as a whole because it would alter the position of the majority in a deleterious way. The extreme elements of this faction constitute a kind of lumpen-bureaucracy, people who are corrupt, perform extreme functions of control, or are afraid of any change lest they lose their positions.

Such people were the sort dismissed at the start of the Gorbachev regime. At the top they were typified by Kunaev, Romanov, and Grishin; at the lower levels, they are the heads of the retail stores and distribution network. The old Stalin supporters are part of this grouping both because they are in favor of repression and because they are corrupt, although these two aspects may not be characteristic of the same person at one time. They are a dying breed not only because they are old and cannot be replaced, but also because their methods have failed. Hence, they are only left with mechanisms of self-preservation, which become ever more repulsive, not to say bizarre, such as Pamiat'.

The contrary faction, that of the bureaucratic persuaders and ultimately the marketeers, has grown increasingly militant and demanding over time. Since the economic managers are not socialist, they can see only a market solution to an increasingly ossified economy, in a world that looks only to a market. The intelligentsia prefer the market because they fondly imagine that they would be better off within a market, as indeed their upper elements would be. They wrongly identify the market with democracy. Whatever the reasons, this faction also consists of different elements: the economic managers, the intelligentsia, and the section of the elite most concerned about the economic decay visible around them.

Nonetheless, there is reason to believe that there are individuals who do not see the system as reformable from above. Clearly this camp will increase as Gorbachev is forced to repress those who want more change while continuing ostensibly to campaign for change. The genuine left could not be in favor of the market, in the way that Yeltsin does indeed stand for the market. It is no answer to say that the wages of some workers will be raised to compensate for the price rises, still less that ultimately the standard of living will rise. The immediate effect is to make the intelligentsia better off and the workers worse off in practically every respect. The touchstone of the left is its attitude to elite control and the privilege that goes with it. In this regard as well, Yeltsin can be seen to be more populist than left-wing. He may be against the special shops, hospitals, holiday homes, transport, and housing for the elite, but these are the automatic concomitant of the exclusive access to the surplus product in the society. The import of what Yeltsin and others are demanding is that direct privileged access be replaced by differences in income as a means of privilege. On the one hand, sections of the elite want to abolish privilege in favor of the market, while on the other, the governing elite is paralyzed lest it lose its privileges and gain nothing.

The Nature of the Party and Political Differences

It was no accident that when Gromyko proposed Gorbachev for general secretary he asserted that Gorbachev was a party man to the core. Gromyko stressed this precisely because those credentials were in doubt. Gorbachev was certainly a longstanding member of the party, but not of its inner core; thus he was ideally suited to reform the ossified apparatus.[13] Although he has directly removed a large number of his opponents, and continues to remove them, not least through the process of guided elections, it is in the nature of the party apparatus that it will not like constant purging of positions.

Of course, he could only perform in this manner if had the support of more than top parts of the party. Clearly, he had the support of members of the Politburo and the Secretariat, but even if he had a majority, that would not be enough to permit him to behave as he did. He must have had the support of the KGB, and with that, dossiers documenting the corruption of important officials that could be used as needed.

By 1990 Gorbachev had established a Politburo much more of his own choosing, and large sections of the party apparatus had been dismissed or reorganized. Nonetheless, the differences between the controllers and the administrative parts of the apparatus have remained, making for a state of tension within the Communist party itself.

Gorbachev could not continue to try to please both factions, so he reversed his line. His 1990 economic plan went back to the old style of "planning." He tried to ban strikes. He sent troops to the republics. But this balancing act only made sense on the basis that the reforms would proceed after a temporary retreat. The conflicting forces to which Gorbachev is subject are beyond the control of the Soviet elite. Gorbachev was compelled to retreat ultimately because of the resistance of the workers. Even the nationalist movements in Lithuania and the other republics can be seen as a way out for local elites, who would otherwise be threatened by their workers. But Gorbachev must go forward if he is to preserve the economy from total disintegration. Return to repression or movement forward to the market are his only options, and yet both ways threaten increasing instability.

Just as the British decolonized gradually by finding a suitable collaborator and a social group to whom they could devolve local power while retaining ultimate power, so the Soviet elite need to find popular leaders and allies among the population.[14] That will only happen gradually. The British succeeded, when they did, by defeating the most militant sections resisting colonial rule and incorporating the moderate elements. This involved a process of trial and error. Yeltsin's mistake was to think that movement had to proceed, when in fact there is no clear path at all, just a process of trial, error, and hope. But Yeltsin realized that only a bold and immediate form of action had any hope of success, and hence decided to precipitate events. He evidently hoped that such a move would contain an unstoppable momentum and the seeds of its own solution. He failed, as he had to fail, because the elite were afraid of the consequences of such an action. Yeltsin was almost certainly wrong in believing that the system could be reformed without major upheavals, or indeed that it could be successfully reformed at all.

The Secret Police

The problem with the bureaucratic apparatus is that it is unable to enforce its will without the operation of the instruments of repression, the secret police and the army, and hence it must always be allied with one or both of those institutions. On the other hand, the secret police is quite capable of reforming the party apparatus from top to bottom. In the present context, then, when the system is in evident crisis, only the secret police can act to maintain the system.

Gorbachev has never hesitated to demand increased discipline, a favorite policy of the secret police. True, their more usual slogan is "vigilance," a word much employed by Chebrikov, but no one could expect the secret police to be anything other than hard disciplinarians. At the same time, they are realists and know that they cannot perform their own function in a declining economy with rising discontent. They need reasonable economic and social conditions to be successful, and these are absent. Logically, they have turned to a solution that is not pure force, and so to leaders who know how to combine force with economic and social change. The KGB does not know the solution, but it does know the urgency of the problems. It should also be noted that the KGB is not spared the general factionalism within the society. By 1990 the general perception of the close relation between the secret police and Gorbachev was such that even Quentin Peel of the *Financial Times* described the "co-ordinated Gorbachev offensive against conservatives" as bearing "the hallmarks of a campaign co-ordinated by Mr. Gorbachev's allies in the KGB."[15]

It is indeed of some importance that the secret police are playing such a new role. Under Stalin they ruled, but always commanded by Stalin (the party was entirely secondary, if not tertiary). The direction of labor required an apparatus of force, necessarily of a hierarchical kind, but directed to a civilian purpose. The role of the secret police was one of ensuring that the economy continued functioning through whatever means. Patently this form of an economy has a limited life and it is not possible to revive it today, nor is it being revived.

The secret police have now emerged in an entirely new form.[16] Through their command over the apparatus of information and their ability to cut through the formalities of a bureaucratized society, they have an unrivaled ability to understand and direct Soviet society. In the time of Stalin they were subject to the elite in formation, personified by Stalin, whereas today the situation is very different. The KGB personnel, their numerous part-time assistants, and their informants constitute an integral part of the society. In one sense no one is outside their network, so that the secret police is the society itself. Only certain persons have specific full-time security tasks, but these same people are integrated into the society in a way that no other secret police has ever been. Outside of the USSR such a secret police would not be effective since it would lack the instruments given it by the nature of the society—instruments such as deportation from towns, dismissal from jobs, eviction from homes, removal of qualifications, and the possibility of virtually total control over communications. The importance of this brief recital of the powers of the KGB over the society is to explain the meaning of their coming to power. Today they are not just the instrument of the elite, they have become its governing section. If the secret police is part of the society, its full-time personnel are in great measure a part of the elite in the USSR. They constitute its praetorian guard.

The praetorian guard is now in power for the same reasons that gave it power in ancient Rome: a declining society has no other way of ensuring the continuance of the ruling group. Clearly, the analogy must not be pressed too far. The real point is that the faction in power is there because of the support of the secret police. Why has this happened and what are the consequences? The reason already given—the decline of the system—requires amplification. The fundamental reason lies in the particular role of the secret police in ensuring discipline and order in the society. Previously that function was applied to all persons in the society, whereas today their discipline is really over labor as opposed to the elite and the intelligentsia. They too are supposed to perform their allotted tasks, but if they fail, they can be dismissed. Thus, from the point of view of the intelligentsia, the security organs are moving in the right direction, away from themselves and against labor.

Gorbachev represents the section of the elite and the intelligentsia who want to ensure their own stability and rising standard of living by changing the relations with the workers in production. Ultimately this would mean the market, introduced in the only manner in which it can be introduced, through direct repression with ostensible democracy. The secret police are the only source of power in the Soviet system that is capable of managing the kind of change the elite needs.

On the other hand, it might be objected that there have been a number of incidents indicating the discontent of the secret police with what has been occurring. That is true. Chebrikov spoke out against dangerous phenomena that could lead to threats to the system. Again, it is evident that the secret police will not look with favor on strikes, demonstrations, or demands to introduce a Western-style capitalist democracy without safeguards for themselves and the elite. Hence, Gorbachev has insisted on the need to proceed through phases. Interpreted, this means that he is only in favor of change if it can be properly controlled.

The Soviet Ruling Group

The term "elite" has been used hitherto to describe the ruling group. Historically, various categories have been used for this purpose: caste, class, bureaucracy, bureaucratic elite, and nomenklatura are all terms that have been employed. Trotsky used *caste* and *bureaucracy*, although he recognized the inadequacies of the terms. He opposed the usage of the category of *class* on the ground that the ruling group was a parasitic section of the working class; in other words, the ruling group had not yet separated itself out sufficiently from the workers to constitute a class.

A number of prerequisites must exist before the term "class" can be employed. In the first place, it is not enough for workers or rulers to have particular positions in the social structure of a given society for them to constitute a class; they must form a collectivity. The structure is defined by the form of the relationship to the extraction of the surplus product. *A class, then, is a collectivity that has a particular relation to the extraction of the surplus product.* In turn, it is this form that provides the dynamic toward the formation of the collectivity.

In other words, one starts from the proposition that the USSR is part of a world in transition away from capitalism. Capitalism was overthrown in the USSR, but the country failed to move to socialism. The social relations were and remain in a state of flux. The social relations needed time to gel. While Trotsky appears to have been wrong in his time frame (he expected the ruling group to be overthrown after the war), the instability of the society has been a permanent feature of the social structure. The use of extreme methods of coercion is always a manifestation of lack of social integration. Put differently, the method of extraction of the surplus product has never had a viable form in the USSR. The elite has consequently controlled the surplus product to a limited degree only. The system is therefore partly driven by the elite's need to become a class. To change into a class, the ruling group needs to establish full control over the surplus product and hence over the extractive process itself.

The instrument by which the elite has constructed its control is the administrative-command apparatus or, as it has been known, "the plan." The essential point, of course, is that the plan has never actually functioned in the manner intended. The elite, therefore, has never been able to obtain the economic results it needed for its own reproduction or for the viability of the system itself. The reason goes back to labor and the lack of control over the labor process, which will be discussed elsewhere.

The ruling group, thus, has an apparent means of extraction of the surplus and thereby exists as a ruling group, but it is not able to have the degree of control over that surplus that is necessary for a class in a mode of production. The consequences of this contradiction within the elite are profound.

In the first place, the elite lacks the coherence required to establish a collectivity. Indeed it lacks any forum or any means of internal communication. Furthermore, the interpersonal elite relation is brutally competitive precisely because of the instability of the position of each individual, consequent on the instability of the elite itself. At the topmost levels this point is obvious, particularly under Gorbachev, where so many have been dismissed.

Objections that, since elite offspring tend to remain in the elite, membership of the elite is stable, are wide of the mark. The incoherence of the elite makes for a smooth transition between the intelligentsia and the elite. It is not clear who should be included in one group and who in the other. The definition of the elite may be further refined by including all those who are in charge of others as their only activity. The intelligentsia, in turn, can be regarded as those who are in charge of others but also alienate their labor power. Children of the elite would tend to remain in either the intelligentsia or the elite, but there is no guarantee that they will stay in the elite itself. While they may obtain a graduate education, they also need to be promoted to particular positions (as factory directors, party-state functionaries, etc.). Two factors militate against automatic entry to these positions. First, the numbers involved have grown relatively slowly since the time of Stalin, in comparison with the numbers in the intelligentsia. Second, the constant economic and political problems of the USSR have forced the elite to use competence as the main criterion for entry into an elite position.

In the second place, as already mentioned, the elite is constantly in search of some means of establishing full control over the surplus product. Ultimately this could only be the market, but in its absence, the elite has tried a series of expedients that have established the nature of the system itself. The purges, the atomization of the society, the constant reorganizations of the apparatus of control, and surrogate forms of the market are all means of buttressing the position of the elite. In other words, the history of the USSR under Stalinism has been a history of the vain attempts of the elite to eternalize itself.

The advantage of the use of the word "elite" is that it permits a description of the instability and incoherence of the ruling group as well as its drive toward its own transformation into a class. The smoothness of the transition between the social groups as compared with the situation in a class society militates in favor of a category that takes account of this aspect of reality.

The term "class," conversely, is inapplicable unless the criteria for the use of the word are purely descriptive. The term "elite" is not correct either if used in the sense employed by Pareto. Trotsky used the word "bureaucracy" instead. The problem with this term is that it requires some qualification. Clearly not everyone who is in the bureaucratic apparatus is either in control of others or privileged. Clerks, typists, and the like are ordinary workers. For that reason some have used the term "bureaucratic elite." The word "caste" is obviously wrong in that there is no real similarity with countries that have had a caste system. The reason for the use of the terms "bureaucracy" and "caste" is that they imply that the ruling group is really a parasitic part of the working class, and so remains confined by the momentum of the original October Revolution. Such categorization does not provide any understanding of the dynamic of the regime.

There are two reasons why there is no term in the English language that can be used to describe the ruling group in the USSR. First, the group, as we have argued, is in transition and so has no clear-cut form. Second, the system itself is unique. Its uniqueness is shown by the fact that it is not a mode of production: that is to say, production relations in the USSR do not facilitate production itself, in the context of the contemporary world (capitalist relations are clearly less inefficient). Worse still, the contradictions in the production relations themselves can reach a level of intensity such that negative production can actually result. Where the product itself is so defective that it becomes a symbol of the system's inefficiency, the system itself can only be regarded as having a limited life. Precisely because it is not a mode of production, its social relations become

NONPOLITICAL POLITICS OF THE ELITE   63

highly ambiguous, reflecting the contradictions at the heart of the society. The ruling group, therefore, can only be described in terms of its own contradictory nature, which propels it to metamorphose into a class.[17] Its contradiction is that of the system, in that the elite exists in an organizational position over the workers without the necessary means of control.

In all modes of production there is a means of enforcing the needs of the ruling group. Under capitalism, unemployment and commodity fetishism (or so-called market forces) act as that means. Under feudalism, the serf is part of a manorial system in which he accepts his lot. In the USSR the worker regards the elite as a usurper to be thwarted to advantage whenever possible. With neither money nor unemployment, the worker cannot be compelled to work as required. Since everyone in the system and indeed every part of the system is in a similar position, the parts of the system constantly threaten the whole. The elite in one sense are engaged in a permanent juggling act to prevent the system from disintegration. That indeed is their function.

The Soviet elite are rent by the systemic contradiction that they possess their position by virtue of their control over the organization of the economy but they cannot fulfill that position except by abdicating it. The rational method of dealing with elite control over the so-called plan is democratically to extend decision making to all those affected, so ensuring both the rationality of the plans and the probability of implementation. Such an extension of democracy means abolishing both privilege in consumer goods and the special access to the means of control over the surplus product. Since such a move is ruled out as long as the elite do not want to be the first ruling group in history to abdicate without a struggle, they are doomed to an unequal struggle with the "planning mechanism."

One method of avoiding the consequences of the nature of the economy is to turn to the so-called illegal economy—in other words, to use private enterprise. The elite do in fact employ private enterprise for their own consumption and obtain the required money and goods through what amounts to another form of private enterprise. The story of Uzbekistan and its transformation into a personal fiefdom, with Brezhnev's son-in-law exercising an important influence, may have been manipulated for particular purposes but it is nonetheless illustrative of the vast scale on which so-called corruption has existed in the USSR.[18] Corruption in the context of the USSR cannot just mean rubles: a few more rubles buy little. Thousands of rubles may buy various things, but even then, certain things cannot be bought without the secret police wondering what was happening to enrich the particular individual. Apartments and cars are registered items. Even the storage of thousands of rubles is a problem. That is why petty and not-so-petty crooks require protection. At the higher levels, the need for money is much more a question of buying support, converting rubles into real money (gold or foreign currency), and acquiring certain services. The elite are able in this manner to reduce their own insecurity to something more acceptable. Money can be transmitted to children or used when in disgrace or defecting to the West. Of course, there are problems associated with this latter course of action, but it does establish some means of defense against the insecurity that all members of the elite suffer.

The real point is that the elite promote what is called corruption. They cannot do otherwise, given their own insecurity and individual lack of power. They promote it individually, while collectively, as an elite, they oppose it, for if corruption were to become widespread it could destroy the system and hence the basis on which they exist. To the extent that they utilize this primitive capitalist sphere, it might appear that they have less to fear from the market, but that is not the case. A capitalist economy would have no use for an underground sphere of financial and other services. They would be legalized and become part of the world economy. The result would be that the primitive forms now existing would be driven to the wall, because they are fundamentally dependent on the deficiencies of the existing system. This sphere of a limited operation of the law of value is dependent on the instability of the overall system. It acts to support the elite and yet to destabilize them. Since 1985 Gorbachev and his group have been attacking corruption hard, not because they are necessarily incorruptible, but because they have the information on their enemies and, what is just as important, they have the power to use it. Where there is a separate sphere of influence, it is easier to establish a personal form of control. Hence the republics, and for that matter the ministries, have been particularly vulnerable.

The high degree of centralization, the Russianization of the country, and the atomization of the population can be seen then as necessary policies of the Stalinist elite. They have ensured the integration of the country in the past. Today these policies are counterproductive and thus the elite is itself disintegrating along with the system and country.

Characteristics of the Soviet Elite

The Soviet elite consists of those in charge of the administration of the country. It therefore includes those who run the enterprises, institutes, and other economic, educational, and political institutions. The party–state apparatus is necessarily part of it, as are the higher officer corps of the army and the secret police. The higher intelligentsia of academicians, professors, and senior research personnel are also part of this group.

Another approach, that of orthodox Sovietologists like Mervyn Matthews,[19] for instance, reduces the elite to little more than perhaps a few hundred thousand individuals. For them, only the very top managers of enterprises are in the elite, only the immediate decision makers are included. On that basis, of course, the executives of companies of all kinds in the West would also be excluded from any ruling class. The definition employed is effectively one of political decision making of a very narrow kind. It is not a socioeconomic definition and really sheds very little light on the real social relations of the USSR. On the contrary, it obfuscates the nature of the Soviet elite by identifying it only with the higher party–state echelons. Yet another approach is one in which the Soviet elite is identified with the so-called *nomenklatura*,[20] which is the list of positions that the center retains the right of filling. While the elite and the nomenklatura overlap, they are not identical. The term "nomenklatura" cannot be regarded as a theoretical description or category applicable to the USSR, since it simply describes the practice of the Soviet elite of supervising appointments to elite positions. Nonetheless, it does have the merit of including much of the stratum in the elite itself.

In 1985 there were some 9.297 million "leaders" in the USSR according to Soviet statistics. Of that figure, 45 percent had higher education and 41 percent had technical, specialized education.[21] With a total 130.3 million persons employed, this represents 7.1 percent who are in the elite. The figure does not include the KGB or the army officers, which could bring the proportion up to around 8.5 percent of those employed. It is also to be noted that the numbers of specialists grew from 20.779 million in 1980, and that of the elite from 8.84 million in 1980. The ratios were then 42.5 percent and 39.8 percent of the elite to the intelligentsia or specialists, including technicians. Clearly, social mobility is declining: 55 percent of the managers are over the age of 40, but only 41 percent of the specialists are over the age of 40. In sexual terms, the division is startling: women constitute 60 percent of the specialists but only half a million of the heads of plants and institutions. A further one million are in charge of various subdivisions in the enterprises. Even if we take the two figures combined, we find that only 16.1 percent of those in charge of others at some significant level are women.

Whereas before and immediately after the Second World War, the elite included many without postschool education, by 1985, 7.973 million of the 9.297 million in the category of leading bureaucrats had such education, and more important, only 4.177 million of those with higher education actually entered the elite. The figures for 1980 show that only 29.4 percent of those with higher education entered the elite, whereas in 1940 potentially they could all do so. In 1980, 80.7 percent of the elite had postschool education and 40.1 percent had higher education. In 1985 the process had gone further and 44.4 percent of the elite had higher education but only 27.8 percent of those with higher education could enter the elite.

Two processes are at work. One has been the increasing monopolization of elite positions by those with postschool education (increasingly, higher education); and second, the decline in the proportion of those with higher education who are able to enter the elite. Since the proportion of the intelligentsia in the work force is not very different from the proportion of the age group able to enter higher education, it would be expected that the intelligentsia would become a self-perpetuating group, squeezing out potential entrants from below but finding it harder to enter the elite. In other words, the intelligentsia is finding itself in an increasingly more difficult position, threatened from below and from above. With a quarter of those with higher education entering the elite and the latter being rather older, it might be expected that a substantial proportion of the intelligentsia have a real prospect of entering the elite. Since, however, the elite is not expanding as fast as the intelligentsia, the question then remains whether the elite offspring do not monopolize entry into the elite themselves. Clearly, such a tendency would be bound to show itself as the numbers of those with higher education expanded quickly and the total in the elite rose only slowly. This has been coped with in large measure through the numbers going into the category of scientific workers: 1.5 million.[22]

In the elite itself there are divisions. In the first place, it is bound to be divided structurally by occupation. There are some 4.2 million persons in industry, construction, transport, and communications. On the other hand, there are 831,000 in the bureaucratic apparatus and finance. The remainder, in health, education, distribution, social services, etc., would be in a lower category, with less influence given the priority accorded to industry. The million or so who run the farm sector are in a still lower category, given their isolation. Those in the army and in the secret police are not known, although the figure must run close to a million.

Various studies have shown the tendency for the elite to be Russian,[23] with concessions to a local elite in the various republics and autonomous regions of the USSR.

In summary, the Soviet elite is largely male, over forty, and Russian, which indeed is what could be expected. It is also highly educated and becoming more so over time.

Predictably, there has been no real discussion on the Soviet elite in the Soviet literature, so there is insufficient detail on its membership, behavior, and constitution. The attacks on privilege have emphasized one aspect of the elite. There is, as is well known (although it is carefully concealed from view), a hierarchical allocation of privileges to members of the elite encompassing special shops, medical facilities, holidays, travel abroad, access to information, and in general all goods and services. This is indicative of the hidden nature of the allocation of part of the surplus product, and of the absence of money as a universal equivalent. Rubles alone will not purchase these goods or services.

One peculiarity of this form of elite remuneration is that it is attached to the particular post. The member of the elite loses his privileges if he loses his job, although he may recoup some of them if he is transferred to a job in a lower level of the elite. This adds to the insecurity of the individuals in the elite and therefore to their desire to go over to market forms of privilege. The hidden nature of privilege does not mask its very obvious existence, but it has prevented the population from knowing the exact forms and from putting forward concrete demands for its abolition.

Probably the most detailed discussion of privilege and the effect of its attachment to the post is in Boris Yeltsin's autobiography.[24] Yeltsin points out that the hierarchical nature of privilege makes holders of elite posts adapt to the demands of their superiors or peers lest they lose those privileges. Gorbachev, he points out, refused to discuss privileges (in the case of the "dacha") at the First Congress of People's Deputies. Thereby he nailed his mast to the defense of privilege. It appears that Gorbachev proposed a rise in Politburo salaries and had a new dacha built for himself. The extent of privilege revealed by Yeltsin is quite large, including a not inconsiderable retinue of personnel to serve the particular individual and his family. Of course, Politburo privileges are more extensive than those attached to generals, ministers, and other state functionaries.

Much has been made of the compilation of letters to *Pravda* on 13 February 1986 which, among other things, called for the elimination of the special shops and other privileges. Indeed, there were even reports that some of these special elite shops were closed down (as mentioned by Yeltsin), but they were only changed in form. Members of the elite can get the same goods, but they now do so through a catalog and a system of ordering. Unlike other services in the USSR, this delivery system is efficient and quick; moreover, it allows the elite to dispense with an obvious target of envy, the special shops.

It is difficult to believe that the Soviet ruling group will be the first in history to abolish its own privileges. The question of privilege has been Yeltsin's own particular target, which he has used to very good effect. In the end, Yeltsin and others are actually saying that it is dangerous to flaunt the ill-gotten gains of the elite. The real meaning of the discussion around privilege is that the workers' hostility to the obviously privileged position of their leaders has to be given a focus, and an outlet. Yeltsin, the man who supported a stock exchange for the USSR, is the ideal lightning rod for an attack on privilege.

The Soviet Elite in the Context of History

The ruling group in the USSR is highly unstable both in the nature of its control and in its individual privileges. It needs to go over to the market, and so to capitalism, but it has been unable to do so from the day it was formed. It came into being through a historical accident, in that the bureaucratic elite of the 1920s was forced to proceed against private property to ensure its own safety. At the time, return to the market would have required repayment of the tsarist debts, compensation and perhaps even the return of property seized, return to the world market when the world depression made it impossible, and a direct confrontation with the workers and left opposition. The solution adopted was a compromise that has never worked. They nationalized all property while adopting forms of the market. They used the market's unequal forms of control and payment, but then had to use discipline, coercion, and commands as the means of administration over the economy. Surrogate market forms in the context of nationalization have force as their necessary concomitant. In other words, it was precisely those forms that led to the so-called administrative command economy and the purges.

Either there is a democratic form of control over the nationalized economy, and so genuine planning, or else there must be some form of compulsion to control the direct producers. Stalin, from this viewpoint, was a necessary result of the introduction of inequality and surrogate market forms into the Soviet economy. The elite could not control the economy in the period 1929–36. The logic of the system was that it return to NEP and the market, or else use a system of direct orders emanating from the center. Logically, that led to a squeeze on all intermediate layers between the top and the workers. In the end, the elite was completely subject to Stalin himself. Members who were not killed were reduced to complete subjection. The old layers of administrators were replaced with controllers, and the elite itself was recast.

It was only when the size and complexity of the economy reached a point where direction from the apparatus of force was not just counterproductive but also dangerous that the elite could emerge in group form rather than as personified by one man. It was Khrushchev's role to facilitate that transition. He removed the secret police from their position of control over the elite and from the conduct of the economy. He admitted the higher intelligentsia into the elite itself.

In the post-1953 period the elite has evolved into a social group that has largely merged with the a section of the intelligentsia. It no longer has to be concerned with its place in a market economy. The managers are increasingly competent while the administrators have become adept at running a crisis-ridden economy. They could transfer to a market economy with considerable skill, provided the conditions for such a transfer existed. It is true that the controlling section of the elite would have more trouble, but a solution could be found for them, given the will.

Notes

1. This point is also made by the Roy and Zhores Medvedev in their book *Khrushchev: The Years in Power* (New York: Columbia University Press, 1976). The crucial fact is that the old secret police was effectively cleaned out by Khrushchev, who not only killed its leaders but also placed the Komsomol leaders of the time in powerful positions over the secret police. Above all, the secret police lost the authority to hold anyone who belonged to the party, without the permission of the party itself.

2. In a *Pravda* interview with a worker running for election in the February 1990 local and regional elections (*Pravda*, 30 January 1990), it is made clear that the worker is the representative of a rare breed. The candidate does not want a special section of the elected body for workers, and he is constrained to state that he is against strikes.

3. To go back in time, a 1986 article in praise of A.A. Zhdanov (*Pravda*, 24 February 1986, back page) was a good illustration of the continued existence of the Stalin faction. In the article, Zhdanov's role in the postwar purges and cultural censorship is supported without being spelled out, not to speak of his prewar role in support of Stalin. Who could wish to revere such a monster? Again, the existence of Pamiat', the reactionary anti-Se-

mitic and ecological group, was another indication of a faction on high protecting its own supporters. It is no accident that Yeltsin was accused, by one of those denouncing him at the Central Committee meeting in November 1987, of being soft on Pamiat', which was described as a group of the Black Hundreds type, that is, reactionary and pogromist (*Pravda*, 16 November 1987). That Pamiat' could be so denounced in the presence of Ligachev suggests that he did not directly support it and that it represented a part of the party–state apparatus that was out of favor. In an interview in *Le Monde* (4 December 1987), Ligachev denounced the purges in no uncertain terms. He had been a supporter of Gorbachev's speech in November on the seventieth anniversary of the Russian Revolution, wherein Gorbachev attacked Stalin, but it appears that he is also critical of Stalin on his own account. Boris Kagarlitskii has described in some detail the battles that have occurred between what he correctly describes as the liberals and the conservatives over the composition of various bodies ("The Intelligentsia and the Changes," *New Left Review 164*, pp. 1–26).

Gorbachev mentioned four factions apart from himself in his speech on 18 February 1988 to the Central Committee plenum on education (*Pravda*, 19 February 1988). The supporters of so-called Marxism–Leninism are seen as supporters of Stalinism, and although Gorbachev cannot in fact attack Marxism–Leninism, he appears to come very close to doing so even while apparently praising Marxism in his speech. These are the so-called conservatives, Brezhnevites, and one-time Stalinists. Then, to his right are those he identifies as wanting capitalism, presumably including many economists who had expressed views that are not only procapitalist but of a rather primitive extreme right-wing variety. (See, for example, Nikolai Shmelev, "Novye trevogi," *Novyi mir*, April 1988, p. 171. Since Shmelev is the major liberal strategic economist, his views are very important.) This faction may have considerable support among managers. Gorbachev also spoke of those who called the reforms cosmetic. Such would certainly be the view of those on both the left and the right who want either capitalism or socialism. Finally, Gorbachev referred to a group of people who wished to go too fast, presumably those who supported Yeltsin. In fact these factions may be renamed as the old-line Stalinists, the right, the social democrats, and those who confusedly simply want change. Gorbachev almost certainly left out the groups allying themselves to working-class demands for a genuine socialism.

In an interview with Monty Johnstone, Roy Medvedev has accepted the general formulation of factional struggles as well as the difference between Yeltsin and Gorbachev in terms of speed of action while being united in opposing the old-line bureaucrats (*Marxism Today*, August 1988, pp. 14–17).

4. Still later, in *Nedelia* (11–17 April 1988, pp. 10–11), Bestuzhev-Lada argued that some one-eighth to one-sixth of the 25 million peasant families had been destroyed, or virtually so, as a result of collectivization. Since the 25 million families amounted to 150 million people, according to him, that meant that up to 25 million people were involved. He then said the Stalinist repressions of 1936–53 involved the same number of people. The actual number of people who were killed as a result of these repressions is still not known. The KGB have produced figures that are very much lower than these—but that could be expected. Until scholars are permitted access to the KGB files in their entirety, the true figures will not be known.

5. It was curious that newspaper accounts in the West ignored the anti-Semitism in the *Sovetskaia Rossiia* letter and the lack of any reply to it by the official organs. The British press and radio conspicuously mentioned only the Stalin question, and even a detailed article in the West German press did the same (*Die Zeit*, 15 April 1988, p. 13). Earlier, in *Pravda* (3 December 1987), Iakovlev denounced demagoguery and scapegoating and so, by implication, anti-Semitism.

6. The liberals have been able to use *Novyi mir* and a number of other literary journals, as well as economic journals such as *Voprosy ekonomiki* and *EKO*. On the other side, the Russian nationalists and anti-Semites have used *Literaturnaia Rossiia, Nash sovremmenik,* and *Molodaia gvardiia,* largely through their control of the Union of Russian Writers. The left cannot express itself except through duplicated sheets, but a distorted version of working-class demands comes through in the newspapers of the trade unions such as *Trud. Pravda* and *Sovetskaia Rossiia* have had different views depending on the editor. Until the dismissal of Viktor Afanas'ev as editor of *Pravda,* that newspaper expressed a balanced and nuanced view of the party apparatus; it printed the views of different factions within narrow limits. These two papers can be regarded as expressing the various attitudes of the factions on the Politburo.

7. Yeltsin raised the issue of privilege at the Nineteenth Party Conference, and Yevtushenko and others did so at the Congress of People's Deputies. Democracy was mentioned by Burlatskii, the editor of *Literaturnaia gazeta* and a former adviser to Khrushchev, who called for various forms of limited democracy in 1987. Multiple-candidate elections were introduced in 1989 and 1990. The Interregional Group then called for the elimination of Article 6 of the Constitution, which guaranteed the position of the Communist party. The democratic demands of the intelligentsia then went through a rapid evolution, partly because of the changes in Eastern Europe. The entire political evolution was toward the formation of a parliamentary-style democracy.

8. The election of Gavriil Popov in Moscow is instructive. Although Popov subsequently resigned from the party, and although the Moscow soviet even removed Marx's name from the square that had it, it would be mistaken to take these anticommunist gestures as evidence of genuine change. What they signal, rather, is the splintering of the elite, and the efforts of one section to challenge the power of the central apparatus. Gorbachev has been remarkably successful in introducing parliamentary-type reforms that in effect consolidated the regime, for the fact is that even the opposition in the Congress of People's Deputies and the Supreme Soviet basically supports the regime. And yet the USSR continues to disintegrate.

9. The elite is not only afraid of the working class, it fears that the nationalities and elements from the intelligentsia could open the way to disorder and possibly to the installation of a regime that would be a client regime of the West. Gorbachev has often spoken in favor of what he calls "the common European home," apparently meaning a kind of European Common Market in which the USSR would be a part. The vagueness of this aim is a true expression of Gorbachev's view. He is pragmatic and shifts according to the relative strength of the factions and the needs of the time. The racialism of the slogan is unconscious but nonetheless real. The Asiatic areas of the USSR are regarded as necessary dependencies. Nonetheless, the common European home is a capitalist home, and Gorbachev has to introduce the market to introduce the USSR into the "European home."

10. There is a whole range of groups, from anarcho-syndicalist to Marxist, that see themselves as being on the left. In June 1988, the club Democratic Perestroika held a meeting attended by 500 persons. The club put forward a number of demands related to the theses of the Nineteeenth Party Conference, some of which were reproduced in *Komsomol'skaia pravda* (7 June 1988, p. 1). These included the abolition of the privileges of the nomenklatura, i.e., the elite, the radical reconstruction of the KGB, and the right to freedom of movement. There were also demands not only for what amounts to a parliamentary system of elections but also for the founding of a National Economic Council of Labor Collectives in order "to draw workers into the real process of management." Since then, a Socialist party has been founded with an associated trade-union body. Additionally, the miners' councils are on the left, at least in terms of their programs (see

"Ekonomicheskaia platforma Soiuza trudiashchikhsia Kuzbasa," *Voprosy ekonomiki*, February 1990, p. 85).

11. In early 1990 Vladimir Kriuchkov, the head of the KGB, characterized the existing political groupings as "left-radicals and social democratic shades to openly nationalist, anticommunist, and even monarchist."

12. Until 1990, factions in the USSR were not yet open or able to function in a natural manner. They were officially banned and hence they had to take the form of spontaneous agreement and of individuals pushing for goals common to a group. The interesting question is that of the social groups represented by Ligachev and Yeltsin respectively. This has been clarified since by the evolution of the individuals, and most particularly by the evolution of the Communist party. A new group, Democratic Platform, established itself by the beginning of 1990, with Iurii Afanas'ev one of its main leaders. It was enraged by the failure of the February 1990 Central Committee Plenum to democratize the party and it considered splitting from the party, which it did, splitting itself in the process. Its leaders then effectively took power in a number of towns, especially in the Russian Republic.

13. See Archie Brown, "Gorbachev: New Man in the Kremlin," *Problems of Communism*, May-June 1985. The article is an exceptionally detailed and informative discussion of the life and career of the new leader in relation to the party.

14. The difference between Gorbachev and his mentor, former KGB chief and party general secretary Andropov, might amount to the judgment that Gorbachev is the poor man's Andropov. Unlike Andropov, he tried to be popular. But by 1989 his appeal had evaporated and the emptiness of his speeches was quite evident. While appearing reasonable, personable, even affable—anything but authoritarian—he also seemed to be blustering, with little to say. Immensely popular in the West, in the Soviet Union he is now considered a good export. Yeltsin claimed popularity purely because he stood up to Gorbachev and the bureaucratic apparatus. With fundamentally the same program, however, he too can only lose his support over time.

In spite of Gorbachev's failures, however, history will record the way in which he also succeeded. Although he failed miserably with the economy, politically he went far beyond what anyone could have imagined. At a time of extreme instability, he maneuvered successfully to introduce the forms of parliamentary democracy, winning a degree of political stability for the elite that had never before seemed possible. Even if these reforms are blunted, they cannot be reversed completely.

15. Quentin Peel, "What's to be done after bankruptcy?" *Financial Times*, 5 February 1990, p. 14.

16. W.R. Carson and R.T. Crowley, in *The New KGB* (Brighton, UK: Wheatsheaf, 1987), note the new power of the KGB under Gorbachev.

17. Indeed, possibly the best term that can be used is the hybrid term *proto-class*, but this is a clumsy, invented word. We have used "elite" simply because it is immediately recognizable as referring to a group that is in control without constituting a class.

18. "Kobry nad zolotom," *Pravda*, 23 January 1988, p. 3. The story of how the investigators went to discover the missing millions and tracked them down in the desert in Uzbekistan shows the lengths to which the elite has to go to hide their ill-gotten gains. More importantly, the article asserts that a considerable proportion of the government apparatus was involved in the nominally illegal system.

19. Mervyn Matthews, *Privilege in the Soviet Union: A Study of Elite Life-Styles* (London: Allen and Unwin, 1978).

20. Michael Voslensky, *Nomenklatura: Anatomy of a Soviet Ruling Class* (London: Bodley Head, 1984). In a book that is descriptive, although it uses the concepts of exploitation and surplus value, Voslenskii effectively identifies the nomenklatura with its innermost sanctum, the party secretariat and bureaus.

21. The figures here and below are taken from *Narodnoe khoziaistvo SSSR za 70 let* (Moscow, 1987), especially pp. 416–22.

22. Ibid., p. 62. In this entry the USSR boasts that it has one-quarter of all scientific workers in the world. This is certainly an exaggeration, although it might be such a figure as a proportion of all those in government-funded research establishments. In any event, it is a very large number.

23. See, for example, George Fischer, *The Soviet System and Modern Society* (New York: Atherton Press, 1968).

24. Boris Yeltsin, *Against the Grain* (New York: Putnam, 1990), especially pp. 127–37.

5

The Intelligentsia

Since it is part of the overall argument of this book that the intelligentsia are the group that has benefited most from the Gorbachev regime, it will be instructive to observe how the position of the intelligentsia has changed.

There were many more members of the intelligentsia in employment in 1987 than in 1941; 15,530,000 as opposed to close to one million. In addition, there is an intermediate layer of specialists, technicians of all kinds, numbering some 20 million.[1] As a result, they are a more powerful social group, particularly the writers, propagandists, and those closer and more important to the elite; but over time there has been a steady decline in the position of all sections of the intelligentsia against those holding manual jobs. Whereas a skilled worker in ferrous metallurgy might be earning around 400 rubles per month, an engineer or research worker could be earning as little as 150–200 rubles.[2] Indeed, semiskilled workers can earn more than those with university education.

Below the level of the elite are the specialists—some 23,347,000 in 1985, of whom 9,622,000 had higher education and 10,776,000 had technical education.[3] The difference in the figures for the intelligentsia and specialists gives the numbers of the intelligentsia in the elite and in the manual work force. There were some 4.1 million in the elite in 1985, and approximately half a million who have become skilled workers.[4]

We have already mentioned the relatively rapid rise in numbers in the intelligentsia relative to the numbers in the elite. In historical terms the picture is as follows: the crucial figure is that in 1941 there were only 909,000 persons with higher education in the economy, as opposed to 15 million in 1986. In parallel, the number of technical specialists rose from 1,492,000 to 19,600,00. With the work force today totaling some 130 million, the two groups combined constitute some 26.4 percent of the employed, compared with 3.9 percent in 1940. For those with higher education the increase has been from 1.5 percent to 11.5 percent of the employed. As discussed in the previous chapter, only 27.8 percent of those with higher education could enter the elite in 1985.

73

The Political Economy of the Intelligentsia

In the USSR the term "intelligentsia" is employed as a category to describe all those with higher education, whether they possess a diploma or not. It therefore includes academicians as well as ordinary engineers working in plants who receive a salary considerably below the average wage of around 200 rubles. Doctors and teachers, who also receive very low wages, are also part of the intelligentsia. Clearly, a better definition is required.[5]

The intelligentsia in the USSR is a social group that stands between workers and the elite. Its topmost layer is in the elite itself and indeed has played an increasing role within the elite. Then there are the 1.5 million research workers in the USSR (whose salaries were quickly raised by Gorbachev in May 1985). They work in institutes closely connected to some aspect of the economy and society. The functionalist role of the "scientific workers" in the USSR is part of the system. Even sociologists perform the immediately useful function of ameliorating the lot of the worker in order that he may perform better. The output of the higher educational institutions could not be absorbed by the enterprises or ministries, and hence graduate employment has been provided by a huge system of bureaucratic relief.

The layer of the intelligentsia that is just below the elite, the middle-level executives of the enterprises and institutes, is male and upwardly mobile. By contrast, doctors and teachers, who are at the bottom of the intelligentsia in pay and prestige, are very largely female. They approximate much more closely to workers, alienating their labor for defined periods of time, and without any control over others. This inferior position of women in the intelligentsia parallels their position in the elite and in the work force. While men are more directly involved in production or forms of control over others, women perform the function of dealing with the social services of the society. As social services have been neglected, women have had to accept poor remuneration, poor conditions of work, and poor job prospects.

The intelligentsia, then, cannot be regarded as a cohesive group. Yet they have tended to behave in a cohesive manner, although their viewpoints may be radically different—some want an authoritarian Russian nationalist regime while others want a liberal social-democratic system. Their attitudes, however, have been consistently elitist, regarding workers as "cattle," to use a favorite Soviet epithet. They perceive themselves as the foundation of the society and the natural leaders, who were repressed by Stalin and the regime itself: "Stalin had always been hostile to and suspicious of the intelligentsia."[6]

From one angle, this is understandable since their position is that of a layer between workers and elite. They aspire to enter the elite, but the workers have overtaken many of them in remuneration. In this they approximate the classic position of the petite bourgeoisie, who are ground between the two great classes of capitalism, the workers and the bourgeoisie. It is not surprising, therefore, that many of theme have turned to anti-Semitism and nationalism.

From the viewpoint of political economy, the intelligentsia may be defined as all those who both alienate their labor power and assist in the process of extraction of the surplus product, usually by being in charge of others. The great bulk of the intelligentsia work in enterprises, in one way or another in charge of workers. Even the so-called scientific workers are often involved in trying to find a way to raise the surplus product squeezed out of the direct producer. While they are not directly in charge of anyone, they are assisting the process of extracting the surplus product.

Doctors and teachers, overwhelmingly female, do not entirely fit into this definition. Of course, they assist the process of extraction of the surplus product by ensuring that the workers are able to function as workers. But in fact it is not their occupational prestige, which is low, but their position within the family, as wives of engineers, academicians, and so forth, that determines their social position. (It is difficult to imagine men who were so poorly compensated and so tightly controlled who would not have joined allegiance with ordinary workers, but then men in such occupations would almost certainly not be treated so shoddily.) The special position of women is very important in understanding the political economy of the USSR. We return to this question later, when discussing the nature of the divisions in the work force and so the forms of control over the workers.

The concept of dependence was discussed in chapter 3. The total dependence of members of the intelligentsia on their colleagues at work for their everyday needs has made for a compliant body of individuals who at the same time are very discontented. For them it is this bureaucratic apparatus in which they find themselves enmeshed that has to be smashed. Paradoxically, they have long demanded freedom of speech, imagining that it would solve their problems. To a large degree they have been granted their wish today, under Gorbachev, with the virtual abolition of the censor. They have found that it is not enough. Like everyone else, they want a higher standard of living, in addition to the kind of freedom possessed by their counterparts in the West. They want the indirect dependence provided by the use of money. That doctors and engineers are far better off in the West is quite clear. Teachers and academics would similarly be better off in a market.

Discussions of the role of the intelligentsia arouse extraordinary passions. On the one hand, there are those who seek to support the Soviet intelligentsia and so ignore their particular social position in Soviet society. On the other hand, the long anarchist tradition, which incorporates the work of Makhaisky, is only too ready to denounce the Soviet intelligentsia as the living proof that the Bolshevik revolution led to the takeover of the intellectuals, who then dispossessed the workers. The work of Ivan Szelenyi has also given the intelligentsia a particular political role in society.[7] Szelenyi has argued that the intelligentsia possess the monopoly of knowledge and so have established themselves in power. The argument of the present book is that only a section of the intelligentsia is actually in power while the rest are divided, although eager to take power.

The intelligentsia, then, is to be seen as a social group standing between the elite and the workers that has historically been used by the elite to maintain its rule. This has been accomplished by dividing them from the workers and using sections of the intelligentsia as a lightning rod for discontent. Anti-Semitism has played the traditional scapegoat role under Stalin and his successors; nationalism has had the functionalist role of separating the workers of different parts of the USSR; and it is the intelligentsia that has developed the role of nationalism and separatism.

One condition for change, then, has to be the disintegration of the intelligentsia itself, with sections seeking their salvation in the historic role of the universal class, the working class. That is precisely what Stalinism has hitherto prevented and Gorbachev is continuing to prevent. Indeed, the turn to parliamentarism can also be seen in this perspective. Threatened by the possibility of working-class action, the elite has moved to incorporate the intelligentsia in a multifaceted parliamentary mold. Anyone who asks for more can be branded with the standard word of modern Soviet abuse: extremist.

The Debate on History and Rehabilitations

The effort to attach the intelligentsia to the elite has involved a three-pronged policy. First, their salaries have been raised. Second, censorship has been curtailed. Third is the process of rehabilitation and introduction of the rule of law, intended to reassure the intelligentsia that they will never again be vulnerable. The move to the market is also in their interest, as argued above, but that is a long-term policy.

Concessions to the intelligentsia reached the Khrushchev-era level by the end of 1985. The release of Sakharov and political prisoners was a further gesture, although Marchenko died in a prison camp and the KGB continued to victimize dissidents. The next step toward incorporating the intelligentsia required that the past repressions be condemned. This began with the rehabilitation of Bukharin and discussion of the unpersonage of Trotsky, the role of Stalin, and more recently that of Lenin. It appears that the struggle around these issues reflects the operation of different factions. Gorbachev's November 1987 attack on Stalin as personally guilty of crimes was an attack on a wing of the elite. By identifying Stalin with terror, Gorbachev threatened the control bureaucracy. He then retreated to speak of Stalin positively in connection with the war, presumably to mollify elements of the elite who either continue from the war period or invoke it to justify the system.

The mistake made by those on the left is that they identify these discussions with a real possibility of return to the politics of Bukharin, or at least anti-Stalinism. In fact, Gorbachev is merely acting to destroy the opposition. By exposing the terror of the 1930s and the reality of an alternative, he weakens both ideologically and personally the position of those who stand only for control. It may be true that Stalin, Beria, Molotov, Voroshilov, Malenkov, and the rest are dead, but those who rose to power under them are not. It is noteworthy, therefore, that Gorbachev was forced to defend the war generation, because these are precisely the group identified with Brezhnev and other so-called conservatives.[8]

The rehabilitation of Bukharin threw into question the whole policy of the 1930s. Indeed, what could be more advantageous than the rehabilitation of Bukharin, the inventor of Stalinist ideology—the man who put forward the concepts of socialism in one country and socialist realism, produced a scholastic Marxism, and above all, appears as a humanist and a supporter of peasants and the market? He is indeed the ideal icon for the modernized Stalinist regime.

Of course, the real Bukharin was much more contradictory. He opposed the existence of the market under socialism, arguing only for its temporary necessity in the conditions of the USSR. He was also on the left of the regime from 1917 to 1921, so much opposing "socialism in one country" that in 1917 he wanted to continue the war against Germany.[9]

Trotsky had to be cleansed of the absurdities flung against him and made to appear, as they now say, a courageous Civil War leader, but indecisive, vain, and ambitious; a man sometimes correct on some questions but wrong on all important issues.[10] Following the February 1988 Plenum of the CPSU, *Pravda* (26 February 1988) opened a discussion of the 1920s, beginning with Lenin's last days and his testament. Stalin is shown as a competent organizer, but crude and capable of abusing power. Trotsky is described as having had considerable support among the workers and especially the youth; he was a good orator and by implication a demagogue. Mention is made of Trotsky's anti-Bolshevism, as a warning that no one should take up his cause. Bukharin, by contrast, is described as having made mistakes when he was on the left, until 1921; thereafter he was approved of by Lenin. Other voices have argued that Stalin was for all practical purposes a pupil of Trotsky in his industrialization policy; in other words, Stalin and Trotsky alike were wrong and dangerous.[11]

The real danger of discussing Trotsky's views is rooted in that fact that even now they are subversive of the regime in their attack on privilege and bureaucratic control, whereas the regime had no fear of politically rehabilitating Bukharin.[12] The history of the USSR is one of left opposition. Hence, it is not impossible that a section of the elite are actually pushing for the rehabilitation of an emasculated but critical Trotsky.[13] The publicity about Trotsky is not explicable simply in terms of cleansing history. It is more likely that a group within the elite can see the advantage of accepting his critique of privilege, his paean of praise for planning and industrialization, and his denunciation of Stalinism. Accepting Trotsky's characterization of the USSR as a degenerate workers' state, they could argue that the task is to regenerate it. They could then abolish official privilege and replace it with differential salaries based on the market. This would amount to a kind of social-democratic reform of the regime, and indeed is the only hope that the regime might have for success, slim as it might be, for it could involve just enough bamboozlement and enough concessions to enthuse potentially left sections of the intelligentsia and working class.[14] Hence, the regime could well open the door wide and find out too late that it had made a mistake. Although the left opposition is history, a working-class critique is not, and the left opposition produced the first such critique.

The Old Bolsheviks were killed precisely because they were Old Bolsheviks. Contrary to the protestations of some, it is perfectly possible that those on trial wished to remove Stalin from power and were plotting to that effect. Indeed there is such evidence for at least some of them. They would have had to be utterly useless had they not been at least attempting preliminary discussions to that eventuality. Stalin was thus correct in his accusation. Any authority takes extreme measures when threatened.

In disposing of the issue of the show trials,[15] the regime thus achieves three goals: it undermines its internal opposition in the elite, who were historically associated with such crimes; it removes the attraction of illegality around the Old Bolsheviks; and it permits the introduction of a new pragmatic language within the elite.

Legality and the Rule of Law

The issue of rehabilitations has been framed as one of legality. The need for the rule of law appears to be crucial for the reformers. *Izvestiia* (10 April 1988) carried an article on the show trials, in which it stressed the terror used by Vyshinsky against the accused, particularly Krestinsky. The article subtly attacks the sections of the police and party apparatus who would prefer to use force, and directly mentions the reintroduction of secret trials under Brezhnev.

Vaksberg's attack on Vyshinsky[16] at first sight appears to be a move to the left in that it completely rehabilitates all the Old Bolsheviks put on trial or imprisoned under the chief prosecutor of the late 1930s. On the other hand, a closer reading shows that the form and detail are of a legalistic and orthodox Western approach. Implicit is a philosophy of the need for a division of powers, independence for the judiciary, and proper rights for defendants, all of which is laudable and would greatly improve matters if introduced. The contradiction is that a separation of powers in the form required is impossible, where a judge is dependent for his housing and privileges on the local soviet and the party.

In any case, the USSR exists on the edge of a precipice. The elite, correctly, perceive themselves as under threat from below. Under these circumstances, it is very difficult for legal reform to have much effect, since the elite are not likely to provide the instruments for their own overthrow. Accordingly, the right of the KGB to deal with internal subversion as it sees fit has been reinforced.

Furthermore, as long as the real dependence of the individual on the structure, and hence directly on other individuals, is maintained, no legal framework will defend the individual against the state or the elite. Where there is no money, as in the USSR, resources for the administration of justice always have to be provided by the state. This always entails personal decisions in relation to both the prosecution and the defense.

Vaksberg has pointed out that there are some one million rules in the USSR that are not laws but have the force of law. Such rules exist wherever there is a bureaucratic form. Obviously, a prolixity of rules is counterproductive in that judges cannot know the rules or how to apply them. On the other hand, rules arise out of everyday need for them. They can only be abolished when sufficient trust exists between different parts of the system. Where, however, there is a necessary contradiction within the elite itself, rules are of the essence of the system and any codification will be quickly overtaken by an avalanche of modifications.

Another function is also facilitated. Vaksberg and the state commission working on codification are really concerned with the introduction of procedures that approximate to a rule of law. An oligarchy that appears to function impartially is much more secure than one that is inefficient and vindictive. Hence, arbitrariness has to be eliminated. Strict procedures are to be followed. Corruption will thereby be rooted out. Yet, there are fundamental reasons for believing that neither arbitrariness nor corruption can be removed from the system, whatever the good intentions of the liberals in the Soviet regime.

Gorbachev has explicitly linked the economic reforms with democracy; hence, the debate around the figure of Bukharin was an ideal way to link the two aspects of the reform program. His rehabilitation is a gesture to truth and more open discussion but also a means to acceptance of the market itself. The real questions of the introduction of the market are how to introduce it without antagonizing the majority of the population and whether the repression necessary for its introduction can be combined with the kind of democratic reforms needed to appease the intelligentsia and sections of the working class. The market has coexisted with mass repression for most of its existence, so that the rather simplistic if not pathetic argument that it must necessarily lead to or require democracy cannot be entertained. What is true is that democracy is essential for the elite and probably also for a considerable proportion of the intelligentsia, but there is every reason why workers have to be kept outside such a democracy if they are not to control the product themselves, as they cannot if there is to be a market.

On the other hand, there are aspects of the society that have to be changed for any level of efficiency to exist. For one thing, deception and avoidance of the truth are not conducive to consistent or realistic planning, while the absence of a genuine discourse (as opposed to a counterconceptual one, such as Stalinism) requires the use of more empirically based language, rather than "Marxism-Leninism."

Indeed, whatever the reforms may be, there can be no hope whatsoever of their success if there cannot be a critical discussion of their progress. This problem, however, is insuperable because any real discussion must come up against the nature of socialism itself—with the majority controlling, work become humanity's prime want, interchangeability of occupations within the division of labor, and hence the abolition of the elite itself. Western economists may accept the eternal nature of exploitation, but workers will not. A new justification has thus to be provided, a task that will not be easy.

Notes

1. *Narodnoe khoziaistvo SSSR za 70 let* (Moscow: Finansy i statistika, 1987), pp. 39, 418; *Narodnoe khoziaistvo SSSR v 1988* (Moscow: Finansy i statistika, 1989), p. 52. The figure for the technical specialists as opposed to those with higher education is 20,161,800 in 1987.

2. *Narodnoe khoziaistvo SSSR za 70 let*, p. 431. It is to be noted that this reduction in the position of the intelligentsia is discussed by Gordon and Kostin, whose articles are cited below. The raising of the salaries of scientific workers soon after Gorbachev took power (*Pravda*, 15 May 1985) is, of course not, accidental.

3. *Narodnoe khoziaistvo SSSR za 70 let*, p. 421.

4. In 1987 some 578,800 persons with higher education were working as manual workers (*Narodnoe khoziaistvo SSSR v 1988* [Moscow: Finansy i statistiki, 1989], p. 53). Note that in spite of *glasnost'*—or perhaps because of it and the attacks on privilege—the USSR has not published the statistics for the elite beyond 1985.

5. It is important to make a distinction between an intellectual and a member of the intelligentsia. These are quite different terms. The intellectual is involved with the world of ideas, usually with a critical assessment of the society of which he is a part, whereas the members of the Soviet intelligentsia are those who alienate their labor power in order to engage in nonmanual work. The anti-Semites and Russian chauvinists of Pamiat' and other organizations, including the Union of Russian Writers, are usually members of the Soviet intelligentsia; whether people holding these views could be termed intellectuals is dubious. The term "intelligentsia" therefore refers to a particular social group in the society. The reason for the confusion between the two terms is that the Russian noun *intelligent* was used to apply to genuine thinking and critical intellectuals of tsarist times.

6. V.N. Dashichev, "Vmesto dogmy—trud uma," *Izvestiia*, 13 April 1988, p. 2.

7. George Konrad and Ivan Szelenyi, *Intellectuals on the Road to Class Power: A Sociological Study of the Role of the Intelligentsia in Socialism* (New York: Harcourt Brace Jovanovich, 1979). No member of the intelligentsia has developed to the point of critically assessing the nature of the Soviet Union as well as capitalism.

8. The newspapers had already printed attacks on Stalin, Voroshilov, and others for their conduct of military preparations for the war, accusing them not only of the purges of Tukhachevsky and the rest of the officer corps, but of sheer stupidity in that they opposed the latter's demands for tanks and planes. See Victor Anfilov, "Ot otstupleniia k pobede," *Literaturnaia gazeta*, 17 May 1987, p. 10. The article is in honor of Zhukov but in fact uses him as an excuse to attack Stalin and his supporters for incompetence of an extreme kind—liquidation of the specialized units and refusal to produce and use tanks and airplanes (presumably to preserve the cavalry and thus Budenny). The message is not unclear. The modern supporters of the old school are antiquated and tarred with the brush of mass liquidation of great revolutionaries.

9. The publication and production of Mikhail Shatrov's play *Onward, Onward, Onward*, precisely on the theme of the peace of Brest–Litovsk, makes quite clear where Bukharin stood in this period. See Michael Glenny, "Glasnost Brings Trotsky Back to Life," *Sunday Times* (London), 29 November 1987, p. 57: "Bukharin in particular is given the full rehabilitation treatment." Glenny correctly points to the political utility of the play in that it appeared to give Lenin's backing for the signing of a disadvantageous treaty just as Gorbachev was doing the same with Reagan.

10. This is how Trotsky is depicted in Shatrov's play. See also Egor Iakovlev, "Pervoe Pravitel'stvo," *Izvestiia*, 12 July 1987, p. 3. In his references to Trotsky, Iakovlev (the editor of *Moscow News*) describes him as someone in the workers' movement for seventeen years, exiled to Siberia, who was appointed commissar for foreign affairs in the first Soviet government. Then he quotes Lenin saying that Trotsky holds no views on the important questions and hence cannot be argued with. This is ambiguous in that it brings out the point that Lenin and Trotsky in fact had few important differences at the time of the revolution, while on the other hand implying that Trotsky stood on the fence. Any intelligent reader will get the point that Trotsky was no agent of the bourgeoisie but an important leader, whose views have to be considered, even though evidently wrong. The main debate around Trotsky at this stage is summarized in the *Guardian*, 28 September 1987.

11. Afanas'ev declared that the rehabilitation of Trotsky by some Stalinists had been handled in such a way as to perpetuate Stalinism (*Literaturnaia Rossiia*, 17 June 1988). Afanas'ev considers Trotsky a genuine Civil War leader but otherwise a demon. In an interview in *EKO* (1989, no. 1), Iu.S. Borisov, a department head in the Academy of Sciences Institute of History, effectively argues that Trotsky is ultimately responsible for the economic system in the USSR (p. 156).

12. The rehabilitations have involved such figures as Chaianov and Kondrat'ev, well known for their propeasant views. To emphasize the importance of these thinkers, Professor Teodor Shanin of Manchester University was invited to the USSR to speak on Chaianov. See *Sel'skaia zhizn'*, 23 January 1988 (the article is by I. Suslov, who also attacks collectivization). In this way, the regime is ensuring that a right alternative holds the stage. Indeed, as the discussants at a *Literaturnaia gazeta* forum emphasized, a new orthodoxy is being established. It is a right-wing orthodoxy. See *Literaturnaia gazeta*, 27 January 1988.

13. By the end of 1989, at least nine pieces culled from the work of Trotsky had been printed, usually with commentaries. The attacks on Trotsky continued but he was also described as a courageous man who was correct on various issues including his attack on Stalin and the bureaucracy. Even permanent revolution was discussed, although in a patronizing and rueful tone. *Voprosy ekonomiki*, the economic journal of the Academy of Sciences Institute of Economics, published an extract from *The Revolution Betrayed*, with a commentary by Academician Emel'ianov that approves of Trotsky's attack on bureaucracy and sees him as a forerunner of perestroika. See *Voprosy ekonomiki*, 1989, no. 12. The issue includes an article by V. Ivanovskii on bureaucracy as a class, written in 1903. The inclusion of the latter article, from the tsarist period, in parallel with Trotsky, clearly indicates the view of bureaucracy preferred by the editors of the journal. Fragments from Trotsky's *History of the Russian Revolution*, with an introduction and commentary by N.A. Vasetskii, were published by *Istoriia SSSR* in 1990, no. 2.

14. Academician Emelianov's critique of bureaucracy and approval of Trotsky (*Voprosy ekonomiki*, 1989, no. 12) has to be seen in this light. N.A. Vasetskii observed (*Istoriia SSSR*, 1990, no. 2, p. 156) that of all the Old Bolsheviks whose works had been reprinted, it was Trotsky who was attracting growing interest. (In 1986 Vasetskii had published *Ot "revoliutsionnoi" fazy k bezrassudnomy avantiurizmu*, devoted to exposing

various "reactionary Trotskyist theories.") Vasetskii works in the Ideological Commission of the Communist party. At the Trotsky conference held in Wuppertal, West Germany, at the end of March 1990, Vasetskii made it clear that he had published what he had had to produce. Incidentally, this conference, in which upwards of twenty Soviet historians and other social scientists participated along with well-known Western specialists on Trotsky and equally well-known Trotskyist intellectuals, marked a watershed.

15. The legal rehabilitation of Bukharin, which took place on 4 February 1988, was accompanied by the rehabilitation of others of less importance but also by the rehabilitation of Christian Rakovsky (see *Pravda,* 6 February 1988). Rakovsky was in fact the second in command to Trotsky in the left opposition in theoretical and status terms. Once the so-called "Right–Trotskyist bloc" was declared blameless of crime, the way was opened to the left opposition. Within months all victims of the show trials were rehabilitated, and then practically everyone else incarcerated or murdered by Stalin. On 21 June 1988 the Soviet authorities took a further step when they restored Bukharin, Rykov, and Tomsky (the right opposition) to membership in the party. They added a number of others, most particularly Rakovsky and Krestinsky, both of whom had been members of the left opposition. See "V Komissii Politbiuro KPSS," *Sovetskaia Rossiia,* 10 July 1988, p. 1.

16. See *Literaturnaia gazeta,* 27 January 1988, p. 13. See also Arkady Vaksberg, *The Prosecutor and the Prey: Vyshinsky and the 1930 Moscow Show Trials* (London: Weidenfeld Nicolson, 1990).

6

The Working Class

The theoretical questions concerning the position of the workers in the USSR are twofold. First, we have to examine the nature of labor power in the USSR. Second, we have to consider the conditions for the formation of the workers as a class, and hence the forms that prevented the coming into being of the class and the nature of the new forms being introduced.

We have argued that the Soviet worker controls his own labor process, but not his product. He is alienated from his product, but he does not sell his labor power. There are two aspects to the nature of labor power in the USSR: First, the worker does not have any choice about working or not working; he has to find employment or accept state punishment. Second, the worker does not wholly relinquish control over his labor power.

The Sale of Labor Power

Every Soviet citizen has to work. The parasitism law ensured that anyone who did not work could be deported to Siberia or receive other punishment. Under Stalin, of course, draconian labor laws meant that workers could be imprisoned for contraventions of labor discipline and they were unable to leave their enterprises without the factory director's agreement. Moreover, a substantial section of the work force was in labor camps. Even under Stalin's successors, workers have been confined to particular localities through the internal passport system, and further controlled through the labor books and personal files held on them. Workers in military-related industries are under military discipline. In short, the labor force in the USSR is controlled.

Some workers, however, are able to move from one factory to another, and they do so in search of better conditions. But this hardly constitutes a labor market. Rather, workers are simply taking advantage of full employment to change their jobs. Real pay differentials have eroded over time to the point where most workers are in a very narrow band within the wage–grade structure. Until recently, they could not be dismissed without another job being found for them. It is no wonder then that Oleg Bogomolov could state that labor in the USSR is semiforced labor. Leonid Gordon has remarked that workers effectively get a pension because they get a fixed wage, whatever actually happens to their employment.

The picture that emerges, therefore, is of a worker who is directed to work. In return he gets a certain reward, which is less dependent on skill or work than on other factors. Indeed, the rationing system, particularly in the post-1988 period, has used factories as the unit of distribution. This further reduces the meaning of the wage. Since money is not money in the USSR, an extra few rubles per month is meaningless and even an extra fifty may be less important than a series of other factors such as contacts, the location of the workplace, and so forth.

Workers in the same sector tend to have similar real incomes, whatever their skill and attitude to work. The real division in pay is between pay for men and pay for women, since women get at least one-third less than men. Since the family remains the basic societal unit, it is family income that must be compared, and that tends toward equality for workers.

We have defined the elite and the intelligentsia in relation to the form by which they control the extraction of the surplus product from the direct producer. Similarly, the workers in the USSR have to be defined as all those whose occupation involves alienating their labor power and only alienating their labor power. In other words, they are not in charge of others alienating their labor power (like the elite), or assisting in the extraction of the surplus product from others (like the intelligentsia).

We therefore argue, along with the modern Soviet economists, that workers do not sell their labor power. They alienate it in a particular form. That form is what is typical of Soviet-style production. We will return to this discussion below in the section on wage reform.

The Labor Process and the Changes Demanded

The term "labor process" has been much discussed using a particular French/Italian paradigm known as Fordism. It is not necessary to accept this viewpoint to accept some of the descriptions of the labor process made by members of this school.[1] Mass production is seen as having certain costs. Workers lose their incentive to work to requirements, quality suffers, and the hierarchical form ensures that there is no consultative/technological input from the shop floor. In addition, workers become specialized to particular occupations and hence flexibility becomes the new watchword. An alternative form, where the production line is replaced with less specialization and hence greater worker control and responsibility, is now more successful, particularly in Japan.

The USSR has its own form of labor process. There are those who prefer to see it in terms of the adoption of Taylorism and so would use this Fordist paradigm to view the Soviet factory. It is true that the USSR very quickly went for mass production and controls over labor of the Taylorist type. Lenin was quite explicit about this. Yet the low levels of productivity and poor quality have been unique for any industrializing country. It is not just not comparable with the West, it is also inferior to the industry of such countries as Brazil or South Africa. The explanation has always been simple. In the USSR there is neither a reserve army of labor nor any money incentive. The controls of Taylorism are therefore absent. Not only does promotion give little to the promoted worker,[2] but for the past thirty years there has been downward mobility of qualified engineers, who do better as highly qualified workers.[3] The system has a contradictory series of steps on the promotional hierarchy, which result from the nature of the labor process.

Since the workers cannot be controlled, as under Taylorism, the result has been an increasing degree of control over the work process by workers, as the system has lost its ability to control and direct labor by force. This is not the same form of control as in mass production in the West, where workers can resist through unions or through collective sabotage.

The labor process has gone through three stages. First, the labor process was a scene of conflict between the system and workers. During this period the worker effectively wrested a large degree of control over the labor process.[4] Second, the worker was controlled through forms of force varying from imprisonment to the use of labor books. In the third stage, which gradually came into being under Khrushchev and was established under Brezhnev, the worker has increased his control over the work process to the point where control over the product itself is being questioned. From this point of view, Gorbachev appears as a reactionary, intent on preventing the workers from advancing to the point of taking control over production itself. It is not a question of the working class acting as a class, but rather of the work force moving from a point of individual negative control over the work process to a more collective form, which could so control the work process that production itself is threatened. As already indicated, the key to the increasing power of the worker lies in his increasing socialization within production.[5]

The overall point that the worker has a high degree of control over his own work process is not difficult to show using Soviet literature. It has been a constant refrain from very early times to the present day. I have argued this point elsewhere.[6] Suffice it to say here that because the members of the norm-setting committee include manual workers, and it is in the interest of the factory management to collude with them in order to achieve an orderly result, the whole drive of the enterprise is toward the acceptance of a rate of work largely determined by the worker. The result is described quite graphically today by various reformers.[7]

The difficulty of introducing new technology in relation to the labor process is not unique to the USSR.[8] On the other hand, the extent of the problem is such that it becomes unique, especially in its very close linkage to the labor process. It is this negative control that threatens the Soviet economy. It is also what Gorbachev must break if the elite is to survive.

In theoretical terms, we may point to the way in which the process of atomization, which involves this particular individualized relation to the work process, has broken up the homogeneity of labor under capitalism. In Marxist terms, we have to argue that abstract labor does not exist in the USSR. In other words, the rate of work is different across the economy. It is determined through an individual bargain in each unit. That, of course, might be expected because, after all, atomized control over the labor process can only mean that there would be a tendency for each worker and each group of workers to establish their own pace of work. One contemporary writer put it this way: "Our research confirms that most general engineering work rates are not homogenized and are not equally taut."[9] He then provides precise details showing the different rates among different sectors of work. The result is that average levels of productivity per man hour indicate little at a micro level. Neither the center nor the individual enterprise can know what effect additional inputs will have in the system. Everything becomes unpredictable. Not only do individual units differ from one another, but they must differ from themselves over time, in unpredictable ways, as both the work force and the machinery change. Real planning is therefore impossible.

Because there is no abstract labor, there can also be no value or commodity production (a point that will be elaborated later). It is this contradiction, between the extraction of a surplus product and the lack of control over the process of extraction, that the elite has to break if it is to survive. The logic of the system is toward the establishment of homogeneity over the labor process, but the only means of doing so is organizational and consequently inevitably flawed. There is no way of controlling workers at the point of production other than through economic forms of coercion or through democratic involvement in the system itself. The market is a particularly brutal way of compelling the worker to comply with the competitive framework, through threats of unemployment and a lower standard of living, but it works. The alternative is a system of self-management from the top of the society downward. There is no third way.

The increasing inflexibility of the worker in relation to the work process is crucial in understanding both the rigidity of the economy and its decline.[10]

The Question of Class

Historically, the Soviet worker has alienated his labor power but has retained a degree of control over the work process. The effect is that the worker is atomized, since he relates to his own labor process individually rather than collectively. This individuation, as we have argued above, prevents the emergence of a class.

In principle, the whole nature of the Soviet regime is determined by its ability to atomize the workers through the particular political economy that came into being in the late 1920s. The combination of a bureaucratized economy, draconian police state, and atomized workers constitutes the basis of the Soviet system. Logically, the growing strength of the workers challenges the system itself in a way that is different from the challenge of capitalism. In the case of the USSR, the increasing strength of the workers is potential. This consists of the following aspects.

First, Soviet workers by and large work in enormous factories—from three to five times the size of West German factories.[11] They often live close by, in the same area and in the same apartment buildings. The very centralization of the system has been conducive to the establishment of gigantic concentrations of the work force. This is because it is easier to control workers when they are in one place than when they are scattered over a number of locations. This form of control is, of course, the exact opposite of the modern form under capitalism, where managers prefer a work force broken into small units.

Second, as we will discuss below, the shortage of labor has increased the need to concede to labor. Clearly, it is impossible to shoot down workers when they are needed for production. Nor can they be redirected from one plant to another once they are skilled and relate to a particular labor process. The rising levels of education and integration of production make it difficult to control labor without incurring enormous costs.

Third, as workers extend their control over the labor process, the question of power assumes increasing importance. This is done in two ways. On the one hand, workers have acted in a more collective way to establish their norms over time. On the other hand, they have begun to go beyond questions of the labor process to demand better conditions of work, more consumer goods, and workers' control over production. This will discussed further with respect to the miners' strike.

The whole dynamic of the system is toward its own demise and overthrow by the workers. For that very reason, the formation of the class is the battleground of the system. Whereas in the West the class has come into being and lost its battles, in the USSR the workers have to fight just to become a class. Once they do become a class, the system will not be able to continue. By 1990 the system was disintegrating, though not dissolving. In the USSR only the intelligentsia stands between the workers and the elite, and that would itself divide once the working class began to advance. The point of the reforms, therefore, is to replace atomization as the means of control over the workers with alternative forms of division.

The crucial function of the regime lies in the division of the work force. It is useful to attempt to analyze the methods by which the regime can establish control over the work force, which it has to do if it wants any level of efficiency higher than the present. The primary method of initiating control has been that of increasing the divisions in the working class. This has to be contrasted with the previous system of atomization as outlined above.

The regime needs to control the workers in a manner such that they will work, if not willingly, at least in a similar manner to workers in the West. Under capitalism the control has been exercised partly through the reserve army of labor and partly through the domination of the commodity. Neither aspect exists in the USSR and hence another form of control must be found, at least in the transition period to capitalism. Worse still for the Soviet elite, modern capitalism can no longer rely on the old forms mentioned above and it has consciously invented new ways of dividing the working class over the past century. We will return to this question after a brief history of class relations in the Gorbachev period.

Reforms and the Process of Establishing Control over the Working Class

Social relations in the USSR are essentially based on the contradiction between the form of control over the surplus product and that over the labor process. Whereas the elite have a large measure of control over the surplus product, their ability to direct labor in the work process is severely limited. Gorbachev's reforms are necessarily directed to removing this contradiction by establishing full managerial control over the labor process.

The attitude to the workers has changed over the Gorbachev period. In the first instance, as already noted, there was hardly a Gorbachev speech in which he did not attack the workers for not working hard enough. In 1988, however, the policy changed. Organizational and disciplinary measures had failed. The market reforms were held up. The workers had to be mollified. Consumer goods production was stressed and the usual faster rate of growth of producer goods ended. By 1989 producer goods grew only 0.75 percent, as opposed to over 4 percent for consumer goods in that year. Shmelev—the Milton Friedman of the USSR as one journal called him[12]—advocated rapid and large-scale imports of consumer goods, a view held more generally, in order to assuage the workers' discontent when the market was introduced. The regime indicated that it would import more consumer goods. It had become clear that no change to the market was possible without the agreement of the workers, whether through passivity or direct consent. The next section focuses on the interaction between workers and the political leaders.

The Position of the Workers and *Perestroika*

Under Gorbachev there has been a definite attempt to appeal to workers, as well as an effort to control them more strictly. This has meant that sections of the apparatus have attempted to represent, comply with, or concede to workers' demands. At the Twenty-seventh Party Congress the head of the trade-union council complained not only of the poor work conditions but also of the difficulty in obtaining housing, particularly when some comrades received many more square meters than others.[13] In 1989 one trade-union representative again articulated objections to the reforms when he argued that the cooperatives were taking scarce resources and paying themselves high incomes. Of course, the fact that the produce of these cooperatives was largely utilized by the elite, as workers could not afford to patronize cooperatives, lay at the back of this reference.[14] The July 1989 miners' strike also led to demands for the abolition of the cooperatives. Gorbachev specifically discussed the miners' objections.[15] These references to the need to do away with privilege and to redistribute income clearly express not just the needs of workers but also the view of a faction in the party.

An early article in the Gorbachev period by Torkanovskii argued (to quote the title) for workers' participation in management as a form of the realization of ownership.[16] In effect, his discussion piece (it appeared in the discussion section of the journal *Voprosy ekonomiki*) tries hard to put the case for more forms of genuine workers' participation in management from direct accountability of managers to greater availability of information. There has, of course, been a long discussion around this theme, but its explicit resurrection in an official journal in this manner shows the way one school of thought, if not faction, developed early on.

There is no doubt that all the references to self-management made by Gorbachev, as well as by others, are fundamentally limited, but they were not intended to be mere window dressing. The regime is now factionalized and the institutions representing workers also want to have an easier life. As the system declines and disintegrates, these puppetlike institutions are acquiring a life of their own and have to receive concessions. Furthermore, unlike some Western economists and Sovietologists, the regime is aware that if it is to implement the economic reforms of which it speaks, it must find a way to neutralize the workers against whom the reforms must operate. Hence, a bow and scrape in the direction of the workers is obligatory. It does look, however, as if the reforms are more than that. The force of the workers is now such that real concessions may have to be made.[17]

In his acceptance speech as general secretary (11 March 1985), Gorbachev explicitly spoke of the need to expand democratic forms. This reference was a departure from the norm inasmuch as it clearly implied that democracy did not exist and attempts would be made to begin a democratic process. Andropov, as argued earlier, also tended this way, but apart from imprecations, nothing really happened. The only real meaning to be attached to the reference is that Gorbachev knows that he cannot only appeal to the organizational side of the elite or the demand for efficiency and so a higher standard of living for the intelligentsia. He has to make a gesture to the ordinary worker, who has no real forum whether as a member of a union or of a workers' collective. Clearly, the intelligentsia saw the reference as giving them more individual leeway as well.

Two years later, in January 1987, democracy was the theme of the Central Committee meeting.[18] Elections became the order of the day, except that elections to the post of factory director were made so indirect as to raise the question of their meaning. Examples since given show that the factory director was selected among candidates approved from above and that the board of selection was essentially the responsible personnel of the enterprise, so excluding most workers.

Even had all workers been able to elect genuine representatives, or, better still, been able to be present at the selection, they could have achieved little in the face of the fact that the candidates came from above. To choose among different oligarchs may ensure a less oppressive regime sometimes, but it is not much of a choice, and surveys showed that workers cared little for these so-called democratic reforms. Again, it is clear that the result is a patched-up compromise, but there is no evidence to suggest a genuine movement to direct election of factory managers by the total work force—a system that exists nowhere, and certainly never in Yugoslavia. The result still meant the removal of anti-Gorbachev forces and hence achieved one of its real objects. That indeed may be seen as the real meaning of the so-called democratic reforms. Academician Rumiantsev put the nature of the "democratic reforms" in a clear perspective: he declared (in a report of an economic conference held toward the end of 1986) that the USSR was moving from "dictatorial democratic centralism" to "dirigiste democratic centralism."[19]

The elections to the newly reformed Supreme Soviet held in February–June 1989 provided a new focus. Indeed, worker deputies did put forward different views. Yet the unofficial opposition, led by Yeltsin, apparently called for an end to the miners' strike, laid great stress on the market, and did not include any demands for greater equality in the system. On the contrary, because it is a marketeer opposition, it supports Gorbachev's campaigns against "leveling." Popular demands, on the contrary, are against privilege of all kinds, whether of the market or of the current bureaucratic form. Indeed, Gorbachev's references to the miners' strike indicate quite clearly that the miners were demanding greater equality when they called for the closing of cooperatives.[20]

No party of a Marxist type could be allowed to exist in the USSR, since it would demand the abolition of any elite and therefore of privilege of any kind. It would adopt Lenin's dictum that no one should receive more than the wage of a skilled worker, and it would call for the revolutionary overthrow of those who rule. Yeltsin, from this angle, is seen as a double-edged member of the elite. He appeals to workers, and hence may unleash a worker revolution against his own will, while on the other hand, he supports a reformed marketized system in which the elite would continue to function. The system has created its own acceptable opposition. From a worker's point of view, however, there is no real representation, even if his grievances are being aired in some distorted form.

The elections elsewhere in the system have meant little real change for workers. They are all still predicated on the principle of selection of candidates from above, although the actual personnel have indeed changed. Nonetheless, the acceptance of the principle of democracy is an enormous change in the USSR. Effectively, what has happened is that the workers have been told that if they behave themselves, they will have not only a higher standard of living but also the opportunity to improve their conditions of work, through being able to control their management by election. The actual change has been minimal but the potentiality appears exciting. Of course, the trouble is that no one really believes that Gorbachev will deliver, since, in spite of all the words and apparent changes, little really does change for the ordinary worker. By the last quarter of 1989 the democratic facade had faded. Election of managers was abolished by the Congress of People's Deputies.[21]

That the June 1989 session of the Congress of People's Deputies meant little except raised expectations was pointed out by Quentin Peel in his article on the miners' strike of July 1989. The miners waited for something to happen after each change introduced by the regime.[22] They listened to the debates in the Congress but these had no sequel. They therefore decided to take action themselves. It is only possible for so long to make promises without actually delivering.

The miners' strike has been the crucial event of the Gorbachev period. We have argued that it put a barrier across the road to market reform. The workers have said quite clearly that they do not want private enterprise, involving as it does higher wages for those who work in it and better supplies for the Soviet elite. Exactly what the miners wanted became an object of debate, with the different sides trying to get the miners to support them. Different manifestoes have been published. Perhaps the most accessible is that published in *Voprosy ekonomiki* in February 1990, wherein the miners demand equality with management, which they want to be directly elected and recallable by the electorate.[23] At the same time, they want some form of the market. It could be argued either that they are confused, since there is a tendency to call for cheap inputs and expensive outputs, or that they are simply trying to raise their incomes in an acceptable manner. It is quite clear, however, that they do not want private enterprise as it is normally understood. How could there be private enterprise if the management of the factory or enterprise were directly appointed by the workers and responsible to it? They explicitly reject all private enterprise other than that based on individual or family labor. The regime, of course, has been evolving strategies of getting around the workers.

The fact that the miners' strike was the first to spread across the USSR since the 1920s, albeit in one industry, is significant. It set a precedent, picked up, it would appear, by the railway workers.[24] The regime is trying to respond by containing the strikes both by law and by making it a matter of confidence in the regime itself. The political attempt to hold back strikes can only further politicize the strikers. Strikes were made illegal in the energy industry, among others, for an eighteen-month period from late 1989. Gorbachev had asked for a complete ban on strikes but got a limited result.

The law was ignored by the workers. Vorkuta miners struck in November 1989 and produced a series of demands including the "abolition of serfdom," which meant that they demanded the right to retain the extra pay consequent on living in the North when they changed enterprises. They also demanded recognition for their strike committees, which were in fact protosoviets.[25]

The next result of the strike was a political one. Although the regime did its best to avoid politicizing the strike, the strike was political in essence. Since all decisions are taken at the center, the strike could only be successful if the political center conceded. And it did. The economic demands could only be successful if policy changed with respect to supplying consumer goods for the ordinary worker, as opposed to the central elite and intelligentsia. However, the strike was actually a political strike, because it opposed private enterprise, something Gorbachev himself took up, as pointed out above. It was political because it set up independent workers' committees, as opposed to the trade unions. Above all, it was political because the underlying demands were for greater equality throughout the system, against the privileges of the elite, and for a decentralization of decision making. Gorbachev and his men managed to distort these demands into an acceptance of market-type reforms that involve more decentralized decisions.

This apparent deflection of the workers' demands into a form inherently opposed to their own interests cannot last very long. At the most it will be an attempt to buy off the miners by providing them with better conditions than are afforded to other workers. Nonetheless, the regime was successful in this deflective exercise. It was also amazingly successful in bringing the strike to an end. It did so by making concessions and by infiltrating the workers' committees themselves. It also has to be said that the normal Soviet forms of repression—controlling the documentation of workers and using the secret police—could not have been absent. The miners were in the fortunate (in one sense) position of living in areas and in housing that could not be worse. Deportation of strike leaders would therefore be no punishment. Incarceration is another matter, but that would be dangerous.

The Nature of Actual and Potential Divisions of the Workers

The regime in the USSR has tried a series of measures to divide and control the workers over the last sixty years. The primary method of control has been one of atomization, as discussed above, but atomization has also involved a fragmentation of the work force. To the degree that the regime, in order to raise productivity, shifts away from atomization and toward a division of the work force, it naturally tends to turn to existing divisions.

These are divisions by sex, by geographical/national area, by sector (including the military/civilian division), by skill, by wages, between the employed and the unemployed, and between mental and manual labor. Let us consider each in turn.

Male versus Female Labor

The political economy of the USSR is predicated on the sex division in a way found in no other economy. A country where 90 percent of women work full time is very different from one where a majority of women do not work. For that reason, the significance of the underpayment of women is different in Western economies than in the USSR. Women in the USSR work by and large in the consumer goods industries, in distribution, in the postal services, in health and education. They are clerks, bookkeepers, teachers, doctors, nurses, cashiers, and counter assistants. They are cleaners, janitors, street sweepers, and field hands in agriculture. They tend, therefore, to perform the jobs that are least well paid and least skilled. Even in health and education, their jobs, although skilled, are badly paid and poorly respected. A society that provides minimal resources to the social services cannot value the workers in that sector.

The consequence of the position of female workers is that they are more dependent within the home. The paradox is that they are paid, but at a lower level than the husband, so that the measure of independence they do have is insufficient to establish equality within the home; hence all the studies that show the burden of housework on the woman. This, however, is the result of the position of women in the economy.

It is difficult to avoid the conclusion that men are relatively better off because women are worse off. Yet this effect is one that operates at a national level rather than through competition between men and women. No studies have shown that women are paid less for the same work or are prevented from taking a particular job at the bottom of the ladder for which a man is competing. But promotion tends to go to men, as can easily be seen by looking at the sex of those in charge of institutions and enterprises or their structural subdivisions.

No plan was ever devised to introduce such a division. It almost certainly came into being in the early 1930s because the priority sectors preferred men or single women who would not be subject to the needs of the family. At the same time, the family was proclaimed to be the basic unit of society.

It is difficult to use this natural division any more than it has been, in a society where men get at least one-third higher wages and occupy the higher ranks of the occupational ladder. Men cannot be used any more than they already are to control women in employment; nor can women, who are in an inferior position, control men. The regime may, of course count on the docility of women, who have to support children, but they might well be disappointed given the history of towns going out on strike, with women playing a crucial role.

On the other hand, it might be easier to apply the market reform to the consumer goods industries, where women are dominant, on the principle that they are second earners and hence could be more easily dismissed. Certainly that viewpoint has been held by various economists for a long time. Indeed, light industry has already had the principles of the reform applied to it, such as they are.

To the degree that the regime changes to the market, however, the existing division could be employed to ensure stability. Women could be dismissed from employment in order to make up the complement of some 15 to 20 percent of the work force estimated to be redundant. Such proposals have long been put forward. If day care centers, nursery schools, and the like are closed down or considered costly in a market environment, then clearly it is women who will suffer.

Of course, if the market is introduced on top of the existing social structure, then questions of pay, promotions, and admission to jobs formerly occupied by one sex will become much more important and sexual competition will become normal. In the absence of any genuine unions and with the individualization of the worker still operative, it is possible that this division will be effective for a period of time. Everything will depend on the relative speed of introduction of the market and of genuine workers' organizations.

Privileged versus Nonprivileged Regions

As noted above, the USSR is divided into relatively better-off and relatively worse-off towns and regions. Since movement between them is restricted, the workers in certain towns remain better off in terms of pay, real income, nature of employment, education, and potential advancement. Such workers are privileged and would tend to accept the regime more readily than workers in other regions. It is noteworthy that one of the demands of the Vorkuta miners was that the "budget and other privileges of the capital towns be abolished."[26] Furthermore, the influx of workers from outlying areas who live illegally in towns like Moscow has created a division akin to the immigrant-versus-indigenous worker antagonism that exists in many capitalist countries. It is noteworthy that Pamiat', the protofascist organization, asked Yeltsin to close Moscow to new entrants. Nonetheless, as long as the system relied on atomization as its means of control, this division played a role only as part of the atomization. In other words, it reinforced the atomization by preventing contact among workers and did not create an antagonistic division among them.

It might well be the case, however, that the workers in the closed towns, where wages, jobs, and consumer goods are superior to what is typical elsewhere in the country, could be divided from the rest of the country once the market was introduced. Thus, the economic experiments could be applied to Moscow with the threat of deportation from the town if there were any trouble. On the other hand, this would be a dangerous step, since such workers would then lose their privileged status and perhaps begin to act in a working-class manner. Hence, it is not all that likely that the regime would apply such pressure except in extremis. Of course, a regime against privilege would have abolished the privileged status of such towns and it is noteworthy that Yeltsin reinforced the status of Moscow, rather than the reverse.

Export and Military versus Civilian Industry

Workers are privileged in particular sectors of the Soviet economy. Historically, heavy industry, military industry, and the export sector have been given priority. This meant that workers in these areas were better paid in reality as well as nominally. In the military sector they were also under military discipline. They were not able to leave the factory without the agreement of the director. The export sector has necessarily to be better paid and provided with better supplies. It also has stricter quality control as well as greater incentives to produce more and better products. Workers in these industries are therefore both better off and more controlled than in the rest of Soviet industry. This division would permit the regime to introduce the market at least for the export sector. Since the military is always, in every country, within an organizational network, it is difficult to see the arms industry within a free market, but demilitarized plants may not find it too difficult to switch. Efficiency is in the interests of the military.

It is therefore not unlikely that the market will be applied in this differential manner. Indeed, the permission granted to enterprises to conclude their own foreign contracts has this effect. To the extent that they retain a proportion of foreign currency earned, these enterprises are orienting themselves toward the world market on a limited profit/loss basis. Workers privileged to work in such enterprises would be expected to support the market. Since many enterprises supply goods for internal and external consumption, the retention of foreign currency could not be limited to the section of the factory involved. The Vorkuta coal miners demanded that they keep 25 percent of the foreign currency earned.[27]

This kind of bridgehead for the market for privileged workers is really possible only insofar as the enterprise relates to the world market.

Skilled versus Unskilled Labor

The Gorbachev regime has quite clearly oriented itself to a section of the workers who would respond to an incentive system. It is clear from numerous articles that this is the way they intend to go. Gorbachev and his fellow politicians have continually denounced the tendency toward egalitarianism, with boring regularity. Thus, the regime attempted to incorporate the more skilled workers who are better paid, are usually older, and sit on supervisory-type boards such as those involved with promotion and norming. The problem with this tactic is that it is not easy to separate out the more skilled. At the present time the majority of skilled workers are in the same wage grades as those who are less skilled, and hence receive no better wages or better conditions than their fellow workers.

The differences between skilled and unskilled workers evolved under Stalin, when a payment system was developed with a range of roughly three to one between the skill ranges. Over time these differences were eroded. In an atmosphere of general shortage, when extra rubles do not buy much, the only incentive that the skilled worker might have lies in the greater control over his work time. If he is placed in a position of limited responsibility over others, then the nature of the labor process in the USSR is such that he would have to collude with the ordinary workers. If he did not, and attempted to force the pace, then his own life would become considerably harder both inside and outside the factory. The aristocracy of labor, which might have existed under Stalin, is more limited today. It would have to be re-created in order to introduce a section of the work force that supported the reforms, whether premarket or market.

White-collar versus Blue-collar Labor

It has been a feature of the Stalinist regime that it placed itself between the intelligentsia, the skilled white-collar group, and the manual workers. It played up suspicion of the intelligentsia as a privileged group, contemptuous of workers. There can be no question that most white-collar workers stand opposed to the ordinary worker.

Here the division is between the intelligentsia, on the one hand, and the manual workers, on the other. It involves both the highly skilled white-collar workers of the factory and the bureaucrats of the regime as a whole. Gorbachev produced the figure of 18 million bureaucrats, which he said had to be cut down to size. Similar remarks have been made of the staffs of factories. It is curious that the regime should have seen fit to attack a section of the intelligentsia in this way, unless it intended to appeal to the skilled workers.

Workers often find themselves involved with three social groups, against whom they may have grievances. One is their supervisors, including the whole hierarchy of staff in charge of workers; a second is local officials; and a third, those in charge of distribution, who are widely regarded as corrupt. It has very much looked as if the regime has been prepared to throw to the wolves the section of the elite involved with distribution, and with them the workers in that sector. The elite calculation that their political concessions as well as salary increases will keep the loyalty of the intelligentsia as a whole, even while they attack sections of the intelligentsia and their own elite, is probably correct. Such populism might indeed make life easier for sections of the working class, in that lower-level bureaucrats might become more responsive and lower factory executives more flexible and hard-working.

Supervisors versus Labor

Within capitalism, the division between foremen and laborers has been the traditional method of control over labor within capitalism. In the USSR, however, complaints about the low pay of foremen and the unattractive nature of the job are rampant. In fact, the foreman or other person in charge of workers cannot easily be privileged under conditions where workers are paid piece rates, and an extra 10 percent, which they have traditionally been given, buys very little. It is only if foremen have the possibility of further occupational advancement outside the range of the workers' contempt that they are likely to function as genuine controllers. With the current low level of social mobility, that is not likely.

Again, in the West the fact of control by capital permits the foreman to arbitrate and for that even to be respected, but in the USSR there is no accepted mode of control. Those who do control are viewed as corrupt usurpers; hence, a foreman can only be regarded as a lackey if he performs according to orders from above. This is really a reflection of the fact that workers control their own work process, with the collaboration of the foremen, and hence any attempt to break this feature of the Soviet social system would put the foremen at the sharp end of the class struggle in the USSR. Indeed, it is clear that the brigade system is intended to achieve just this objective. The new norming decrees of December 1986 did place pressure on those in charge of workers to increase the speed of the production line to conform with the potential of the machinery. By changing the pay structure and the position of those in charge of workers, the regime hopes to obtain crucial allies among the skilled, supervisory, and ambitious workers. It is utopian, however, to imagine that, short of the introduction of a reserve army of labor, workers will voluntarily surrender their existing control over the work process. We have stressed this aspect of the reforms because the reforms themselves will only have a possibility of success if this section of the workers is prepared to collaborate.

The Necessity for Control Measures

The upshot of this discussion of control over the working class is that the regime relies very heavily on a particular form of appeal, which requires a lot more attention if it is to have any chance of success. Given that the regime is unable to take on the workers directly, measures to establish an alliance with skilled workers probably involve a direct defeat of the ordinary worker. This is most unlikely, although that does not mean that the regime will not continue to muddle on with its policy. It has also to be noted that such a policy would involve downgrading the other divisions that are now counterproductive. The introduction of the market, or more market-type measures, does not change the need to use many of the measures examined above and new ones discussed below, such as the brigade system.

The regime needs both to divide the workers and to introduce further measures to control workers. In principle, a pure capitalism would rely on the domination of the commodity to establish control. But such a capitalism has long ceased to exist and hence modern capitalism has used similar expedients to those discussed above. While quality control under capitalism is far better than in the USSR, it is significant that it exists at all, that it is not enough to rely on the good sense of the worker.

New Measures Introduced to Control Workers

Quality Control

Gospriemka, the quality-control system introduced in January 1987, failed for the simple reason that the plan would have been massively underfulfilled had it been strictly implemented. It led to a decline in production in January–February 1987, with the overall increase in production for the first nine months of 1987 at just 2.5 percent. In fact, this was a reflection of the refusal of workers to raise their standards.[28] This policy has been particularly cited as leading to working-class discontent. The regime was consequently compelled to retreat, and reports indicated that failure to pass the tests did not necessarily lead to lower pay of workers. Production was allowed to pick up when the strict testing of quality was relaxed. Officially, the campaign goes on, but it has failed, as it had to fail. When there is no competition, whatever is produced can be disposed of, and consumers require the goods even if they are not quite what is required. Above all, workers will not work harder merely because of exhortation from above. The whole approach was idealist in expecting results simply by decree.

Some description of quality control has been provided in the journals and newspapers.[29] The picture that emerges is of a separate apparatus with a member of the intelligentsia in charge, with considerable authority to inquire into the workings of the factory. Refusal to accept production is his only real sanction, a sanction so drastic that it is not an option.

Indeed, the plan results for *gospriemka* for 1988, the first year of its operation, were hardly encouraging, with only a trivial amount of goods rejected.[30] Given the scale of the problem, there ought to have been huge quantities of rejects. In fact, the leadership quailed before the scale of the operation and retreated. There can be no question that the total quantity produced would have been a fraction of what it was if high standards of quality had been maintained.

The failure of the Soviet regime to produce goods of reasonable quality is at the heart of the system's failure. Examples abound: in 1986, 31 percent of the cost of refrigerators was spent on repairs to refrigerators returned (the figure might well be much higher if the relevant trading organizations accepted more returns and if consumers were more demanding; after all, it is better to have a refrigerator that largely works than none at all); and one in three color television sets was repaired within the period of the guarantee.[31]

Injunctions and Disciplinary Campaigns

As under Andropov, exhortations, campaigns, and disciplinary methods could work for a time but not for very long. After a certain point the injunctionary effect wears off and bureaucratic methods of dealing with the controls evolve. Plant personnel can be frightened for a period of time, but after that, unless camps are set up, the campaign loses its meaning. In a certain sense this is the very nature of the system itself. The system and so the elite have the alternatives of applying maximum pressure to production, and so the workers, through organizational methods or using the market.

In the end, strict quality control, so-called scientific norms, and similar measures are forms of organized pressure that can only work as long as workers accept the pressure. Once they do not respect their superiors, for whatever reason—whether because they are no longer frightened or they hold them in contempt as corrupt and corruptible individuals—their productivity is irrevocably affected in a deleterious manner. Hence, the regime has tried to use workers' participation as an alternative, while it has also tried to clamp down on the natural alternatives of moving from factory to factory, absenteeism, alcoholism, and other responses. Nonetheless, these forms of control can only diminish with time.

The Question of Workers' Participation

The alternative mode of proceeding involves more substantial concessions to the working class in the direction of workers' self-management or workers' participation in control over the enterprise. There has been a long debate on this issue, but thus far it has amounted to very little. On the other hand, modern production, with its high level of integration, requires consultation, not command. The need for greater consultation has been a theme in Soviet sociological and economic journals for some time now.[32]

As argued above, however, the democratic maneuvers hitherto have amounted to little more than a cosmetic exercise. Furthermore, they can never amount to more than such an exercise. Workers the world over have found to their cost that control over management within a market is worth very little, since control over the plant is really exercised by the process of accumulation itself. If they control the plant manager, they might make the regime more humane, and indeed that is worth something. On the other hand, competition may simply be such that the maintenance of jobs comes to depend on self-exploitation, as it may be expressed. In such a case, the workers may actually be worse off. The only democratic concession worth the game is one that involves direct control over the central economic planners, such as is now held by the Politburo. That is not on offer. Hence, all the discussions around self-management really only amount to an exercise in propaganda and possibly also to an attempt to further the incorporation of the skilled working class by putting them on more committees with a measure of decision making, especially over their fellow workers.

Nonetheless, the link between planning and democracy is crucial. I have argued at length that planning is not possible without democracy.[33] While the more general discussion of this question is important, it is logically placed with the theoretical section below. The interesting point here is the way in which it is now seen in the USSR. It is worth quoting the reports of speeches at a conference of the Economics Institute of the Academy of Sciences of the USSR. One Dzarasov, now head of a department of political economy, had this to say:

> The economic position of the person leads to an economically responsible relation to business. Lack of participation in management, its bureaucratization, when formal fulfillment of the plan becomes more important than the actual result, when waste is tolerated instead of achieving economies, when control from below is excluded, and theft and corruption take on a socially dangerous form—in these circumstances a situation is created when workers lose their position as masters of production and responsibility for results.[34]

In other words, some Soviet economists not only see the need for workers' participation as instrumental in raising productivity, but they are also aware of the impossibility of achieving genuine planning without control of the central economic planning system by all those involved in the economy.

The reforms consequent on the adoption of the Law on the State Enterprise involved the election of managers. In fact, such elections were from a panel chosen from above. There could be no real discussion of different policies in the absence of different political tendencies among workers, and hence the result was at most the election of a director who would be more responsive to complaints from below. In the worst case, the result would be largely, though not entirely, cosmetic. There ensued a fight over the election rules. The logic of the law was that it had either to be abolished or to be extended to the point where everyone in the factory could elect the factory director by secret ballot. Nominations would come from below and the different candidates would put forward different platforms.[35] In the first case, the factory directors would be assuaged, and in the second the workers would begin to have some power. The factory directors, however, were totally opposed even to the very limited form of the change. By September 1989, the elections were dropped by decree of the Council of Ministers, something much appreciated by the Supreme Soviet. Even though the election of managers achieved little from the point of view of the workers, it did make the elite and managers, in particular, insecure.[36]

By the beginning of 1990, then, the Gorbachev regime had given up on attracting workers with direct democracy. They recognized that it could not work unless they went the whole way, which would imply the abolition of the elite itself. Hence it was dropped. Its failure was an indication of the fact that Soviet society could not go the German way, with supervisory boards, or the Yugoslav way, with workers' control or any other form short of genuine workers' self-management, because workers would demand the whole hog and not some cosmetic device.

The Anti-alcohol Campaign and Its Failure

The anti-alcohol campaign had particular importance for industry. Although the campaign had some effect, it was not sufficient according to the statements of the Central Committee and reports in the press.[37] The incidence of absenteeism and drunkenness at work may have been down but not to the degree required. The extent of alternatives to official purchase can hardly be underestimated. Alcohol made in private stills was plentiful. Some success has been achieved, but in the long run alcoholism is a consequence of stress within the system, and only to a secondary degree a cause of the stress itself. In the end, the regime was compelled to remove its controls over alcohol—an inevitable result since by addressing alcoholism as it did, it was tackling the symptoms and not the disease.

The stress within the system is crucial. Since the worker is atomized, and so tends to relate to his own work process, he is doubly stressed. He lacks control over his product and over the enterprise, and his response is to work at his own rate and in his own way. Productivity is thus lowered and the worker is deprived of whatever creativity he or she might otherwise have enjoyed. The unpredictability of production, the constant shortages and breakdowns make production a hazardous affair. In addition, the worker is deprived of forms of collective action. To turn to drink is a natural response. This is not unknown in the West, but to a much lesser degree. In every culture there is a particular historical form of stress relief. In Russia it has been concentrated on drink. Soviet commentators have stressed the particular rise in alcoholism under Brezhnev.[38] The real point, of course, is that the level of stress under a system in decline could only rise. While physical conditions were much worse before, people were killed, imprisoned, or otherwise disciplined. There was also a hope for the future.

One might anticipate that drink might have been used as a means of control over the workers. Indeed, this was so under Stalin, when liquor kiosks were specially constructed outside factories. The problem is that the system could not tolerate a still lower level of productivity. In the West, drink and drugs provide a means of relief even if they are officially frowned on or declared illegal. The paradox, in the USSR, is that these forms, which are in widespread use, have to be actively combatted, in order to raise productivity.

Decrees on Norms or Controls over Labor in Production

The publication of labor norms represented an attempt to establish controls over the speed of the production line, overmanning, and wage drift, which resulted from worker domination over the labor process.[39] But the establishment of tighter norms is only possible if sanctions are available, and these are absent. The Soviet Union has been trying to apply them ever since it came into existence. Stakhanovism, so-called socialist emulation, the use of camp labor, and threats of imprisonment have all failed to achieve any real change.

The struggle between workers and management has been largely conducted around the question of piece rates and hence the speed of the production line. This has become symbolic of workers' attitudes to production. Zaslavskaia estimated that a third of workers work properly.[40] In fact, the reason why workers are able to control their work process ultimately lies in their relative strength against the management. It always pays the management of the enterprise to collude with workers to have a defined output, even if it is considerably below the potential level.

There are only two ways around this problem. One is to go back to the use of prison camps and so terrorize the workers, but such a gross incentive system functions only to a limited degree. Since there is only a limited positive incentive, the quality of production under such a system is usually low. It is therefore not suitable for modern production. The second solution is that of the standard capitalist incentive system of unemployment plus real money. Modern capitalism, however, has been compelled to use a battery of workplace controls in addition to the penalty of firing or the reward of more money. The trade union relationship with management has evolved into a form of collusive control over the workers. Promotion procedures play a critical role in many companies.

How can the USSR evolve into modern capitalism with powerful trade unions without giving away too much to the unions? Can promotion be so arranged that it proceeds in a less corrupt way than could be expected? Can the enormous plants and enterprises be broken up to prevent the workers showing their strength? If the answers to these and other questions of the same kind are negative, then even with a reserve army of labor and consumer goods in the shops, it is highly likely that the worker's existing control over the labor process will continue. The only way to make the answer to these questions positive would be to introduce a very large reserve army of labor, permit emigration, and allow a large section of Russian industry to be transferred to foreign ownership. It does not seem likely, therefore, that control over the labor process can be transferred to management.

This question, which is one of establishing strict controls over the production line to establish a uniform and optimum speed within an enterprise, is discussed in more detail in the next section.

Wages, Norms, and the Campaign against Egalitarianism

The campaign against egalitarianism is part of both an attempt to raise salaries, which is being done by decree, and a decision to widen wage differentials. According to the deputy chairman of the State Committee on Labor, workers' pay rates are being raised by some 20–25 percent on average, compared to the 30–35 percent raise allocated to specialists. The specialists (i.e., the intelligentsia) have lost out, however, because enterprises have only paid them some 20–22 percent more, having insufficient funds, and some specialists have been placed in lower categories after reexamination.[41]

According to the wage reforms of autumn 1986, the wage scales were altered to increase the differences between grade six, the top of the scale, and grade one, the first point on the wage scale. In the food industry, the bottom was increased by 16 percent but the top by 33 percent. In engineering, the system was so altered that three wage scales replaced the previous wage scale, introducing much greater differences between someone at the bottom of the lowest wage scale and the highly skilled worker at the tip of the highest wage scale. Bonuses were also supposed to be paid according to position on the wage scale, so that someone on the top would get a higher percentage of salary from bonuses than someone at the bottom. Finally, workers not performing as scheduled, in terms of quality or quantity, could be reduced in grade. On the face of it, these wage reforms were a very considerable step toward greater inequality among workers.[42]

In fact, however, Shcherbakov, the head of the wages section of the State Committee on Labor, reported that they had failed to "achieve the main object, the surmounting of egalitarianism in the payment of labor."[43] He goes on to point out that in some instances specialists are being allocated pay up to 24 percent less than that of workers in the same factory. In turn, worker differentiation is not being imposed. Norms are also not being raised. He gives one instance where 180 percent fulfillment continues. This all sounds familiar except for one fact, hitherto not mentioned. All these instances are occurring *after* the introduction of the new conditions under which pay is to be allocated. Shcherbakov depicts a situation where the position has actually deteriorated after the reforms on issue after issue. Bonuses are not allocated, specialists and workers are not being examined for their tasks. Brigades do not function at all in industry, even though they do in agriculture and construction. Above all, surveys have shown that increases in productivity have occurred through the dismissal of workers, even where it is unjustified in cost terms. In areas of labor surplus, such dismissals make no sense, as he points out. He is not slow to imply that the real reason for the failure lies in the absence of *glasnost'* or democracy. In other words, the workers have resisted the changes and management cannot go too far in opposing the workers. Hence, they prefer simply to issue orders to workers to transfer to other jobs, not wishing to get involved in protests. It is obvious that a massive reform of this kind will not work unless the workers are somehow induced to take part in its operation. If they oppose it, there is no hope at all. Such indeed is the case.

There has also been widespread discussion of the extension of systems of payment by results. The problem, however, cannot be solved by simply raising the money differentials, as the absence of goods makes such money differences among workers of secondary importance. In addition, the nature of the payment system appears to be such that it automatically erodes differentials. Under Stalin the wage system was reduced to chaos. There was no one in the first two wage grades and there were huge rates of overfulfillment. The reforms of 1957 onward were supposed to take care of this. Indeed, they did, in that the number of wage grades was reduced and overfulfillment of norms was greatly reduced. Nonetheless, during the Brezhnev period the same phenomenon reasserted itself. The lowest wage grade became meaningless and overfulfillment of, say, 28 percent in engineering became normal. At the same time the differences in pay according to skill were greatly eroded.[44] Finally, in this regard it has to be pointed out that workers have not historically been easily divided on money lines in the USSR.

Nonetheless, the decision to try to ally with the skilled working class has meant a need to reform the wage structure and come to grips with the old structure. In an exceptionally open article, Leonid Gordon of the Institute of the World Working Class Movement in Moscow has portrayed the Stalin period as one of forced industrialization with the appropriate wage structures. Gordon has pointed out that wages remain at subsistence level, but that until 1965 they were below that level. Furthermore, he argues that as a result workers remain discontented with their wages. He argues forcibly for the introduction of greater wage differentials, pointing out that in fact workers are now virtually given a guaranteed income approaching the status of a pension and that wage differences between skilled and unskilled are down to a ratio of 1.4 to 1, and hardly exist between semiskilled and unskilled.[45]

These features reinforce the view, argued above, that workers do not in fact sell their labor power, a necessary consequence of such statements. Gorbachev in fact confirmed this view in his speech to the 1988 February Plenum of the Central Committee, when he said that it was well known that many people just get paid for reporting for work.[46] They alienate their labor power, but that is another matter. The essential point is that if wages are given automatically and there is little difference between one worker and another, there is in fact no labor market. There is a certain movement of labor; such movement however, is not based on payment for labor power but rather on a question of workers' convenience, and it is subject to state controls.

The entire reform structure hinges on this question of turning labor power into a commodity and the consequent removal of the automatic wage, the destruction of the workers' control over the labor process, the introduction of substantial differences in pay between skilled and less skilled, foremen and workers, and finally removal of the right to employment.

Workers' consciousness is overwhelmingly in favor of an egalitarian solution. While in the first instance this represents an attack on privilege, and so on the elite and sections of the intelligentsia, it is also a statement of a desire for relatively small differences in pay among workers.[47] It is only to be expected, however, that workers would be confused both by the official line and by their immediate situation. Miners, for instance, as indicated here already, were opposed to cooperatives and the inequality involved, but on the other hand, they

THE WORKING CLASS 105

wanted higher prices for their own goods. There is a contradiction between the collective interest, which is egalitarian, and the immediate interest and consciousness.

Unemployment

The absence of a reserve army of labor has been a feature of the USSR since 1929, although the presence of prison camps may be regarded as partially fulfilling that role during the Stalin period. The reason for this has to do with the increasing absorption of resources into an economy that permanently and increasingly malfunctions. There have been a large number of articles of various kinds arguing for the introduction of unemployment in the USSR. This would serve to reduce overmanning and act as a spur to workers in employment.[48] It has been explicitly ruled out as a method of proceeding, but this retreat is more likely strategic than of substance. Soviet economists have been speaking for too long about the need for unemployment for the demand to be dropped. The problem is that it is not enough to introduce a small reserve army to have an effect; a large reserve army, however, would destroy such stability as now exists. Hence, any move in this regard can only be gradual and surreptitious. That indeed is the real meaning of Aganbegian's favoring bankruptcy but not unemployment.

The decrees on redeployment in the new labor laws produced in January 1988 are one more step toward the establishment of a reserve army of labor. Workers are given one month's pay on dismissal and up to three months on full pay to obtain another job. While this law establishes a social security framework, it does not introduce unemployment. Its contradictory nature is contained in the permission given to enterprises to continue employing pensioners. While such pensioners might act as competitors, the decrees are really restating the intractable problems of a labor shortage.[49] Nonetheless, the decree is crucial in confirming the removal of guaranteed employment. By a decree of 17 September 1987, some workers from late 1986 on could be dismissed without being found other jobs by their factory directors.[50] In the report cited above, Shcherbakov refers to the redeployment of workers as the main means of raising productivity and indeed gives examples of hundreds of thousands of workers being redeployed. While such movement of workers might raise productivity, it is not unemployment. As he points out, such worker transfers are being misused, so that instead of increasing production, workers are removed from the plant to provide higher productivity statistics. This again is only to be expected. Wherever there are indicators, they will be abused.

While the overall shortage of labor continued, the possibility of dismissals combined with the relative deprivation of the non-European areas of the USSR has meant relatively high levels of unemployment in such areas as Azerbaijan, which, in any case, had the lowest average wages in the USSR.[51] These areas had relatively little industrialization, a high peasant population, and high birth rates. The effect of the reforms in this sphere, as in others, has been toward further disintegration. If, indeed, the policy of driving up to 20 percent of the population out of their existing jobs were implemented, the results for these peripheral areas would be disastrous.

The Brigade System

The brigade system is the one obvious measure, particularly for agriculture, that appears unique to the regime, not in its invention but in its role. It amounts to an interesting attempt to inculcate discipline by breaking up large enterprises into small units under responsible controllers. It has never been clear, however, how modern production can be so fragmented that profits can be allocated to such units. In practice, not many enterprises were able to establish brigades genuinely based on so-called economic accounting. In any event, there was evidence that workers resisted these forms of control. Since the control was direct and not really through economic forms, the social and physical pressure on the foreman or brigade leader has been considerable, in particular over the question of norms. In other words, the regime sees the brigade leaders and foremen as a tool in controlling the worker and as a bridge to skilled workers, who might ally themselves with the regime.

The brigade system appears to be an alternative form of control. It seems to be a cross between the "Volvo"-type experiments, which break up a factory into small work groups with their own decision-making process and responsibility, and a Thatcherite attempt to increase the rotation of jobs, decrease overmanning, intensify the work process, relate work done to reward, and increase the overall degree of control over the work process.[52] Aganbegian seemed to see the brigade system as the ideal solution, as noted above.

Much has already been written on the brigade system, but the essential point is that although officially 70 percent of the work force is now on the system— that is, they belong to small work units—only 31 percent are actually on the so-called economically accountable brigades in industry. In construction and agriculture the proportion is much higher, although in transport it is much lower.[53] Indeed, how could it be otherwise, since it is not believable that modern factories can be broken up into separate economic units. There is no way that Gorbachev will succeed in using brigades unless he wants to break up the enormous concentrations of industrial plant in the USSR. There is no question that he might want to go that way, as witness the articles to that effect under Andropov. Still, the idea of brigades is not only utopian, it is absurd. The integration of modern production necessarily prevents any attempt to reward any part of the factory separately, while the regular failure to receive supplies on time, lack of spare parts, and machinery breakdowns reinforce the management's inability to determine the efficiency of any part of the factory. The system has to be reformed as a whole or not at all. That is the lesson.

It is true that in those parts of the system where the labor process is most independent, as in agriculture, construction, and repair/maintenance, the brigade system might operate as a mode of control, but here the attitude of workers is crucial and the evidence is that they ignore the instructions of their brigade leaders or even physically assault them. There is little reason to expect that the lack of goods, will be overcome specially for such brigade members, and in the absence of goods monetary rewards become meaningless. Finally, there is no difference in the lack of supplies for the different sectors of production, however independent they might be. Thus, the brigade system can only have a limited effect in certain sectors.

It is all the more interesting that Tat′iana Zaslavskaia should have written what amounted to the editorial on the front page of *Sovetskaia Rossiia*, 7 January 1986, arguing that the solution to the problems she outlines lies in the brigade system. Her article argues in effect that there is no incentive system operative and that the workers are lazy, whether as a consequence of the system or for genetic reasons is not clear. Her earlier article, the so-called Novosibirsk Report, justly well known, had also placed the blame on the lazy workers, but with more finesse.[54]

Economic Reforms and Their Effect on the Worker

Price Reform

The raising of prices to reflect costs, and in particular the removal of agricultural subsidies holding down the price of food, is essential if any market-type incentive system is to be introduced. The obvious attack on the standard of living of the worker has never in any regime been mitigated by wage rises for the lower paid. Gorbachev's promises are useless in this respect. It is obvious that the whole point of the price rises is to bring demand and supply in alignment. If this is done, the waiting lines and rationing must end, and the advantage that goes to those who can line up and can get the ration will disappear. Then those who have money will be able to buy goods and those who do not will be worse off. The rich will be richer and the poor will be poorer. It is no argument that bureaucratic allocation gives advantage to the bureaucrats and speculators. It does so, but a percentage of ordinary people will lose out when they have to pay higher prices, which they will not be able to afford.

The raising of prices to reflect costs, and in particular the removal of agricultural subsidies, so increasing the price of food, has been on the agenda for at least three of the first five years of Gorbachev's tenure. As chairman of the State Commission on Prices, Valentin S. Pavlov argued this case. Even though he insisted that consumption would remain the same, the political impact of such a measure is so great that it is difficult to see it ever being really implemented. The effect of price increases in sparking off social unrest in Poland has not gone unnoticed. Indeed, Pavlov explicitly referred to the previous price rise effects within the USSR. That has not prevented Gorbachev speaking at length about the effect of the necessary rise in prices, or Soviet and Western economists producing a chorus about the absolute necessity of raising agricultural prices. Clearly the regime will have to change prices if it is to have any economic reform at all, but it cannot do this and destabilize the system at the same time. Hence caution again is the key word. Pavlov spoke of decentralizing all but 10 percent of prices, but since he spoke of some 22 to 25 million prices, 2 to 3 million key prices will still be controlled, and he is quite clear on that front.[55] By 1990, the regime had retreated numerous times from its declared intention to introduce cost-based prices. Each time it attempted to raise prices, the objections from workers and the official trade unions forced a retreat.

Reformers argue somewhat disingenuously that the subsidies go more to the wealthier than to the poorer sections of the population. That, of course, is true, but it ignores the obvious fact that the poorer will suffer more from the removal of subsidies and the richer groups will gain more from a situation where they can purchase goods in the shops rather than being rationed. A transitional hybrid with both rationing and a progressive increase in prices appeared as a possibility. This only puts off the evil day when the workers confront the reality of higher prices.

Decentralization

Decentralization was first officially discussed at the Central Committee plenum at the end of June 1987. If fully implemented, the result would be a decentralized control system using the wholesale-trading organs. Everything would then depend on the nature of the organization of those wholesale-trade units, as well as their coordination. The problems associated with such decentralization were partially discussed by Gorbachev at the June 1987 plenum. Nonetheless, there appears to be no real method of implementation. Even if wholesale organs are set up and obligated to work on a market basis, for the system to work there have to be competitive firms, delivery of goods on time, and freedom for each enterprise to determine its output. The establishment of the wholesale-trading organizations and the attempt to make firms relatively independent will undoubtedly put pressure on the workers of the plant to work harder, but like all reforms, it will in due course run to sand when the workers see that there is no need to continue to obey the injunctions, as no change is likely.

An editorial in *Kommunist* offers the following appraisal:

> The "Law on the State Enterprise" envisages economic management on the basis of "democratic centralism." . . . the widening of the rights and responsibilities of enterprises and labor collectives will in no way be accompanied by a weakening of centralized planning and management. . . . Norms of distribution

of profit between enterprises and society, amortization norms, percentages and rules for credit, etc., etc., ... all these are forms of centralized plan directive and are no less strict and much more effective than the direct apportionment by volume indicators. Planning, investment, and financing indicators also remain the prerogative of the state.[56]

Thus centralization remains. Many observers found it difficult to see how the volume basis of so-called planning could be removed on the basis of the 1987 reforms. Thus, the prominent Soviet economist V.D. Belkin pointed out that "if the system of directive centralized planning remains in its present form, then ... wholesale trade will be a toy."[57] He asserted that there was no official body set up to deal with the reformed supply system.

Whatever shakes up the system tends to have an ameliorative effect, but it wears off quite rapidly. Indeed, if Aganbegian is correct in his statement that there was an absolute decline in productivity in 40 percent of industrial enterprises after 1979,[58] then a rise in industrial production was not difficult to achieve. When industry is working below capacity, as Gorbachev indicated for the construction and other industries (June 1987 plenum), then a shake-up can clearly be beneficial. The real question was not whether he could succeed, but what he was to do once these effects wore off.

In March 1990 Gorbachev declared, yet again but with more determination, that he was going to introduce all the necessary aspects of the reform, including competition, market-determined prices, etc. He really had no alternative, since the reforms to that date had failed and he had either to return to the old system or to attempt to force through the market. If he fails, then his whole attempt to reform the economy and so society will have failed. It does not require much perspicacity to see that he has only a very small chance of succeeding. He has the political ability to force the changes but not the political support.

Reform of the Banking System

Hitherto enterprises have found it easy to obtain and renew credit. It is now suggested that unsuccessful enterprises may not be able to do so. Since banks are not threatened by bankruptcy or takeovers, etc., as they are under capitalism, it is not likely that the banks exercise the ultimate sanction of withdrawing credit. Furthermore, the act of doing so would lead to the bankruptcy of the enterprise with all the attendant bureaucratic problems, which no organization is likely to welcome. Again this matter was discussed by Gorbachev at the June 1987 plenum when he pointed to the fact that money in circulation had more than twice exceeded the money level of goods produced in the period after 1972. He correctly pointed out that this is not authentic money. However, he provided no real solution. In the reform program the application of strict controls over finance was to take place first, in the period 1988–90, but it is predicated on the conditions already discussed.

The banking reforms and the creation of a central bank with independent commercial banks under its aegis is essential to any market reform. The barrier lies in the absence of a capital market. Under existing conditions, the banks have to lend money to enterprises that might otherwise cease to operate. The ultimate reason, therefore, lies in the fear of mass protests against unemployment.

Foreign Trade

Decrees on direct contact with external agencies have not been genuinely implemented. Indeed they could not be unless the control over currency were relaxed. Joint ventures have been introduced, but at first only Finland took up the challenge. Subsequent progress has been slow.[59] By March 1990, only 6 percent of 1,200 joint ventures were actually operating.[60] The USSR is applying to join international trade and financial bodies, but it cannot really abandon the monopoly of foreign trade without destroying its own industry. Nor is a policy of permitting international competition to raise the level of unemployment any different from a deliberate policy of raising unemployment. It is significant that in Eastern Europe, Western capital has preferred to go into property, finance, tourism, or even fast food rather than into manufacturing.

On the other hand, joint ventures may well bring in foreign currency, which will permit purchase of foreign goods to pay the skilled workers with useful goods. Foreign bankers are now wary of Eastern Europe, given its high level of foreign debt, and the USSR has been raising its debt levels quite rapidly in the Gorbachev years. Only an overall detente-type deal with the West could provide sufficient foreign funds actually to provide the wherewithal to reequip industry and provide the consumer goods required.

The logic of the introduction of joint ventures is toward ever more concessions to the foreign partner. Foreign investors want to invest in the USSR to take advantage of the internal market, but the Soviet "planners" want foreign investors to invest in plant and equipment that can export goods to the West. For that reason, Soviet controls have ensured that only that part of profits which is earned in foreign currency can be exported. Whereas the East European economies have been prepared to hand over much of their economy to Western firms, the Soviet elite is not prepared to sacrifice itself in the same way. While the introduction of special economic zones may tempt investors, it is not clear how many Western firms will come. It appears more as a panacea seized on by promarket intellectuals.[61] Even the acceptance of Western control and management has not been enough.

Nonetheless, foreign firms or joint ventures would attract Soviet labor, which would have to work in a way similar to workers in the West in order to make the firm profitable. To the extent that they were better paid and could be fired easily, such workers would indeed be radically different from the ordinary Soviet worker. The addition of substantial numbers of foreign firms with the right to

THE WORKING CLASS 111

hire and fire, together with the so-called cooperatives and private agriculture, might add up to a substantial market sector. The foreign firms might, therefore, constitute a wedge in the Soviet economy for private enterprise and greater control over Soviet labor.

The Necessary Failure of the Economic Reforms

The reason for the lack of success of the reforms is the same as that given by the Hungarian reformer Reszö Nyers for the failure of the earlier reform program in that country. "At the root of the party's hesitancy over reforms," he noted, "lay the fear of conflict and social tensions in Hungary." Further, "Hungarians would not even accept a small amount of unemployment which would inevitably result from meaningful economic reforms."[62] It is this question of the attitude of the working class about which the Soviet regime is most concerned. The USSR is not Hungary, and could not even contemplate a limited attack on the working class.

Gorbachev gradually moved over, in his speeches in April 1985, June 1985, March 1986, June 1987, and October 1987 in Murmansk, to openly expressing the need for a market-type solution. Nonetheless, he has never produced a completely open speech in which he calls for the whole gamut of aspects of the market, which he clearly would prefer. Measures proposed have shifted from economic accountability to direct trading between enterprises, and by June 1987 the establishment of wholesale trading as the basic form, together with possible bankruptcies, while in October 1987 price rises were crucial.

There is a natural progression. He has already incorporated the need to be part of the world market, on the way toward the complete acceptance of a labor market and capital market. The question is whether Gorbachev can actually get there and take much of the intelligentsia and the elite with him. The almost certain reply is that he has no hope. It is too late. Two forces stand against him. The first is the enormous growth in size and class character of the work force in the last two decades, so graphically demonstrated by the mine workers' strikes of July 1989. The days of the intelligentsia are numbered; it is probably no longer possible for the intelligentsia to take a share of power, even if the coalition referred to would take shape. But it is the only strategy left for the elite, and even if they are unlikely to succeed, this strategy is better than nothing, especially when it is realized that they are unlikely to perceive the absurdity of going to a market during a period of world market failure. And this is the second reason why Gorbachev is likely to fail: the necessary subsidy from the Western capitalist class cannot come, given its current banking and industrial crisis.

It remains necessary to stress that even if the attempt is doomed, that does not mean that it may not be made. The Soviet regime is in a real crisis, mitigated only by the more general world crisis.

At this point it will be useful to consider the whole nature of Soviet political economy, in order to understand the need for the economic reforms.

Notes

1. A modern description of this school is provided by R. Kaplinsky in "Restructuring the Capitalist Labour Process: Some Lessons from the Car Industry," *Cambridge Journal of Economics*, 1988, no. 4, pp. 452–70.
2. The wage-grade system used has meant that most workers, skilled or unskilled, remain in wage grades 3 or 4. The few that move up to grades 5 or 6 effectively do so through age and contacts.
3. In 1987 there were 578,800 workers with higher education (*Narodnoe khoziaistvo SSSR v 1988*, p. 52).
4. Rather interestingly, in a general discussion of the nature of the Soviet working class, V.S. Levchuk and L.A. Gordon argue in terms of the "peasantization" of the Soviet worker during the 1930s and 1940s. The worker, they say, lacked the necessary discipline that goes with proletarianization. See the roundtable in *Voprosy istorii*, 1988, no. 1, pp. 3ff.
5. For a discussion of the evolution of the form in which workers relate to the work process, see Donald Filtzer, *Soviet Workers and Stalinist Industrialisation: The Formation of Modern Soviet Production Relations, 1928–41* (London: Pluto, 1986). Filtzer has taken my basic thesis, originally put forward in the journal *Critique*, and employed it to good effect in relation to the workers struggles in the 1930s.
6. H.H. Ticktin, "The Contradictions of Soviet Society and Professor Bettelheim," *Critique* 6, pp. 35–38.
7. N. Rimar, "Novye usloviia—novye trebovaniia," *Sotsialisticheskii trud*, 1987, no. 10, p. 61. Rimar points out that many workers overfulfill their work plans by 130 to 150 percent. He states that the average level of possible plan fulfillment is understated by 25 to 30 percent. Fifty percent overfulfillment is normal. In fact, workers tend to work up to a certain limit, beyond which they do not go in case their norms are raised.
8. Kaplinsky, "Restructuring the Capitalist Labour Process."
9. M. Buchalkov, "Sovershenstovovat' sistemu trudoykh normativov i norm," *Sotsialisticheskii trud*, 1987, no. 10, p. 55.
10. V.D. Kozlov, "Pochemu rabochie ogranichivaiut vyrabotku," *Sotsiologicheskie issledovaniia*, 1990, no. 2, pp. 50–56, discusses the issue of why and how the worker in the USSR restricts the rate at which he works.
11. G. Kulagin, "Trudno byt' universalom," *Pravda*, 9 December 1982. The author argues for small plants, for control reasons.
12. Stuart Anderson, "Nikolai Shmelyov: The Russian Milton Friedman," *Bloc*, 1989, no. 1, pp. 25–29.
13. *XXVII S"ezd Kommunisticheskoi Partii Sovetskogo Soiuza. Stenograficheskii otchet* (Moscow: Politizdat, 1986), pp. 519–20.
14. Speech by V.I. Bakulin at the First Session of the Congress of People's Deputies, *Pravda*, 2 June 1989, p. 3.
15. *Pravda*, 19 July 1989. Gorbachev refers to demands that cooperatives be closed down and states that he is against speculation but questions whether demands for higher wages and social reforms without considering the effect on the performance of the enterprise are the best way forward. He then caves in to the miners and says that where cooperatives are against the social policy of the regime, they can be closed down. He faces both ways.
16. E. Torkanovskii, "Uchastie trudiashchikhsia v upravlenii forma realizatsii sobstvennosti," *Voprosy ekonomiki*, 1986, no. 2, pp. 52–62.
17. For a useful empirical discussion of the workers under the reforms in the USSR based on discussions in Soviet newspapers and journals, see David Mandel, " 'Revolu-

tionary Reform' in Soviet Factories," *Socialist Register* (London: Merlin Press, 1989), pp. 102–27.

18. *Materialy Plenuma Tsentral'nogo Komiteta KPSS, 27–28 ianvaria 1987* (Moscow: Politizdat, 1987).

19. "Politiko-ekonomicheskie osnovy uskoreniia," *Voprosy ekonomiki*, 1987, no, 3, p. 52.

20. *Pravda*, 19 July 1989.

21. *Pravda*, (6 April 1990, p. 2) reported that a new law on the appointment of managers, which would remove their election, had been prepared by the Council of Ministers, to be passed by the Supreme Soviet.

22. *Financial Times*, 24 July 1989.

23. "Ekonomicheskaia platforma Soiuza trudiashchikhsia Kuzbasa," *Voprosy ekonomiki*, February 1990, p. 85.

24. See the article attacking the miners' strike in *Izvestiia*, 7 September 1989, in which a complaint is made that production has become more irregular because of the failure of the railways to deliver, consequent on strikes.

25. "Shakhta: Zabastovka zakonchilas'. Shto dal'she?" *Ogonek*, 1990, no. 3, p. 3.

26. SMOT Information Agency (Paris), *Information Bulletin*, Special issue: Materials of the Vorkuta Strikes, no. 30 (December 1989), p. 1.

27. Ibid., p. 2.

28. An example of the failure of *gospriemka* was given at the Moscow Regional Party Committee Plenum in August 1987. Thus, "Of the 59 enterprises operating under *gospriemka*, 24 have shown an overexpenditure above plan production costs of 16 million rubles in the first six months of this year." The workers are blamed for not taking *perestroika* seriously. See "Trudnyi pereval," *Kommunist* 1987, no. 13 (8 August), pp. 27–37.

29. "Ne bylo ni grosha, da vdrug million," *Pravda*, 8 January 1988, p. 2. This article is discussed below.

30. *Pravda*, 24 January 1988.

31. *Narodnoe khoziaistvo SSSR za 70 let* (Moscow, 1987), p. 197.

32. See the article by Joel C. Moses, "Worker Self-Management and the Reformist Alternative in Soviet Labour Policy, 1979–85," *Soviet Studies*, April 1987, where he gives an account of some of the discussions around greater worker participation. Also see Torkanovskii, "Uchastie trudiashchikhsia."

33. H.H. Ticktin, "Towards a Political Economy of the USSR," *Critique* 1 (1973).

34. "Politiko-ekonomicheskie osnovy uskoreniia, *Voprosy ekonomiki*, 1987, no. 3, p. 50.

35. V.I. Gerchikov and B.G. Proshkin argue this case in "Vybornost' rukoviditelei, pervyi opyt, pervye problemy" (*EKO* 1988, no. 5).

36. R.W. Davies gives an account of the reform in "Gorbachev's Socialism in Historical Perspective," *New Left Review* 179, pp. 22–23. He cites Aganbegian's remarks about the introduction of the election of the factory directors in order to motivate workers: "the further we go the more obvious the negative sides of this system." Davies then says, "More recently, workers' self-management was severely restricted in a number of ministries by a Council of Ministers decree, leading to a 'very negative reaction in the population' " (here quoting a speech by A.A. Sobchak printed in *Pravda*, 10 October 1990).

37. The Central Committee issued a decree that noted that the decree of 5 May 1985 "On Measures for Overcoming Drunkenness and Alcoholism" and other related measures have led to a "healthier moral atmosphere in society and a strengthening of law and order." The decree asserts further that experience of the last three years has shown that

where educational, economic, medical, and administrative-legal measures were implemented in accordance with the principles laid down by the Party, there were positive results. The coordinated efforts of Party, Soviet, and law-and-order organs and social organizations have led to a marked reduction in instances of drunkenness at work and in public places. The situation inside families has improved and there has been a reduction in the number of accidents. Also, drink-related crime has decreased. However, "radical changes have not as yet been achieved." This is due in part to the failure to take advantage of the wide possibilities for combating alcoholism and drunkenness in a sufficiently sustained way. See "V Tsentral'nom Komitete KPSS: O khode vypolneniia postanovlenii TsK KPSS po voprosam usileniia bor'by s p'ianstvom i alkogolizmom," *Sovetskaia Rossiia*, 26 October 1988, p. 1. I am indebted to Walter Joyce for this summary.

38. Valerii Kondakov, "Trezvost' i tol'ko trezvost'," *Sovetskaia Rossiia*, 30 October 1988.

39. Bulletin of the State Committee on Labor, December 1987.

40. T.I. Zaslavskaia, "Chelovecheskii faktor razvitiia ekonomiki i sotsial'naia spravedlivost'," *Kommunist*, 1987 no. 13, pp. 63–64; quoted in V.D. Kozlov, "Pochemu rabochie ogranichivaiut vyrabotku," *Sotsiologicheskie issledovaniia*, 1990, no. 2, p. 51.

41. L.A. Kostin, "Perestroika i zarplata," *Izvestiia*, 11 September 1987. Summary provided by Walter Joyce.

42. "Perestroika sistemy zarabotnoi platy," *Ekonomicheskaia gazeta*, 1986, no. 43, pp. 6–7. It consists of an interview with Gladkii, the chairman of Goskomtrud, the State Committee on Labour.

43. V. Shcherbakov, "Novye usloviia oplata truda: kak organizovat' zavod," *Ekonomicheskaia gazeta*, 1988, no. 7.

44. L.A. Kostin, "Perestroika systemy oplata truda," *Voprosy ekonomiki*, November 1987.

45. L.A. Gordon, "Sotsial'naia politika v sfere oplata truda (vchera i segodnia)," *Sotsiologicheskie issledovaniia* 1987, no. 4.

46. M.S. Gorbachev, speech to Plenum of CPSU Central Committee on 18 February 1988.

47. E.A. Mel'n. Speech at an editorial roundtable, *Sotsiologicheskie issledovaniia*, 1989, no. 6, p. 43. He found in a survey of workers that they were against "leveling" when asked their opinion of it, but when it came to concrete measures they did not want a difference in pay between the lowest and highest paid workers of more than 1.7. Since everyone in the USSR would be careful in opposing the official line in favor of greater differentials, this result may not be unexpected.

48. In a review of a work by one T.A. Iugai, G. Popov reported with obvious approval that at the moment workers who are displaced are given work elsewhere in the enterprise, but that in the Eleventh Five-year Plan it is intended that unqualified workers be dismissed, while in the Twelfth Five-year Plan it is intended that there be dismissal of workers of average skill. See *Social Science Abstracts*, seriia 2, ekonomika, 1985 no. 2 (Abstracts), 42. The well-known essay by Nikolai Shmelev, "Avansy i dol'gi," in *Novyi mir*, 1987, no. 6, argues precisely for a reserve army of labor and quotes approvingly the economist Shatalin who argues for the same in *Kommunist* 1986, no. 14. It is true that they are only arguing for a limited amount of unemployment, but they are quite clear that it is as a form of control over the worker. Kostakov, Director of the Scientific Research Institute of Gosplan, argues in *Kommunist*, 1987, no. 14, that labor must be redeployed now, as present practices are retarding productivity, but that technical progress requires some 16 million persons to be dismissed and redeployed over time. Nevertheless, he argues that there will not be unemployment. His real intention appears to be the same as that of the above two authors: that dismissals are essential and a small reserve army will

be introduced with the statement that unemployment will not be tolerated. Since most of the 16 million will be reemployed, the argument is not illogical. *Kommunist,* 1987, no. 18, also discusses unemployment.

49. *Pravda,* 19 January 1988, pp. 1–2. Decree issued by the Central Committee of the CPSU, the Council of Ministers of the USSR, and the All Union Central Council of Trade Unions.

50. *Ekonomicheskaia gazeta,* 1986, no. 44.

51. The average wage in Azerbaijan was 138 rubles per month in 1987, as compared with an average for the USSR of 192.5, and 155.4 for Moldavia. Armenia's average wage was 159.8 while Estonia had the highest at 242.1. See *Trud v SSSR* (Moscow: Finansy i Statistiki, 1988), p. 157.

52. See "Brigady v usloviakh eksperimenta," *Ekonomicheskaia gazeta* 1985, no. 2, and similar articles in practically every issue of that journal since. In this particular article the bureaucratic avoidance of controls by workers is also described. If the work is overreported, then the attempt to make people work harder must fail.

53. *Narodnoe khoziaistvo SSSR za 70 let,* p. 108; while the figures moved upwards in the *Narodnoe khoziaistvo SSSR v 1988,* p. 67, the overall point remained valid, that a minority of the workers were on self-financing brigades. This point is made in some detail in an article by Iu. Rytov, "Idem na podriad," *Izvestiia,* 9 July 1988.

54. "The Novosibirsk Report," *Survey,* Spring 1984, pp. 84–107.

55. V.S. Pavlov, "Perestroika i tsenoobrazovanie," *Izvestiia,* 30 August 1987, p. 2.

56. *Kommunist,* 1987, no. 11.

57. *EKO,* 1987, no. 6.

58. See *Inside Perestroika: The Future of the Soviet Economy* (New York: Harper and Row, 1989), p. 146.

59. See, for example, *Financial Times,* 10 March 1990, p. 24, for a report on the disappointing record of joint ventures.

60. *Financial Times,* 12 March 1990, p. 15.

61. See A. Cherepanov, "Svobodnye ekonomicheskie zony," *Izvestiia,* 14 August 1988, p. 5, for a typically upbeat discussion of the topic.

62. *Financial Times,* 19 June 1987.

7

The Nature of the Soviet Political Economy

Control over Labor in the Brezhnev Period

All problems go back to labor.[1] The slowness of the introduction of new technology, egalitarianism in pay, overmanning, and the large repair sector are all a consequence of the inability of enterprise managers to do anything but concede to workers. The special character of the Brezhnev period lay precisely in these concessions. It was a period of social peace because the elite preferred to concede to the workers rather than take them on. The initial reforms under Kosygin were dropped in favor of partial attempts at control, which only increased the size of the controlling apparatus while having little long-term effect. This was a considerable contrast with the attempts made under Khrushchev to find organizational forms of control. It was even more of a contrast with the Stalin period, when direct force was employed. From the point of view of the elite, workers can be controlled by compulsion, through an incentive system mixed with administrative measures, or through the market. They have tried all three at different times and there can be no doubt that the market is the preferred solution. The problem is that it means a direct confrontation with workers—or peasants, when the latter had any economic power.

The regime used force with the peasants and workers under Stalin, although it used other forms of control as well. But once the scope of force as a mode of control was reduced, an alternative had to be found. Under Khrushchev the removal of direct force initially had its own incentive effect. Nonetheless, pressure was being applied to raise output through administrative measures. This was extended under Brezhnev, but in such a half-hearted way that little change in fact occurred. The economic reforms were abandoned, the Shchekino experiment ultimately failed,[2] fulfillment of plans through realization in money terms meant little as long as volume quotas remained. Through all the talk of the Brezhnev era, the situation of the workers did not materially worsen. Gorbachev is very different. He stands for a confrontation with the workers. The Brezhnev group preferred a strategic retreat, whereas the present regime sees attack as the best means of defense. Aganbegian and the forces around him are attempting a rollback of the position of the workers as far as possible. This is not a new position, but the considerable gains made by workers under Brezhnev, just because of the nature of the socialization of industry and the cowardly nature of the elite, give the issue immediacy.

The Laws and Contradictions of the System

The fundamental contradiction of the Soviet system lies in the form of control over the workers, through their atomization. This necessarily leads to a decline in productivity and hence to a lower standard of living for the workers than would otherwise be the case. It also means that the elite are deprived of the power to direct the productive forces in a manner they would regard as efficient. This contradiction intensifies over time as the socialization of production increases workers' power. As a result, efficiency actually declines even if output goes up. The nature of the waste changes. In the early period, workers directly sabotaged production, took time off, had high labor turnover, whereas in the post-Stalin period the norm became the focal point of the struggle. This represented a movement from a more individualistic to a less individualistic form of struggle. The logic of this movement is that workers will collectively decide on the norm, instead of having it decided on the basis of bargaining between management and skilled and older workers. Hence, the new regime has decided that the norm has to be decided by more reliable elements.

It is easier to deal with workers who act on an entirely individualistic basis, but more difficult when they begin to act, even if unconsciously, in their own class interests. Hence the Brezhnev retreat. There appears, then, to be a law of the Soviet regime. It is not one of increasing waste as put forward by Antonio Carlo,[3] since the waste of the 1930s with the death of millions from starvation is incomparable, but is rather a law of increasing inefficiency, or a growing gap between potential output for the consumer and actual output. Thus, the inefficiency of department one as documented by Soviet figures is perhaps graphically shown by the simple fact that expenditure on capital repairs of machinery and equipment came to 8,670 million rubles in 1986 as opposed to just 288 million for light industry.[4] These figures also graphically bring out the real expenditure on the different sectors. As indicated above, light industry had a lower percentage of incomplete projects and a worse increase in costs-to-output ratio. This leads to the conclusion that department one has an enormous expenditure on repairs and incomplete projects. It also, as a result, appears more efficient in its "capital"–output ratios. Since these figures also reflect pricing policy, not too much can be read into them except for the fact that light industry is the Cinderella of the regime. A society engaged in producing ever more machinery that has little impact on consumption, even for the elite and the intelligentsia, is a peculiar phenomenon. The real point is that it is of this kind for one reason only: its own inefficiency makes it very difficult to produce the machinery required for light industry.

The fundamental law of the regime is one of a conflict between organization and the individual interest of the unit. Put empirically, the regime itself is one where there is a permanent and endemic conflict between the need of the center to control and develop the system in the interest of those who control, and opposition by all units below it. The problem is that there is no inbuilt mechanism for reconciling this conflict.

It is useful at this point to summarize the argument provided elsewhere. This starts from the view that the USSR is rent by two conflicting laws: a law of organization and a law of self-interest. The term "law" expresses the objective and necessary nature of the two features of the regime. There is, therefore, no method for the center to achieve its object by subordinating its units, and so the workers, to its needs. A law is a description of the process of movement of the poles of a contradiction. The two opposing poles of the law of self-interest are the atomized worker and socialized labor. The law of organization has as its poles central control and the specific interests of the elite. In a socialist society the law of planning would be dominant, and here the contradiction would lie in central planning as opposed to the concrete requirements of the individual citizen. The development of the USSR has been specific in that the original laws of value and planning have degenerated into the new forms described above.

The difference between the USSR and a planned society is that the USSR has centralized control in the interests of a small group—the elite, bureaucracy, or ruling group (the term is of no importance). In a socialist society, on the other hand, the centralized control is in the interests of the society as a whole. The immediate effect of the difference in the nature of a socialist society and that of the Soviet Union is that an insuperable opposition is created between those being "planned" and the planners. As a result, the central "planners" have to take this into account and compromise and hence, rather than control, they have to organize and bargain, often to the detriment of the interest of the elite itself. The interest of the elite then expresses itself and a dynamic is set up to provide a mediation, which quickly breaks down. For instance, it is in the interests of the organizers to have higher norms, or at least ones that conform to technical specifications, but they know that such pressure is counterproductive and thus they normally bargain for a practical figure. The result is that the economy is worse off, goods are not delivered, discontent rises over time, and the position of the elite is threatened. A new solution is required.

It is in the interests of the elite to maximize control over the surplus product for their own ends, which can be reduced to their need for occupational stability and for access to privileges. This can only be achieved if each member of the elite has individual control over a portion of the surplus product. Since they do not have such individual control, they exist in a position of permanent instability and constant attempts to exert centralized control over the direct producers. In principle, the achievement of full control over the surplus product and so the labor process would then achieve the stability required and permit the division of the surplus product among individuals depending on their personal degree of control over that product.

As a result, the law of organization expresses the permanent tension that exists between the need to organize the economy on a centralized basis and the real needs of the elite. This may appear to contradict the view that the elite often introduce measures that increase the degree of centralization rather than the reverse. However, the reason for this paradox lies precisely in the fact that since their "planning" of the economy conflicts with the interests of the direct producers, it also conflicts with the interests of all units in the system. Hence, the latter constantly reinterpret all commands in their own interests. Logically, this has led to attempts to avoid such reinterpretation by concentrating as much detailed organization as possible in the center. This was the economic meaning of the purge period, and it has led to the emergence of a section of the elite that is more interested in enforced control than in organization. Such a movement, to total control, is a chimera that has failed and must necessarily fail. Hence, this group of controllers can only be regarded as a retrogressive section of the elite, constantly re-created by the nature of their unstable position, growing weaker as the economy itself grows more industrialized. The law of organization, therefore, shows itself in constant attempts by the elite either to centralize or to decentralize, depending on the time and the degree of strength held by one or another faction of the elite. The reason for this hopeless position lies in the fact that elite control is opposed by the direct producers.

The elite, thus, stand in a peculiar position, unique in human history. They control the surplus product but do not control the labor process. As a result, they find that they cannot fully control the surplus product. In turn, to assert control over the surplus product, as today, they try expedients to dominate labor, whether through quality control, raising norms, unemployment, or whatever. The exact form is of no consequence. They cannot succeed in their attempts to control labor, but the history of the USSR is a history of such attempts. Struggle as they may, they are impaled on their own contradiction. Their own interests cannot be ensured through centralized control that can only be maintained for a limited time. The more they struggle to centralize control or organize the economy, the more they socialize the workers and the more difficult it becomes to run the USSR centrally. If they decentralize the organization of the economy, then the law of self-interest takes over and the individual units ignore the center, creating either chaos, the market, or an evolution toward democracy. In fact, events appear to follow the above sequence. The more decentralization proceeds the more chaotic the regime becomes. Order is only maintained through individual units organizing direct trading. Such events challenge the system in its social relations. The workers then become restive when prices are raised against them, unemployment rises, etc. This kind of result appears itself to be a law of history. Thus, for instance we may read the following:

> The [World] Bank estimates that 10 percent of the industrial work force will be laid off as uncompetitive enterprises collapse. This will only increase the unemployment caused by the liquidation of parastatal enterprises. While food prices rise, wage increases will be contained. Labor code modifications demanded by the Bank will allow employers to hire cheap labor ineligible for social security benefits.[5]

Such drastic action, now being applied to Senegal, a small African country, is exactly the medicine being taken by the USSR. The great difference is that the working class of the USSR is incomparably stronger and the elite weaker. This remedy is indeed the only method of ensuring a successful economy with a ruling group in control. Yet there is no way that the workers can be either forced or tricked into accepting it. The very existence of the control over labor provided by nationalization has established an elite or ruling social group in a number of countries over. The problem is that the control can only be maintained by direct force, and therefore creates its own dynamic. The difference between the USSR and all other similar countries is not only that it is the first to perform in this manner but, more importantly, it is the only one to have been based on the working class and it now has a massive working class opposed to it. It is not enough to possess control over labor, because the instruments of control must also be present to ensure that the alienation of labor power can be enjoyed. Force is too blunt a method of control to succeed under industrial conditions.

Thus, the elite is necessarily driven first one way, toward maximum force, as in the time of the purges, and then another way, toward bargaining and organizational forms, as under Khrushchev. In so moving, they have split themselves. The third way, back toward the market and, ultimately, capitalism, becomes ever more attractive as the factions of the elite demonstrate their impotence. The factionalization is only a symptom of the failure of the use of force and its concomitant, the squeezing of ever more labor time to ensure growth, including the intensification of labor.[6]

The need for the direct producers to act lies in their alienated position as workers who alienate their labor power and hence do not control the surplus product that they themselves produce. Without interest in production, life is made tolerable by establishing control over the work process. From the point of view of the elite, this is acceptable insofar as it enforces the atomization of the direct producers, who relate to their own individual work process and not to the society as a whole or even to the factory as a whole. The problem is that it stands opposed to the real social division of labor, and hence lowers productivity and above all elite control to an unacceptable level. As a result, the elite then attempt to centralize or decentralize depending on political exigencies.

THE POLITICAL ECONOMY 121

The problem, then, is one that is insuperable in the context of the USSR. It has to be noted that the two laws of the USSR are a degeneration of the law of value and of the law of planning, but in a scrambled form. No new synthesis or supersession can result from the conflict of these laws, only stagnation. The conflict has given rise to a process of stagnant growth, stalemated social relations, and constant attempts by the elite to find a way out. On the other hand, since each law is itself an expression of a contradiction, it is being superseded. The elite must either give way to central planning or abolish central planning. The workers have to take control over socialized labor or be atomized under commodity fetishism (i.e., the market). The complexity of the USSR is expressed through the existence of two conflicting laws and the contradictions of the society expressing themselves differently in each law. Of course, the USSR is part of a wider world, where indeed centralized organization, planning, or direction is in fact increasing, whatever Reagan and Thatcher may have attempted. In capitalism this is an inherent contradiction: the increasing socialization of production standing opposed to the ever smaller numbers in control over surplus value. Value is nothing if not atomized spontaneity, but to exist today it must organize, must use bureaucratic instruments, and must have a long-term policy. This is complex enough, but in the USSR this same inexorable process has taken on its own more contradictory form.

The socialized division of labor has been, as it were, split apart. On the one side, it requires planning, which has become the exclusive province of the elite, while on the other it stands over but not above the worker. Under capitalism, by contrast, the socialized division of labor stands opposed to the capitalist, expressing the nature of both the working class and the future society. In the USSR the socialized division of labor has to be utilized by the elite and becomes a form of control over the worker. Whereas socialized labor provides the basis for the strength of the worker, in the USSR it has been turned into its opposite. From the point of view of the elite, it is their method of appropriation of the surplus product, and from the point of view of the workers, it is the method of control over them. The latter, however, is achieved by splitting the surplus product from its labor process, so that the worker controls the labor process, but not the product, in an individualized form. Thus, the worker is doubly controlled: his product is held by others and his work process is such that he is separated from his fellow workers.

The dynamic in the society is provided by the movement of the process of socialized production. The more socialized the nature of labor and so production (i.e., the more integrated the division of labor), the more difficult it is for the worker to be atomized around his labor process and the more difficult is it for the elite to obtain compliance with their commands. Democracy becomes an ever-present necessity. The elite are driven by their position as organizers of the economy to expand it, in order to buttress their own control. This is done both by assuaging the demands of the workers for more consumer goods, more jobs, more creative jobs (i.e., social mobility), etc., and by their own needs to maintain control.

Growth and Disintegration

It is, of course, a common view that the elite prefer to produce heavy industrial goods because this provides them with untrammeled power. There can be no question that producer goods, unlike consumer goods, are not rejected by millions of consumers and therefore appear to be less subject to democratic process. This may be true, but it is insufficient to explain why department one expands faster than department two. After all, the elite could maintain themselves as controllers of large car plants rather than as the directors of large construction works or energy plants. That cars would have to be better than machine tools is questionable. There is no democracy in the market at all. Under capitalism, the poor put up with shoddy goods and the very rich get goods of the highest quality. Under conditions of shortage, everyone is glad to get what they can, however unreliable.

The machine tool industry is enormous in the USSR, but this is in large part a consequence of the unreliable nature of its products and the technologically backward nature of the industry. It has indeed been counterproductive to have a gigantic industrial machine that is greater than any other in its producer goods sector but that consistently produces a consumer goods mouse. Thus, light industry grew by 9 percent in the period 1980–86, and engineering grew by 46 percent in the same period.[7] The greater absurdity is that, in spite of the growth of the producer goods sector, technological equipment for light industry grew by 31 percent, and the stock of metalworking machinery is actually aging.[8] Clearly, this has nothing to do with the need to find places for managers, but everything to do with the supreme inefficiency of a system that has no place in history.

Obviously, if industry cannot keep pace with the demands of its own heavy industry, there is no hope whatsoever of providing goods for light industry. It is logical to expect that the problems of the relations between sectors will worsen over time. After all, the needs of the producer goods department can only increase. It needs technologically newer goods, more sophisticated repairs, and—given the nature of the USSR—even more repairs than before. It requires new plants, more construction for newer divisions, and newer sources of raw materials. In principle, there is no need for department one ever to produce any goods that are deployed for the utility of the individual, which even under capitalism is the ultimate destiny of goods and services. The growth in technology, repairs, and construction is never-ending, as long as the surplus product is controlled by a few against the many. The many workers have no interest in their alienated product and the elite have no individual interest in a product destined for others. Collectively, the elite is interested in more and better goods, but individually their interests are best served in smoothing the system along, permitting themselves to be seen as happy and successful bureaucrats. The reason, then, for the lack of consumer goods lies in the fact that they are the end-product of a process of production that never reaches its logical end.

The split in the division of labor, then, has shown itself in the detailed working of the economy. Production is split from consumption, consumer goods from producer goods, the product from its repair, new technology from old technology, and newer plants from older plants. In every respect, a dichotomy appears that cannot be bridged. The capitalist contradiction between use value and exchange value is replaced by antagonisms in every aspect of society. This is as it should be, because it is in the nature of value that it provides a solution to otherwise antagonistic relations, whereas in the USSR such relations coalesce to support the two conflicting laws of the society. With such a conflictual society, there is a special role for the organizers to hold it together. But since they cannot hold it together, the society begins to disintegrate.

We may summarize this analysis by referring to the process of growth. The elite are themselves based on the necessity of growth precisely to avoid the disintegrating nature of the society. Growth is the only means whereby some consumer goods can be produced, some mobility ensured, and stagnation avoided. As long as the absolute surplus was expanding, their problems were containable. Once the relative surplus ceased to expand, they came up against insuperable problems. Society simply had to be fully integrated to allow the relative surplus to expand. The worker had to be subordinated to achieve the object. There is no third way of controlling workers other than through value or through their own self-management.

The elite has no place in history and unfortunately it knows this. It has therefore been more insecure and thus more prone to the use of force than probably any other modern ruling group. Growth is not simply a response to popular dissatisfaction, since the Soviet elite has never been reluctant to deal ruthlessly with the population. Growth is forced on the elite in order to avoid their own loss of power. In the initial NEP period they found that the peasants held them to ransom in the absence of industrial goods. They therefore turned to industrialization, but then they found that an apparent high rate of growth failed to produce the necessary goods of the right quality at the right time and place. That too threatened their rule. On the other hand, no growth would exacerbate the problems of industry, ending the juggling act through which they maintained power. It is a juggling act because they effectively employed the surplus produced to patch up the problems of each period.

Once the surplus ended, the system entered a terminal crisis. The system has necessarily to alternate between the use of direct command or force, and bargaining and persuasion over time, since neither method actually works in the long term, although the alternation is useful in producing an increase in production and in damping the degree of dissatisfaction. Growth is thus a pragmatic response. Insofar as it proves to be counterproductive in preserving their position, the elite would stand opposed to it. Today the increasing intensity of the problems in the economy does raise the question of the necessity of growth, but they cannot dismiss the employed work force without massive internal unrest.

The term *growth* has to be defined. As ordinarily understood, it might signify an increase in the net product of the society. More properly, it refers to an increase in the surplus product produced. If defined in the first sense only, then no indication of future growth would be obtained, since in the extreme case the total consumption of the surplus would lead to stagnation. In the USSR the increase in the net product is formal. More goods may be produced, but they may be useless for production. Thus the existence of numerous uncompleted construction projects testifies to apparent growth, but these projects cannot be utilized.

Similarly, tractors that break down quickly or are used for purposes for which they are not intended can only mean that the USSR requires many more tractors than the United States, as is indeed the case. Indeed, the figures are startling. The USSR produces many more tractors than the United States because it needs 585,000 tractors per year, whereas the United States needs 150,000 per year. Nonetheless, the USSR has far fewer tractors per hectare in service than the United States. The Soviet tractors break down sooner and more frequently. Service and repairs cost four times the cost of production. Labor costs of service and repairs come to four to six times the original costs. Costs of production continue to rise by 4 to 5 percent per year.[9]

How then do we judge growth? The production of more goods that are useless does not permit future growth. Growth in the Soviet sense, therefore, does not necessarily mean an addition to the surplus product. Rather, it signifies an increase in total goods produced, which is a very different thing. In other words, the sum of use values diverges from the sum of goods produced. This indeed is the phenomenal form of the contradiction in the society. Thus, the elite are based on apparent growth, a growth that may employ more people, have more production, but not yet deliver the goods as real use values; these are really the elite's chimera.

It is now possible to see Gorbachev's real problem more clearly. His aim is to turn the elite from an emasculated ruling group, terrified of losing power at every turn, both individually and collectively, into a class that is firmly in control of the surplus product.

The pristine function of the elite, holding together a system that has no basis for being held together, can no longer be served. One might ask, if this is a function, whose purposes does it serve? The only possible answer has to be that of the wider interests of the old order. The elite are, in fact, the despised yet tolerated partners of the bourgeoisie. The capitalist class would prefer them to surrender and transform the system back to capitalism, but the elite cannot do this itself, nor is it certain whether it is worth doing. To have an international diversion preventing the emergence of the new order is certainly preferable to a little more surplus value. The problem, however, is that the system can no longer be held together. The conflict of the laws is too sharp for it to be sustained for much longer. An orderly transition is required.

For this purpose Gorbachev has to turn on the working class, but unfortunately for him, there is no obvious method of proceeding. Only the market will ensure the evolution of the elite into a class, but such a weak ruling group cannot easily establish control over the working class. Hence Gorbachev has to proceed one step at a time, and if it is not Gorbachev, then it will be his successor who will act in similar fashion. There really is no choice but to proceed cautiously. On the other hand, the whole elite and intelligentsia are not aware of their historic choices. Indeed, many decent individuals in the intelligentsia are demanding the market in the mistaken belief that it is the only path to democracy. Despairing of genuine or revolutionary change, they necessarily turn to reform; despairing of the working class, they turn to the intelligentsia; despairing of the concept of socialism, they turn to self-management within a market economy. As a result, most of the members of the contending factions stand in a confused position, as does Gorbachev himself, as explained above.

In the final analysis, then, the elite are based on growth because of the inefficiency of the regime. Its instability and constant destruction of use values requires ever more use values. If the product were not contradictory in having use values that are only partially useful, then the elite could have a much lower growth rate.

It is useful to follow out this train of thought. Clearly, the economy is an industrial one. The elite, themselves, were never based on the peasantry, as in China, and hence their power has always rested on modern industry, however backward it might be on a world scale. Industry does have its own dynamic. In this case, it is the socialization of labor, which demands solutions. Workers have to be better controlled as they become more powerful, and technical improvements assist in this process. Hence, the classical Stalinist school is in favor of total computerization. The world division of labor demands that the USSR install new technique and control labor better. Since the USSR has been insulated from the world market, this latter aspect has played a secondary role until the present. This internal dynamic might, however, have been slowed down, since it is contradictory in its operation. The cure for the increasing power of labor cannot ultimately lie through more industrialization, which itself increases the power of labor. As a result, an alternative policy is one of adopting modern methods of control. This involves smaller plants, competition, smaller work groups, and the like, all of which amount to an attempt to replace the existing atomization with a frontal attack on the form of socialization itself. This in turn logically means a considerably reduced rate of industrial growth. At first such a reduced rate would actually produce more real use values, but over time this effect would be played out. Then further growth would be counterproductive. Only direct pressure by workers for improved conditions of production and consumers for a higher standard of living would cause growth. Under such conditions, the elite would vacillate between palliating demands from below and ignoring them, or perhaps even repressing them.

The conclusion from such a look into Soviet dynamics in the absence of the defective Soviet product is that growth rates would vacillate and be quite low. If this is indeed the case it is probably true that this tendency is present today for the reasons given above, but it is masked by the real situation of the economy. Even now, the Soviet industrial growth rate of around 3–4 percent is high by world standards. The inefficiency of the economy incorporates the need for an enormous and growing repair sector, an ever-devouring construction sector, and a constant need for new products to replace the old ones that have failed. Failure here refers both to the breakdowns of the products, such as tractors, and to the unusability of the goods for the process intended, such as a particular machine tool. In turn, the stocks of the different items grow either because of shortages and potential shortages or because of their lack of use value.

On this basis, clearly, growth can be enormous, with little impact on consumer goods. Nonetheless, the elite are driven by the nature of Soviet political economy to this high rate of growth. The contradiction is becoming absolute as modern integrated production with modern specific skilled labor demands precisely modeled products, delivered on time, to fit in with the modern highly tuned labor processes. Solutions are demanded that are being provided on an ad hoc basis, but this basis is becoming less and less effective. A strategy is demanded.

Today the nature of the growth rate is much more in question. Arguments that the USSR was a workers' state or expressed some element of superiority over capitalism through its high growth rate can no longer be sustained for empirical reasons. Soviet economists now argue that the USSR has expanded in GNP by seven times over the last sixty years, and not ninety times as Soviet statistics show. Furthermore, the inflation rate is now conservatively estimated at around 3 percent per annum in relation to the cost of living. It is higher for department one goods and construction. If the inflation rate is 3 percent and the growth rate is 2.4 percent, what is the real rate of growth of GNP?[10]

There is an argument that the USSR and the East European economies go through a cycle.[11] To the extent that resources are increasingly absorbed in department one or the repair sector without reappearing as a usable product, the system has to wind down in order to restore the rate of growth. The more realistic discussions on the nature of the economy, which began first in Hungary, showed that the internal bargaining process necessarily led to an explosive growth that inevitably wound down. The problem with their viewpoint, however, was that it lacked any theoretical basis. It simply described correctly a bargaining process under which investment, and particularly investment in new construction, went on increasing. The question was why it was permitted to do so. Their answer was that the elite required expenditure on defense, and the economy also needed to grow in order to escape its backwardness, while the power of the elite depended uniquely on a large heavy goods industrial sector.

None of these arguments is sufficient. In the end, as history has shown, the elite did not succeed under any of these heads. A strong elite, after all, would leave the process to its enterprise heads, trusting their judgment. The enterprise directors in the USSR, however, are themselves too weak in relation to their workers to enforce the necessary labor discipline. The consequence is that all production is necessarily indeterminate in both the quality of output and the time for completion. As a result, the central elite, at this level, can never calculate correctly since the local enterprise itself cannot do so. Worse still, it is not in the interests of the local enterprise to tell the truth, as the center itself cannot cope with the truth. Since no one in the system knows the real situation, the center can only accede to requests to the maximum degree, in order to avoid a worse disaster. As argued above, it needs growth because it has such an enormous disparity between real use values and the apparent use values. The reason is not growth itself, but the failure of the elite to maintain control over the surplus product. But if it cannot assert control, it can only do the next best thing, which is to permit the system to operate by itself and intervene at the crisis points. Hence, as Tamas Bauer has put it, the center is too weak.[12] But what *is* the center? It is the centralized economic arm of the elite itself. The elite is too weak, not just because it has to accede to the increasing demands from below, since it cannot discriminate and determine what is necessary and important, but really because it prefers weakness.

In theoretical terms, the contradiction between the real and apparent use values within the system leads to a cycle of explosive investment intended to break out of the contradiction. In principle, if growth could lead to the point where sufficient technologically advanced consumer goods were supplied to the population and improvements in technique could be self-sustaining, the elite would be stabilized. This hope rests on the possibility that workers would accept their fate as workers in return for a rising standard of living and relatively free life. In fact, the controls over labor have never been lifted, while the standard of living has risen too slowly to achieve the object. Hence, every dash for growth has failed. The instability of the elite leads to an unstable economy.

As long as the increased investment did lead to the introduction of new techniques, more spare parts, and more factories, even if at enormous cost, the cycle was functional. The system itself provides a spontaneous solution. In the Stalin period it simply absorbed more labor time, whether through employing more workers or using labor more intensively through coercion. Imports have also been an alternative, particularly in the 1970s. The problem arose once the costs rose to such heights that low growth became the order of the day. That, in turn, meant that a halt could not easily be called. Under Khrushchev, there was a moratorium on new projects, but the subsequent unemployment was among the reasons for his fall. It became politically difficult to introduce the downturn phase. Instead, the process has led to permanently low real growth, even if total investment has continued to increase. Once investment itself could no longer serve as the instrument for temporarily overcoming the fundamental contradiction of the regime, the system had no choice but to abandon the system itself. It had to turn to the market.

In a situation of acute crisis the elite have tended to retreat, and hence we witnessed a decline in quality standards in the 1980s. On the other hand, it might be possible to apply more pressure to the workers, through discipline (as under Andropov) or unemployment of a temporary kind (as under Khrushchev's moratorium). The point is that the Soviet elite do not have to assert control over surplus value but rather over the labor process, from which stems their instability. As the system struggles from crisis to crisis, it can now be seen that each period is characterized by the form of the crisis and the manner in which it has been handled. Under Stalin it was dealt with through the purges, camps, and forced labor. Under Khrushchev an attempt was made to operate a bargaining system. Under Brezhnev the market began to be introduced, failed, and was succeeded by a social peace punctuated only by attempts to find market-type surrogates to halt the system's manifest decline. Stalin represented direct force, Khrushchev organization, Brezhnev peace, and Gorbachev the market. None of these solutions has long-term viability, but each has performed a role in preserving the system. It can be seen, however, that the cycle has a drive toward more general change.

The four aspects of the division of labor, discussed above, and the subsequent theoretical discussion on the nature of the USSR, point to the inevitable conclusion that the USSR has reached a point where no economic reforms will work without concessions to the direct producers. An illustration of the problem is given by Gorbachev's expressed desire to end the emphasis on the construction of new plants. Over ten years earlier, at the Twenty-fifth Party Congress, this point was made and put on the agenda. The Soviet economist Sonin pointed out that labor discipline was the ultimate cause of all problems. He argued, in 1977, that the only way labor discipline could be tightened was to increase the level of mechanization in existing plant. He also insisted that the construction of new plants had to be radically cut back.[13] The same point is being made today, only more forcefully and more repetitively.

The immediate solutions devised, as indicated above, have been to increase investment in existing plant, as opposed to new plant, and to increase the proportion of investment in the producer goods industries, as shown in the Twelfth Five-year Plan. This cautious solution was hardly in accordance with the constant stress on the need for more and better quality consumer goods. But then, without radical change, Gorbachev has no solution other than the appearance of change. Of course, the immediate solution has been followed by plans to introduce market-type reforms, but as of 1990, they remain very much a question of decrees and intentions, rather than a reality, as indicated in our discussion on the contradictions of the reforms.

Notes

1. M. Sonin, "Problemy raspredeleniia i ispolzovaniia trudovykh resursov," *Sotsialisticheskii trud,* March 1977, p. 94ff. Sonin puts the issue of economic problems squarely in terms of labor. Because Sonin is an establishment economist, the conclusion must be that the essence of the problem is obvious in the context of a system that does not have commodity production.

2. Bob Arnot, *Controlling Soviet Labour* (London: Macmillan, 1988).

3. Antonio Carlo, "The Crisis of Bureaucratic Collectivism," *Telos* 43 (Spring 1980).

4. *Narodnoe khozaistvo SSSR za 70 let* (Moscow, 1987), p. 149.

5. " Senegal Revives in Freer Economic Climate," *Financial Times,* 6 January 1988, p. 3.

6. Since 1979 and indeed somewhat earlier, labor turnover and labor discipline have considerably improved. See *Narodnoe khoziaistvo SSSR za 70 let,* p. 140.

7. Ibid., pp. 167, 187.

8. Ibid., pp. 167, 170.

9. S.L. Averbuch, "Skol'ko nuzhno traktorov?" *EKO* 1988, no. 4, p. 108.

10. Alec Nove, "A Further Note on Hidden Inflation and Its Consequences," *Soviet Studies,* January 1988, pp. 136–38. Nove has summarized in this useful note the arguments of a number of Soviet economists, but most particularly that of Khanin and Seliunin in their article "Lukavaia tsifra" (*Novyi mir,* 1987, no. 3). Nove brings out the point that real wages did not increase in the period from 1976 to 1985. This article is a sequel to his earlier one, "Radical Reform: Problems and Prospects," *Soviet Studies,* July 1987, in which he provides an account of the arguments of Soviet economists.

11. Joseph Goldman and Karel Kouba (*Economic Growth in Czechoslovakia* [White Plains, NY: International Arts and Science Press, 1966]), discuss the cycle for Czechoslovakia, Hungary, Poland, and the GDR, basing themselves on the prior work of Michal Kalecki, in particular. For them, the basic causes lie in a lag between industry and the raw material base, as well as a voluntaristic aspect. In addition, there is a runaway investment problem, which is tackled using Keynesian analysis. Later analyses like that of the Institute of Economics of the Hungarian Academy of Sciences, as exemplified by K. Soos and also Tamas Bauer ("Investment Cycles in Planned Economies," unpublished manuscript), placed more emphasis on the fact that investment was not in fact controlled from the center and the voluntaristic aspect was secondary. Their descriptions conform more to reality, although their explanations remain purely empirical.

12. Bauer, "Investment Cycles in Planned Economics."

13. See "Problemy raspredeleniia i ispolzovaniia trudovykh resursov," p. 96.

8

The Present Economic Crisis in the USSR

In the West a crisis manifests itself in an obvious decline in the total of goods and services produced. Crisis in the USSR has not taken the form of an actual decline in total production until recently. Rather, crisis has existed in the form of an apparent growth in total production despite intractable problems in the economy. The similarity between the two systems is that both involve pressure on the standard of living, the waste of large quantities of goods, and above all—and this is what makes it a crisis—a need to reestablish a social relationship of control. In the Soviet context all internal and external observers agree on the steadily declining growth rates, a relatively low (and recently declining) expectation of life, a rise in alcoholism, and a relatively static or declining standard of living for many, particularly in relation to food.

On the question of the standard of living in the USSR, Leonid Gordon is quite explicit that the standard of living is below that expected by the population.[1] However, unlike the situation in a Western depression, this goes along with greater production than ever. Gorbachev pointed out in his 11 June 1985 speech that the USSR produces more steel than anyone else but that it is of poor quality and goes to waste, that the USSR continues to build ever more factories rather than reequipping old ones, that the factories take forever to build and that their completion is unpredictable.[2] There are similar reports about cement. The USSR produces more cement than anyone else but it both has a shortage of cement and does not supply the housing needs of the population.[3] The trebling of investment in housing from 1960 to 1986 has only led to a decline in the actual number of houses constructed.[4] Brezhnev complained in 1976 about the 700 million shoes produced and yet they had a shortage of shoes. Eight years later Chernenko got around to having a decree on shoes.[5] That even the Politburo had to have a special discussion on shoes is itself instructive. Now Aganbegian is discussing the problem of shoes also.[6]

Too much produced, too little output for the consumer is the endemic problem

THE PRESENT ECONOMIC CRISIS   131

of the USSR, although the USSR could not always boast the first place in the world in machine tools, steel, cement, etc. One Soviet writer described the economy as follows. "In life, unfortunately, there is something else: an economy torn by the sharpest contradictions, with its horrifying waste, colossal inefficiency, and total lack of direction in relation to its development."[7]

What then is the meaning of growth with such a low final output? What kind of growth is it that leads to increasing shortages of industrial goods? Can one call it growth at all? The USSR is not like an underdeveloped country, in that it does have a developed industrial base and its industrial production in total quantity compares with that of a developed Western country. Soviet waste, however, is not the same as that of a capitalist country. The problem is not one of unemployed workers or resources, as in the West, but one of goods that are of low quality, the use of outdated technique, and the employment of vast numbers of people and huge quantities of raw materials to achieve results that are a fraction of what was either planned or attained in the West. Long ago, at the time of the First Five-year Plan, Rakovsky discussed these problems of the Soviet economy as follows.

> A rail is a rail; and if, let us say, its formal production cost goes down by several percent, this does not mean that the economy has benefited by this same amount. The fact that this rail looks outwardly just like a pre-war rail deceives no one: nor does it eliminate the fact that our contemporary rail lasts not even five years, while a pre-war rail lasted forty. And this is happening not only with rails. Whole factories are being erected out of defective construction materials and equipped with machines made from defective metal. Today's decline in production costs will turn into tomorrow's ... colossal losses for the national economy.[8]

Since then the same question has become the basis of any understanding of growth in the USSR.

The crisis in the USSR is manifested in the need to establish a new form of social control. Put differently, the elite find that they can no longer manage the society in the old way. Its immediate and phenomenal form has been one of declining growth rates, under conditions where growth has always been contradictory.

In a certain sense, the USSR has always been a country of crisis. Shortages of food and consumer goods have been endemic. In fact, it is quite possible to interpret the history of the USSR as one of lurching from one crisis to another. After all, the New Economic Policy failed under Bukharin and Stalin and was replaced with the disastrous period of collectivization, overaccumulation, famine, and plunging living standards in the towns. In the postwar period, agriculture remained the Achilles heel of the economy, while industry remained locked into production for its own sake. The interpretation of the USSR as a regime of permanent crisis is common and is not without validity. Clearly, the problem with such a view is that the USSR is now in a new kind of crisis from which it cannot emerge in the same form as it has existed for the last sixty years. In short, the word crisis can be overused.

The rationale behind the view that the USSR is in permanent crisis lies in its expression of constant conflict among social forces in the USSR. This has taken such forms as the attack on the peasantry, the purges, anti-Semitism, and indeed an overall chauvinism that is now reaping a harvest of national disintegration. It has involved an atomization of the working class, which was suppressed if necessary with direct force. In economic terms the crisis showed itself in the antagonism between the ruble and goods, or, in other words, in permanent shortages and the absence of money, and in the consistent inability of the center to achieve its goals or plans. Enormous levels of obvious waste and transparent inefficiency have always characterized the regime and it has moved from one form of economic control to another in order to raise levels of productivity.

Yet, whatever the lurches of the regime, it has until recently succeeded in industrializing and urbanizing the economy. If the standard of living is low, it is still considerably higher than it was under the tsarist regime. What it might have been under another system is another question, because the issue under discussion here is only whether the USSR is undergoing a crisis at the present time. Clearly, if there has always been a crisis, then the present crisis is simply a natural aspect of the regime itself. This book argues, however, that the regime has functioned in its own way but has now reached a natural end. It appears to be in permanent crisis because it has no long-term future and because it functions at a higher level of contradiction, or, as the above quote shows, through the sharpest contradictions.[9]

The point is that the USSR is both in permanent crisis and in a terminal crisis. But a system in permanent crisis is a system of permanent crisis and hence interest centers on the form of the system itself and its decline. In other words, the word "crisis" provides an insufficient description of a system that exists over a long period of time with its own mode of existence.

The central issues that have to be addressed are the nature of growth, the reasons for that growth and its ending, and the relationship of the social structure to that growth. The solutions provided here are both simple and complex. The economy did grow, but in a very special form, which, because of its form, could only continue for a limited time. The terminal crisis of the present time is then inherent in the form of growth.

To understand the special form of growth, we have to start from the nature of production itself and so the nature of the Soviet product. Just as under capitalism the fundamental contradiction of the system lies in the opposition of exchange value and use value, or in the opposition of human needs and the form in which they are satisfied, so in the USSR the contradiction must lie in the form of the satisfaction of human needs.

THE PRESENT ECONOMIC CRISIS 133

The Law of Value and Its Absence in the USSR

What the USSR clearly does not have is a market economy. At a superficial level it is obvious that a regime intent on moving to the market cannot have a market, but some people may object that they do have black markets, rubles, sale and purchase, etc. Clearly they do, but capital goods cannot be bought and sold, land cannot be bought and sold, and the transport system, construction, and housing for the individual are all virtually allocated or so heavily subsidized as to make all talk of purchase and sale a mockery. Soviet economists, as we have seen, do not see a labor market in existence either. Bogomolov, indeed, talked of semi-forced labor.[10] If there is neither a labor market nor a capital market, and many consumer goods are directly allocated or subsidized while the rest are obtainable largely through a rationing system, exchange value has been wiped out.

There is a distinction to be made between the existence of the law of value and the existence of exchange value. In principle there could be exchange value without value. Thus, the black market has exchange value without value because there is no basis on which to establish costs. In the USSR the decay of the "planning mechanism" has meant the growth of so-called markets. But they are obviously not based on costs so much as on what the seller can gouge out of the buyer. From the point of view of orthodox economics, there is no difference between this kind of parasitic market and one based on a regular supply system, except for the absence of competition. Yet from the point of view of either Marxist economics or the perception of the Soviet person in the street, there is a considerable difference. Production in the USSR in the main proceeds through the system of bureaucratic organization, and goods are essentially allocated to outlets. The final consumer obtains goods through a modified rationing system.

For the few who have foreign currency or large quantities of rubles and the right contacts, there has been opportunity to purchase goods at a price that reflects only risk and scarcity. With the Gorbachev reforms and the introduction of the cooperative movement, there is a legal market for those who have the rubles, but in the absence of competition, and with the shortage of supplies, which have to be either specially allocated by the "planning system" or obtained by semilegal means, production or the supply of services in this "market" sector takes on a hybrid form.

If there is no value and thus no money in the USSR, the nature of the contradiction in the USSR has to be sought outside of value itself. Indeed it has to be sought in the nature of the Soviet product. A product that is of low quality, does not serve the purpose intended, and is technologically backward is a product, but it is defective as a product. If it is unreliable in operation, the matter is still worse. Yet these features are normally present in the Soviet product either singly or in combination. If a pair of trousers is produced, it can be made with one leg somewhat longer than the other. It can be worn, even though it may be regarded as somewhat inelegant. If trousers were all of one size, most people could find a way of wearing them, even if they looked odd. The trousers thus continue to have a use value, but their real use value is quite different from the imagined or intended use value. In other words, the contradiction lies between the imagined nature of the product and its actual nature. Put differently, the contradiction lies between the bureaucratic or organized nature of the product and its real form.

This difference between the apparent form and the real form is at the heart of Soviet reality. Technically, the USSR is "planned," but in reality the so-called plans are arrived at by a bargaining procedure between the relevant institutions. The targets are adjusted over time. In the next section we will go into more detail on the defective nature of Soviet use values.

The Nature of the Contradiction within the Product

Value represents a particular mode of social organization of production, distribution, and exchange. Its alternative in the USSR is direct organization of those features of the economy. Such organization could be planned or administered. In the USSR it is administered. The contradiction within the product is then between the administered form of the product and its use value. The additional complication is that the contradiction leads to another level of contradiction. The use value produced is defective, and so a contradiction is established between the potential use value and its real use value. To cite one statistic, on 1 October 1987, in a climate of general shortage, one author provides as evidence of poor quality the fact that "unmarketable and old stock came to 1,439 billion rubles."[11] Since this is only goods that are unsalable, it is just a small indication of the larger problem. In the context of the USSR, the term "defective use value" means a good that is not what it appears to be. A jacket is a jacket but a jacket with one arm shorter than the other may or may not be said to be a jacket. A machine tool that breaks down frequently may be considered to be an occasional machine tool: a contradiction exists between its ostensible function and its actual operation. The contradiction in production and circulation is between the form in which production is organized and the use value itself. It results then in the alienation to the consumer of a product that, uniquely in world history, has a contradictory use value.

The waste in the USSR then emerges as the difference between what the product promises and what it is. The difference between the appearance of planning and socialism and the reality of a harsh bureaucratized administration shows itself in the product itself. Marx points out in *Capital* that whether the use value is imaginary or real does not alter the fact that the product is a use value. For purposes of purchase it makes no difference, but in use it does make a difference. In a capitalist society the crucial question is exchange value, and hence the real operation of the product can be secondary. If the Japanese managed before the

THE PRESENT ECONOMIC CRISIS   135

Second World War to sell watches without insides and pencils without lead in the middle, they would nonetheless have accumulated capital with which to make high-quality watches and other items. In principle, if the economy had a whole series of plants that operated poorly, but the products were bought by other plants that also operated poorly, the accumulation process could proceed without hindrance. In practice, if the use value does not live up to specification, further similar products will not be bought and hence a plant that used inadequate machine tools might find its profits reduced. On the other hand, it is quite possible to imagine a section of industry, like the military industry, where use value efficiency and the product actually mean little in the absence of the real possibility of war. In fact, under capitalism the shoddy goods are bought by the workers and the unemployed in particular. Indeed, firms like IBM see to it that their products are so differentiated that the out-of-date and less reliable models are designated for the less fortunate.

In the USSR, on the contrary, all goods are salable and to this day—the promised Gorbachev reforms notwithstanding—profits in fact mean little. It is the use value that counts both in operation and in appearance. As a result, the enterprise has to consider both aspects of the use value, its apparent use and its real use. In producing the good, the superficial specifications are what count. Too much emphasis on quality can only lead to an increase in costs and a decline in the total produced. But in obtaining a product from another enterprise, it will be the real utility of the good that will count. The contradiction in the product therefore sets up an antagonistic relation between producer and consumer enterprises. It also establishes a conflict between the worker as consumer and the elite as a controller of enterprises. At one level it would appear as if the worker stands opposed to himself in that his two sides as producer and consumer conflict. This is only true superficially. The worker as consumer is an individual responsible to himself, whereas the worker as producer is responsible and directly under the control of the factory management and so of the controlling elite.

The two sides of use value (its imagined or intended use on the one hand, and its use in operation on the other) are in contradiction with each other. If the term "contradiction" is used in the sense of an interpenetration of opposites, then it is of interest to note the development of that contradiction.

On the side of the producers, two solutions are provided. In order to compensate for the low quality, more and more has to be produced. Replacements, new products, and spare parts do compensate to a limited degree for the defective product. The society also forces the producers to raise the quality of production. The enterprises, in turn, are compelled to demand more resources to achieve that object, which leads to an increase in costs of the product. Both solutions lead to a greater industrialization and so socialization of production, which because of its greater integration actually leads to the potential of an even worse product when any link in the chain breaks down. For instance, some years ago the then–Soviet prime minister pointed out that irrigation canals had been built in an area of southern Russia that was then flooded accidentally with sea water. The agriculture of that area was obviously ruined. If a crucial machine tool breaks down, the whole factory or a whole sector might be held up. The usual alternative to no product at all is an inferior product. The wheat irradiated by the Chernobyl disaster ought to have been discarded, but it is quite clear from Soviet statistics that it is being used. The crucial machine tool can be replaced by a machine tool that fails to do the job properly.

The dynamic of the contradiction is a process of growth that is ever more precarious. In principle, one could imagine a society that had apparently enormous rates of growth but produced no worthwhile final product at all. Since this is impossible, the real logic of the regime is one of cycles in which very rapid growth alternates with periods of little or no growth. The latter period occurs when the paradox of overindustrialization confronts its own underdeveloped nature. This occurs in two ways: the sectoral division becomes progressively more out of line with demand and the system exhausts its source of labor over time. The natural logic of the system would be one in which all enterprises were crippled through lack of resources, unless the central planners called a halt and introduced measures to reorder the sectors and stop the growth of particularly resource-absorbing parts of the economy. Looked at another way, the system has a natural tendency toward anarchy and chaos unless the center establishes maximum control. The paradox, of course, is that it is in fact the overcentralized nature of the economy, or the bureaucratized nature of the product, that causes the chaos in the first place.

Since the center attempts to administer everything, and it necessarily lacks both the apparatus and the knowledge to do so, the individual plant is forced to find its own individual method of coping with the so-called plans. The plans in fact have the same contradiction as the product in that they are a unity of the imagined and real. The plan itself is imaginary but its imposition does have the effect of organizing the system and preventing chaos.

The contradiction between the imaginary product and the real product, then, is fundamental to the system in the USSR. All categories are subject to it, in the same way that the contradiction between use value and exchange value governs capitalism. At the same time, this contradiction only arises on the basis of a prior contradiction between an administered form of the product and use value.

Consequences of the Defective Product

The administered form of the product is one in which the life-cycle of the product is governed by direct command rather than spontaneity, based either on value or on democratically agreed and internalized rules. The administration of use value is necessarily contradictory for the reason given above. There is no way that a center of any kind can have either the knowledge of the nature of use values or the means of implementation of decisions over use values that corresponds to real situations. The direct producer must have a degree of autonomy to produce a good that conforms to needs. He must also have an incentive to do so. Direct instruction does not provide such an incentive, unless accompanied by a democratic process of decision making. Put differently, behind the administered product form lies a form of control over labor. Labor power as a product has the same form as other products in that it performs below specifications. The imagined performance of labor power is one thing, its actual utility is another. The result, however, is that labor negates the category of abstract labor and becomes organized labor. As organized labor, the worker stands in contradiction to himself as concrete laborer. He works at his own rate with a measure of control over his work process, so establishing an individuality for himself and his work process. In turn, his product becomes individual and so different from other products.

Administrative logic dictates the replacement of humans by machines to avoid all mistakes. Its aim must be total computerization, and so totally centralized control. On the other side, the consumer is led to demand complete freedom of choice in purchase and so competition in suppliers, who will only be rewarded on the basis of real sales with the least cost input. In other words, the consumer is led to the market.

The Soviet regime is actually forced by the nature of its product to vacillate between the market and total centralized control. It stresses one or the other or both, depending on the nature of the particular crisis.

The defective nature of the Soviet product is both a cause and a result of the system of production in the USSR. It results in the formation of an enormous spare-parts sector and a hypertrophied construction sector developed to supply parts that have failed in one form or another or to complete construction projects that seem never to reach their natural conclusion. Additionally, more raw materials are required both to supply the expanding industry as well as to supply the defective goods that unnecessarily guzzle inputs. The vicious circle is developed further with the need to have an ever-expanding producer goods industry, as the defective producer goods absorb ever more resources, most particularly in the spare parts and construction industries. As a result, the consumer goods sector is starved of those resources. The worker receives a below-subsistence wage and has even less reason to work to capacity, and every reason to permit the overabsorption of raw materials and to produce shoddy goods. The bureaucratic apparatus is then expanded to control all these features, which is in turn a further drain on resources. Hence the state has to step in to control the massive discontent simmering below the surface. The worker has to be atomized. An enormous and incredibly wasteful apparatus of force is set up to maintain control. All of these qualities of the Soviet product lead, therefore, to two immediate consequences: a massive waste of resources and an immense shortage of goods.

There is a third consequence that follows from these results. There is a limit to the quantity of goods that can be spent on the resource-absorbing sectors without causing overall breakdown, and, as a result, a halt has to be called to growth at specific points in time. In other words, a cycle develops that is not spontaneous, in that the Politburo has to intercede. Yet, the reason why they step in, the hypertrophy of the construction sector and disproportionate absorption of resources by department one, is beyond their control.

There is also a long-term result. As long as labor can be absorbed from agriculture, the home, and other countries, the expansion of the absolute surplus masks the potential real rise in costs. Obviously, if enterprises keep needing more raw materials, more spare parts, and more replacement machinery, costs will tend to rise, all other things remaining the same. However, as long as labor can be used for repairs or as an alternative to machinery or spare parts, costs need not rise. Furthermore, new techniques can help to alleviate the rise in costs, as long as new plants can be constructed with cheap labor.

The Underlying Reasons for the Crisis

What is it that has changed in the USSR? Four things have altered in the past two decades.

The fundamental aspect of change, underlying the other forms, is that the growth of the absolute surplus has come to an end because the work force can no longer be replenished from the farms, the home, or elsewhere. Thus, the natural increase in the work force was only 600,000 from 1985 to 1986 on the basis of 130.9 million employed in 1986. On the other hand, there was an increase from 106.8 million in 1970 to 125.6 million in 1980. In other words, the employed population increased by 17.6 percent over the ten-year period to 1980, but only by 0.4 percent from 1985 to 1986. Over the five-year period, 1980–85, the relevant figure is 3.7 percent.[12] It is noteworthy that in 1988 the employed work force actually declined by 1 percent.[13] The agricultural population declined from 39 percent of the work force in 1960 to 19 percent in 1986, but hardly changed from 1980 when it was 20 percent of the work force. As regards women, they constituted 51 percent of the work force from 1970 to 1986. However, they are today only 43 percent of the kolkhoz workers engaged in the kolkhoz itself, as opposed to 50 percent in 1970.[14]

This means that it is not possible to continue the rapid building of new factories, since there is not the labor to do it. That leads then to a decline in the introduction of new technique, since it is through new plants that new technology has historically been introduced. This has the effect of the factory using out-of-date equipment, which is more labor-intensive and of lower quality than its possible replacement. As a result, such factories tend to produce goods that are less reliable and less durable. As a consequence, there is increased pressure on the repair and spare-parts sector. This sector had already grown to giant proportions, given the nature of the USSR, but it has had even greater burdens placed on it.

The increasing demands of the Soviet economy have placed an intolerable

THE PRESENT ECONOMIC CRISIS 139

burden on the raw material sector. Thus, the USSR now produces 161 million tons of steel and 617 million tons of oil, not to speak of 744 million tons of coal and 712 thousand million cubic meters of gas.[15] These are enormous figures, outdistancing the United States. They are indeed curious in that the United States produces much more consumer goods than the USSR. For instance, the USSR produces only 1.3 million cars as opposed to the ten million or so made in the United States, even though the latter now produces only half as much steel as the USSR. Again, U.S. oil consumption is not very different from that of the USSR, even though the USSR does not need gasoline on the same vast scale. Thus, the USSR produces an increasing quantity of both raw materials and processed raw materials such as fibers, but the demands of its industry are insatiable.

This would not be a problem if both labor and resources were infinite, but since they are not, and more importantly the USSR cannot innovate to the degree required, it is a necessary result that the raw material sector acts as a constraint on growth. It has to be emphasized that the constraint is not of the kind spoken of by the regime itself, taking the words from orthodox Soviet studies experts in the West, of an extensive growth necessarily reaching its logical end. The absorption of raw materials occurs because of the deficiencies of the Soviet system. It requires, as indicated above, more raw materials for the same job than under capitalism. Furthermore, the level of demand for such raw materials seems to be growing faster with the expansion in the economy, reflecting the increasing disproportions throughout the economy.

Thus, the failure to place new processes in old plants means that more cement, bricks, glass, and artificial fibers are required for construction purposes. The use of old equipment and processes itself means that more raw materials are needed, both because of the faulty nature of the machine and because of the outdated nature of the technique. For instance, today steel has been replaced by plastics, which do not rust. When machines malfunction the steel may be rendered faulty or the part imperfect, and more steel is needed. With plastics on the other hand, the processes are simpler. When the machine malfunctions it is easier to produce a new molding for the purpose required than to go through all the processes essential to produce the correct kind of steel and weld it together. The effect is that more raw material is needed both because the steel gets used up more quickly and because it is inherently less suited to the product.

The point, however, is that the USSR's demands for raw materials would be a fraction of what they are if the system functioned efficiently.[16] Obviously, if fewer products were needed, less raw materials would be required. Improved quality, a reduced spare-parts sector, and a diminished construction sector would greatly assist in alleviating demands for raw materials, and improve the environment as well. Labor cannot substitute for raw materials, but correct usage of labor would mean less demand for raw materials, whereas increasing antagonism, or what has been called lack of discipline, has meant increasing inefficiency. The rise in costs of raw materials following on exhaustion of traditional supplies may have been inevitable but it is very much more than it needed to be. Hence, it is not the problem in the supply of raw materials that is the constraint; rather, it is the nature of the social relation in production. To make the point still clearer, it has been the case historically that raw material problems were met with substitution either of the raw material by an artificial source or of a new technique. These methods are greatly reduced in scope because of the difficulty in introducing new techniques.

The construction sector in turn is under greater pressure to remedy the situation, but given the shortages, it becomes more and more difficult to complete projects. By 1980 Soviet economists congratulated themselves on having reached a point where the USSR no longer was spending all its resources in the construction sector on completing projects already begun. In fact, in 1980, 87 percent of capital investment was going into uncompleted projects, but this had declined to 79 percent in 1986. Nonetheless, Gorbachev was complaining in 1989 of the usual failure to complete projects. It should be noted that the figures mask a vast difference between light industry, where the figure for 1986 is just 64 percent, as compared with a startling of 142 percent for electricity generation or 133 percent for the chemical industry.[17]

The question of the decline in growth rates is reasonably openly discussed in the economic literature today. Thus, Sorokin[18] speaks of a decline in return to funds invested of some 75 percent, growth of amount of goods remaining in circulation of 15 percent, and 15 percent growth of incomplete projects, over the Brezhnev period. Over the same period, 1965–84, the coefficient of utilization of machinery declined by 13 percent, while the rate of return to that machinery declined by 34 percent.[19] The figures also show a considerable and important difference between light industry and engineering. In the period of 1980–86 there is a rise in the ratio of fixed capital invested to output of 23 percent for light industry and 13 percent for heavy industry.[20] The engineering ratio of output to funds invested only declined by 8 percent from 1970 to 1986, whereas light industry declined by 45 percent.[21] To add to the causes of declining returns, he points to low quality and the use of old technique. At the Twenty-seventh Party Congress Gorbachev gave a precise example of a factory that upon completion proceeded to produce outdated machinery. Little of this is news. Ever more production at greater cost, of technically outdated goods that are of low quality, but that everyone has to use because there is no alternative, is of the essence of the Soviet economy. What is different is the spiraling decline.

How can this be explained? The absurd statement that state capitalism requires the accumulation of capital explains little, particularly as really existing capitalism does not have such absurd ratios. Capitalism is simply nowhere near as inefficient. That is the real point. The whole stress of Gorbachev and his coterie is correctly placed on inefficiency as the cause of the economic problems of the USSR.

We have already identified the problem of the introduction of new techniques.

THE PRESENT ECONOMIC CRISIS 141

The problems associated with the question of technique and the nature of Soviet investment are considerable. One Soviet commentator, Pervushin, saw the USSR as suffering not from overaccumulation but from a surfeit of fixed and circulating funds. He argues that the machinery introduced may be inferior to the old machinery, and the total effect of the introduction of the new technique is not necessarily positive in economic terms even if the machinery is superior to that which it replaces.[22] The point then is that even if new technique could be introduced quickly and efficiently, which it cannot, the end result is dubious. Pervushin actually states that the introduction of new technique can cause a decline in productivity and make things worse, not better.

The second cause lies in the vast overmanning of the system. This has already been discussed above, but it warrants a separate section. Figures of 15–20 percent dismissals required are bandied about today. This would lead to some 20 million layoffs. The question is not just the fact of overmanning but its worsening over time. Why are plants more overmanned than before?

The higher education of the personnel means that more people are employed in executive grades than before. More people (some 1.5 million) are involved in research than ever before. The bureaucratic apparatus has become more bloated. This was why Gorbachev could speak of reducing the 18 million in the apparatus. In fact, this is a response to two pressures: the need to employ the intelligentsia and the need to control increasingly fractious workers. If production is poor, the answer has been to set up yet another body to oversee quality control or norms. Hence, bureaucratic employment increases. Here there is a contradiction between the short-term interests of the state and the long-term interests of the ruling group.

In the second place, it pays every plant manager to retain workers, particularly under conditions of labor shortage, in order to use them when needed, rather than to have to find them later. The change has been that the increasing labor shortage has increased the need for hoarding of workers from the point of view of each plant, but not from the viewpoint of the society.

What is also different is the extensive discussion of the details of the economic failure. Thus, when we are told that only eighteen out of forty-five kinds of goods in the RSFSR light industry had their plans fulfilled in 1985, and other examples are given in the same issue of *Ekonomicheskaia gazeta* of plans nominally fulfilled,[23] which involved a considerable decline in production, the very heart of the matter is being touched. The so-called planning mechanism does not work. Some plans are considerably overfulfilled while for others the reverse is true, but nominally the total results show ever-improving production. Since this same problem has been true ever since the first Stalin plan, although never discussed so frankly, the inevitable conclusion is that the system does not work. Such is the intended implication wrapped up in the ideology of changes needed because of a shift into intensive production.

These are issues I have discussed extensively elsewhere.[24] What is different now is that Gorbachev put this issue at the center of his program, as evidenced early on both by his speech of 11 June 1985 and by the preliminary outline of the new (Twelfth) Five-year Plan, where the new investment was now to go only half instead of three-quarters into new plants. We will return to this point below. The Congress speeches just put the seal of approval on the already agreed view.

There is another reason for the failure to complete projects. Under Khrushchev, a moratorium was declared on the construction of new buildings, but this was not repeated after his fall because of the consequence: massive unemployment. It could not be repeated also because there were ever fewer new projects. In other words, the slowdown of the system created its own momentum. It was socially increasingly risky to take decisive measures, and it was more difficult to take a risk because there was less and less leeway. Behind this problem lay two fundamental changes in Soviet society. These were the increased socialization of labor and the consequent growth in power of the Soviet work force. Both are also closely related to the decline in the supply of labor outside of the industrial economy.

The second feature that has changed and led to the Soviet crisis is that the increasingly urbanized economy, based on manufacturing production and not on advertising, finance, corner shops, retailing, and other forms of absorption of labor in the West, is far more integrated than it has ever been. The paradox is that it is an economy with giant plants, trusts, and "central planning" that cannot supply or repair itself with any regularity, so that its potential virtue is in fact its Achilles heel. Today, the ramifications of failure to deliver on time, construct to specification, or repair as requested are much greater than ever before. The costs are multiples of what they were twenty and more years ago. The effect is to magnify the failure of the Soviet economy.

The integration of the economy is ultimately reducible to the integration of the division of labor within the USSR. This, in turn, is composed of two elements: (1) the greater specificity of labor in two senses—attachment to locality (factory, home, town) and the particular development of skills; and (2) a tightly organized production process. The latter cannot be altered without reducing productivity, an evident result in the USSR, while the former, Braverman notwithstanding, cannot be overcome without massive costs. Labor that has been trained can, in principle, be retrained quickly if there is a reasonable incentive to retrain. Where there is little incentive, it will not happen without considerable disruption. We have argued many times that the basis of the political economy of the USSR rests on the absence of abstract labor in that country, and in this context it implies the lack of fluidity of labor inherent in a system with a labor shortage, and a highly specific relation to the production unit.

The third aspect of the crisis is associated with the increasing distance between the West and the USSR in the level of technology employed in production. We have already discussed the question of the introduction of new technology and will discuss it again below. Here we outline the increasing intensity of the problem feeding into the Soviet crisis.

The problems with labor have led to the forced introduction of new techniques and particularly technology imported from abroad. In the context of the USSR, it is to be noted that new technology actually raises costs rather than the reverse. This is because in the USSR new technology leads to the use of new fuel or more fuel in many instances, higher maintenance costs (even if less time is spent, it usually requires more skill), a higher depreciation cost, more breakdowns in the initial learning and development stages, and more auxiliary costs. None of these problems is specifically Soviet. What is Soviet is that they are all exacerbated to a considerable degree and above all not compensated by a reduction in the work force, higher output, and the greater reliability and precision of the new machines. Obviously if a new machine is introduced, it might be expected that it would cost more, but the cost is usually offset by the higher throughput of goods. If the norm is controlled by the workers and they do not permit such a higher output, or if they do permit a higher output but it is so far below potential that per-unit costs rise, then the introduction of the new machine actually raises costs rather than reducing them.

Since the new machine is not reliable, but it performs more tasks formerly performed by manual labor, it will cause more holdups in production than before. Furthermore, it will cause the continued hypertrophy of the repair sector, which in turn will require still more labor and more spare parts. Unless the auxiliary aspects are mechanized, the demand for labor actually increases. The storage and portage facilities can be handled through production lines or by the use of manual labor; by and large the USSR continues to use unskilled female labor for these tasks. Since the production of new products, new spare parts, and new processes requires warehousing, both construction and labor demand rises. The need for transport facilities inside and between plants continues to expand. The problem for the USSR is that such transport facilities are often custom-made and it is not easy to obtain such facilities in the USSR.

The end result, therefore, of the importation of new technique from abroad has been predictable. It has led to demands for the introduction of a system that can cope with the new technology. Much of the machinery imported from the West lay idle in the 1970s. At the same time the need for new technology, computers in particular, became overwhelming during the 1980s. It was not just a question of competing with the West: Soviet production had reached the point where computerization was demanded by the logic of production itself. Yet the failure to produce computers became a feature of the regime.[25]

In fact, the problem with technology was itself a result of the previous two aspects. The ending of the labor surplus meant that new enterprises could no longer be built in order to incorporate new technology in the old way, and the integrated nature of production demanded a much better form of technological coordination, which itself needed computerization, at all levels of production.

Finally, as a direct consequence of the previous points, the strength of the work force could only grow, as it has grown, to the point where the elite are afraid of it and make concessions. That time is now: the elite know that they cannot introduce the market without a revolt, that they cannot introduce a reserve army of labor, and that they have to accept continual growth in nominal wages. The effect is to make the elite cautious of any change, since anything that would reduce the degree of atomization in the system would make the situation very unstable.

The increasing power and negative action of the workers has shown itself in five respects. First, blue-collar wages in industry have been rising steadily over the years, from 66.1 rubles per month in 1950 and 88–90 rubles in 1960 to 216.4 in 1986 and 235 in 1988, making an annual percentage growth rate of 2.41 from 1960 to 1986,[26] while the salaries of the engineering and technical personnel (intelligentsia) have gone up at a much lower rates, by 1.76 percent, from 135.7 rubles per month in 1960 to 239 in 1986.[27]

Second, the control over norms became more weighted in favor of workers in that period. The degree of overfulfillment increased, at the same time that the norms in fact eased in relation to potential.[28]

Third, alcoholism also increased.[29] Alcoholism is a response to stress more than anything else. For the USSR it has played a special role in quenching potential revolt through a solitary solution, made easier by the individual relation to the work process.[30] It is particularly the atomized form that demands that the worker find an individualized, separated relief. In the last period the stress had become greater than previously, leading workers to pay less attention to their work and more attention to their psychological requirements.

Fourth, the nature of performance in the labor process has deteriorated, evidenced by the poor quality of work, even when it appears that the goods are hardly touched by human hands.[31]

Fifth, the number of strikes is increasing and the effect of the strikes has become more dramatic. In particular, the strikes in the mines, in the national republics, and elsewhere showed themselves in terms of the plan results for 1989 and for the first quarter of 1990.[32]

Clearly, the increased power of the workers has increased costs—and the number of bureaucrats required to control such costs. To this has to be added the additional costs of campaigns, and indeed of the dismissals of supervisors to be replaced by trainees.

The Problem of Technology in Historical Perspective

It is important to consider further the problems of the introduction of new technology. It is clear that a rise in labor productivity over time would alleviate the problems of the Soviet economy. Yet, on the contrary, it has become progressively harder to introduce new techniques.

If we consider the problems in the introduction of new technology, they reduce to two issues. The technology produced in the USSR may itself be defective. As a result the costs of introduction are unacceptably high. On the other hand, even a nondefective technology may not be acceptable to the plant because the existing production relations are threatened. Hence, the introduction of new technology goes back to the same issue as in the case of any product. Labor controls the work process and hence produces a good or process of its own kind and prevents the disruption of its time-honored pattern of production.

It has, therefore, to be noted that the nature of Soviet technique is thus a reflection of the nature of the Soviet product. The origins of the Soviet product itself lie in the original conflict within the goals of the regime. On the one hand, in 1929 the aim of collectivization and industrialization was to raise the relative surplus, that is, to increase the surplus product over consumption, by reducing the amount of labor time required to produce goods. On the other hand, it was only the rise in the absolute surplus that permitted growth in the relative surplus and so a rise in productivity. This point will be explained below.

The Soviet elite were faced in the late 1920s with the problem of how to raise the necessary surplus over consumption to ensure sustained "accumulation." There were necessarily two components of this issue. The first was how to obtain the initial surplus; the second was how to sustain the reinvestment of that surplus in the new technology required. They acquired the surplus product through squeezing the standard of living of the direct producers—peasants and workers—and obtained the necessary labor through the flood into the towns induced by the starvation in the countryside. This process, analogous to primitive accumulation, raised the absolute surplus product. In other words, the surplus was raised through the extension of labor time or the reduction of the standard of living.

On the other hand, the process was intended to raise the surplus product by raising the standard of living and either keeping work time constant or reducing it. This could only be achieved through raising productivity through the application of the new machinery and hence new technology, which was being produced with the acquired surplus. As indicated above, the regime has always had considerable trouble with the introduction of the new technique. In the 1930s, the new technology was certainly introduced but only through this process of raising the absolute surplus, that is, using vast quantities of extra labor. That was the weakness of the regime. Its paradox was that, in order to raise the relative surplus, the absolute surplus had to be increased. In other words, the regime has always had to increase the number of workers employed in order to introduce new technology and so raise productivity.

The apparent success of the regime was achieved through an interpenetration of the two above forms of surplus. The workers resisted the introduction of forms of extraction of the relative surplus, as a method of reducing the extraction of the absolute surplus. They worked poorly or took action to contain the effects of the introduction of new technology. The result was overmanning, technology that was outdated even when introduced, high costs of installation, and little savings from the introduction of the new machinery. On the other hand, had the new machinery not been installed, nothing would have been produced. The growth in the absolute surplus then masked the failure to raise the relative surplus by itself or even in itself for considerable periods of time. More concretely, the use of alienated labor to produce machine tools meant that the machine tools were outdated, unreliable, very costly, and of the wrong kind for the job. As a result, the savings anticipated from the use of the new tool were not realized. But the product itself might not have existed apart from the machine tool. Furthermore, there was initially at least a rise in the relative surplus product, as a result of the employment of the machine tool. Problems arose when it was a question of replacement of one tool by another. Then savings became more problematic, with a possible increase in labor costs, increase in raw material costs, increased risk of breakdown, and so on. As long as these costs could be contained, through the employment of more labor to construct new factories that would not have the usual obstacles, or more labor to make more spare parts or more processed raw materials, the question of costs was secondary.

There are two aspects of the extraction of the absolute surplus: the extension of labor time and the reduction of the wage. The reduction of the standard of living, or at least its containment, also permitted a considerable expansion of producer goods, but it was bound to end with the increasing socialization of production and consequent increased power of the work force. There was also a limit to the exploitation of the countryside. Once these three aspects came together, the real increase in the relative surplus was clear. Put differently, the real increase in productivity was shown to be low. At this point it is necessary to be careful, since productivity here must refer to productivity for the purpose of raising the surplus product.

In the USSR it is quite possible ostensibly to increase production but to have no effect on the surplus product. The product may be useless or be a worse replacement for another product. Under capitalism a useless product may create surplus value, but in the USSR the surplus product is in the form of use values. Hence, it is quite possible to have a formally large surplus product that is nonetheless incapable of being used for reproduction and therefore is not genuinely part of the surplus product. It is potentially possible, therefore, for a formal improvement in technique to lead to a decrease in the surplus product. As long as the expansion of the absolute surplus continued, the dubiety of the increase in the relative surplus was masked. Its ending has begun to show the problems. The primary problem is one of ending the control over the work process established by the worker during the 1930s. The method of extraction of the surplus product during this period, which was one of virtually pure coercion, established the nature of the relative surplus product. This is the real point.

In effect, the stability of the regime (to the extent that it can be called stable) was established through this marriage of relative and absolute surplus labor. The different problems in the introduction of new technology are all traceable to this synthesis. Because the worker defended himself against further incursions on his necessary labor time by individually establishing control over his work process, he resisted any change that might alter the particular relation in the factory. Indeed, the factory manager colluded, since it was not in his interest to engage in a long-drawn-out battle that might only benefit his successor, and anyway might never show up as increased production. Hence, new technology had to be tried and tested in newly constructed factories; it had to be specially adapted for poor handling; and a considerable amount of labor time had to be allocated to deal with the problems that would necessarily arise.

It can be seen that new technology was introduced and the relative surplus was raised, but only as long as the absolute surplus product was also increasing. Once that situation ended, the regime faced a crisis. In principle, the regime can solve its crisis by reducing the most blatant examples of overmanning. This, however, would only be a temporary solution, even if it were politically possible. The extra labor would be quickly used up.

Furthermore, as long as that labor is contained under a regime of terror, as under Stalin, labor remains cheap. Indeed, the view that labor is cheap in the USSR and has been so has become the dominant viewpoint among Soviet economists.[33] Cheapness, under conditions where money is not money, cannot just mean that total ruble costs are low. It really means that it is easier to employ workers than to use machines, and that fewer resources need to be devoted to consumer goods, welfare, education, and the factory environment. Both factory managers and "planners" prefer to employ more workers rather than design an automated plant to replace existing plants.

Once, however, the source of labor dries up, then the economy has even greater difficulty introducing new technology and it therefore has a low growth rate.

The Contradictions between Departments One and Two

Gorbachev quickly moved to improve the production of machinery, in terms of total output, level of technology, and quality. The measures have had little result.[34] The situation was better than previously but nowhere near the stated or necessary goals. While the regime has consistently overproduced department one goods (as described above), the producer goods remain antiquated, with average ages going back twenty to thirty years. In the post-Khrushchev period economists complained that machine tools could be found that went back to the turn of the century. Even the defense industry discovered that it was inexorably being left behind by the West. The paradox of a regime that invests too much in producer goods yet produces neither sufficient machines nor machines of the right quality and technical standard must be explained.

The absorption of resources in the construction sector, spare parts sector, replacement sector, among others, is enormous. The producer goods sector can expand indefinitely through the need to expand production, introduce new technology, etc., but costs at the present time have simply escalated. The result is that resources are absorbed in additional output, whether real or not, while the old forms of production remain at their old levels of productivity. The new technology from the West has remained underutilized, and increasingly new technology is simply not introduced at all. The old plant absorbs more and more resources as it ages, while the costs of introducing new techniques also rise.[35]

It is clear that the theorists who argue that the regime just ignores the consumer are themselves ignoring reality. The fact is that the regime cannot produce goods as required. Resources are absorbed by two features. First, the old plant needs replacement, and also spare parts, on a daily basis. Second, the new technology goes into new enterprises, plants, and factories, and so absorbs still more resources through construction needs. As department one has grown, so has the need for spare parts and replacements, as well as the demand for new technology to replace the old. The trouble is that the new technology does not go into the old plants. Since there is a shortage of machine tools and of department one goods in general, it follows that the old sector always has a demand for its goods. It is therefore a law of the Soviet economy that the primacy of department one over department two is correlated with an increasing demand for department one goods. The faster department one grows, the greater, paradoxically, is the demand for department one goods. Department one has to supply machinery not only to itself but also to department two. The demand from department two is really limited only by the supply of goods from department one. It would, of course, be constrained by the supply of raw materials or labor if it had a considerable expansion of machinery, but the latter is not the fundamental constraint. The demand from department one itself is also apparently unlimited. Its expansion requires apparently unlimited inputs for the reasons given above. If, therefore, department one is given primacy, as it has been since 1929, it will grow explosively and in a manner that not only sucks in ever more resources, but also maintains its own backwardness. It has also been pointed out above that increased investment can actually lead to a decline in output. Under these circumstances, department one's expansion can be seen as a paradox of the regime, in which it is driven to expand department one in order to increase the output of consumer goods but is simply never able to reach its goal. No one gains through increased investment in an enterprise that simply leads to a decline in output or to a rise in costs with no increase in output. It cannot be attributed to bureaucratic inertia or support for the heavy-goods sector.

If, on the contrary, as in 1988 under Gorbachev, consumer goods production is given preference, then the lack of machinery in department two will eventually show itself and the system will demand increased inputs for department one. The Gorbachev gamble is that the workers will be encouraged to work harder under conditions where extra money for promotion or bonuses will mean real goods. The problem is exemplified most graphically in the case of cars, where the

THE PRESENT ECONOMIC CRISIS   149

annual production of more than a few hundred thousand cars for general distribution to a population rapidly approaching 300 million requires massive retooling. Even if private cars were rejected as a mode of transport, the public transport system is overloaded and requires enormous investment. The supply of everyday consumer durables from automatic washing machines to video recorders is woefully inadequate. Their production can only be marginally expanded by the present decrees requiring every plant to supply consumer goods. Such central demands are reminiscent of the "small is good" Maoist line, with all that it implied. Under Brezhnev there was only one year when department one was overtaken by department two, but that was all it was. There is no way out of this vicious circle within the confines of the so-called administrative-command economy. It is precisely because of the blood-sucking nature of department one that the social services such as education, housing, health, and welfare have had to be starved. And yet it is all quite rational. Department one cannot supply the goods unless it has the necessary resources. The trouble is that the so-called capital–output ratio has been worsening; in other words, the absorption of resources per unit of output by department one has been rising.

As already discussed, the reason for the worsening ratios of unit of investment to unit of output lies in the increasing socialization of labor and the ending of the period of excess labor. As long as labor could take up the slack when a particular tool failed to perform as required, the costs were relatively low. Once the labor was no longer there, costs escalated. This has been exacerbated by the increasing integration of production, which now magnifies the effects of unevenness of production and the failure of machinery. Then, too, costs of labor have increased considerably with the increasing power of the work force. This involves not only higher pay but also decreasing flexibility of the work force in relation to the labor process.

The Increasing Power of Labor and Its Effects

The Soviet worker has been moving from a position of total defeat to one of increasing strength, which has a series of ramifications throughout the economy. Wages have to rise, as they have done since the 1960s. Consumption demands become ever more pressing as a result. Resources are switched to the consumer goods sector and as a result the producer goods sector deteriorates, immediately affecting the consumer goods sector. New technology becomes more difficult to introduce into old plants as the norm bargain struck with management is difficult to change. Workers work to rule. In turn, the deteriorating economy leads management to pressurize workers, who then become more stressed. They may turn to alcohol or other forms of individualization, which reacts still more unfavorably on the nature of the product. For a time, the product can even deteriorate still further but a halt has to be called to the falling levels of quality control, just to maintain production.

When labor can no longer be used to replace or supplement defective parts, exhausted machinery, or indeed machinery as such, department one has to be further expanded, and this absorbs still more resources. Factories have to invest in more equipment, spare parts, and new extensions. Capital expenditure (so-called) rises. The constant refrain that the USSR uses too much manual labor, particularly in things like porterage, has been heard for the last decade.[36] An intolerable conflict is established between department one and department two, in which the latter has to expand to deal with the increasing power of the workers but cannot do so without the infinite expansion of department one. The dog wants to catch its tail but the only way to do so is to run around so it runs around never catching its tail. In capitalism one or the other sector would be subordinated through the movement of value, most particularly in extremes, through crisis. In the USSR it cannot be done. The elite possesses no mechanism to subject the economy fully to their own control. They can only manage it, administer it, and fail to administer it as it goes into insoluble conflicts.

The economy then finds itself rent, in an even more extreme way than has been the case since 1923, between consumption and production, between demand and supply, between machinery and labor, between the quantity of "money" and the amount of resources available, between new plants and old plants, between the need to improve quality and the need to maintain quantity. Every problem becomes insoluble. The economy progressively falls apart. Dissolution sets in. Hence, Gorbachev and his men are the saviors of a disintegrating economy. No solution can work except the introduction of the market. Yet the very reason for the introduction of the market is the reason why it cannot be introduced: the strength of labor. Thus, the regime has to find temporary solutions for each problem in turn.

The regime has used centralized interference as its prime method of restoring balance in the economy. Under Stalin the purges played a crucial role, while under his successors it was organization and reorganization. Gorbachev is in the same tradition. He has in fact continued to centralize. Yet the centralization inevitably fails to do more than hold the system together. Since the center cannot actually hold all the required information or levers in its own hands, the more centralized the system is, the more independent the peripheral areas become. This is a paradoxical law of the system. A vicious circle sets in. The independence of the periphery has to be curbed and more centralized control established, but the center becomes so bureaucratically overburdened that it progressively loses more control over the units over which it is in charge. This is what led to Gorbachev's original cry that the system required both more centralization and more decentralization. The problem is that the centralization/decentralization as it now exists is chaotic, with both insufficient real centralized coordination and insufficient real direct local initiative for the purposes of the economy. On the other hand, it is the only method of control that currently exists for purposes of organizing the system. In fact, all measures hitherto introduced amount to methods of facilitating this relationship.

That has really been the message for the post-Stalin period. Already under Stalin, in his notorious *Economic Problems of Socialism*, the official doctrine had been changed to argue in favor of the market for consumer goods. Ever since, the regime has been discussing the implementation of some type of market reform. Since they have never done it, they have used the alternative of market surrogates, such as planning on the basis of amount realized rather than total quantity produced. These forms have all worked to a limited degree and then failed.

The bureaucracy has reached its ultimate point when it can no longer organize, but only organize itself to organize. It has to reorganize itself constantly to secure the economy. Stalin by contrast liquidated the layers that are today being reorganized in order to establish direct control. He failed, and his successors have tried to implement new forms of control over themselves. They have also replaced one group of administrators by another. The drastic step of killing all the administrators or replacing them in a more humane manner is unlikely to achieve anything other than limited goals and the regime has therefore been compelled to find ever new forms of reorganization. The bad workman always blames his tools and the elite blames its organizational form rather than the reality of conflict with the direct producer. None other than Joseph Stalin himself began the fashion of attacking bureaucracy in order to preserve the bureaucratic elite.

Gorbachev's acceptance of this point marks a new stage in the Soviet crisis. He proposed that the soviets should manage the administration of the country while political and ideological functions would remain with the party. This would appear to mean that the party economy would function independently of the party. The elite, however, are impaled on the horns of a dilemma: They can introduce genuine democracy and be voted out, so losing all, or they can create an imaginary democracy, which may buy them time but will whet the appetite of the population for real democratic forms. The latter is the way that they are going. On the one hand, they are afraid to go too fast in case they lose all, and on the other hand they have to install a temporary alternative that does indeed prolong their tenure as members of an elite. Until 1990, at least, they had succeeded in maintaining their own position while introducing a semidemocratic parliamentary institution, with an executive president who would not run for popular election until 1995. The examples of Eastern Europe are only formally similar, since they were always either occupied countries or very much dependent on the USSR. The elites in those countries were always disposable by their ultimate supporters in the USSR. The only question for the Soviet elite is whether it can maintain itself in power while converting to the market.

Notes

1. L.A. Gordon, "Sotsial'naia politika v sfere oplata truda (vchera i segodnia)," *Sotsiologicheskie issledovaniia*, 1987, no. 4.
2. *Pravda*, 11 June 1985.

3. M. Krushinskii, "Khvatit li resursov?" *Izvestiia,* 14 July 1988, p. 4. Krushinskii deals with the whole question of housing and points out, among other things, that piles of cement are hoarded by enterprises, that buildings are constructed that are unnecessary, and that priority is given to projects that have greater total plan results. In this case the ministry and enterprise might prefer a dam to housing construction.

4. *Ekonomicheskaia gazeta,* June 1985. *Pravda* (1 October 1987) carries the statement of the Central Committee promising an individual flat to every family unit by the year 2000. The statement admits that there is a severe housing shortage and criticizes existing corruption in allocation. The actual number of flats constructed reached a peak of 2.6 million in 1960 but was down to 2.1 million in 1986 and not quite 2 million in 1985. It has to be said that the size of the flats has increased over this period. Nonetheless, capital investment in residential construction has trebled in the period from 1960 to 1986 (from 10.8 billion rubles to 30.9 billion rubles, with inflation officially taken into account) (*Narodnoe khoziaistvo SSSR za 70 let* [Moscow, 1987], pp. 510, 514).

5. *Pravda,* 22 February 1985.

6. *Izvestiia,* 25 August 1987, p. 2.

7. Kastutis Jaskelavičius, "Summa slagaemuemy sil'na," *Litva Literaturnaia,* 1989, no. 4, p. 141. This article is an argument for the economic independence of Latvia. The author points out, in the context of the above quote, that the grounds for maintaining the economic integrity of the USSR are greatly weakened by the failure of the economy. He then cites the example of two adjacent factories in Kaunas, the one supplying the inputs needed by the other instead to factories in the Urals, the Caucasus, and the South. There is, he argues, no unified plan, only a mess.

8. Christian Rakovsky, "The Five-year Plan in Crisis," *Critique,* 13, p. 24.

9. See the discussion of contradiction in chapter 1.

10. "Deputaty-Ekonomisty o radikal'noi ekonomicheskoi reforme," *Voprosy ekonomiki,* 1989, no. 9, press conference given by Popov, Bogomolov, Lisichkin, Abalkin and Tikhonov, 16 June 1989. For Bogomolov's remark, see p. 5.

11. Iu. Rytov, "Sdvigi est," *Izvestiia,* 1 October 1987, p. 1.

12. *Narodnoe khoziaistvo SSSR za 70 let,* p. 411.

13. *Ekonomicheskaia gazeta,* 1988, no. 5.

14. Ibid., pp. 417–18.

15. Ibid. pp. 163–64.

16. V. Rutgaizer, Iu. Sheviakhov, and L. Zubova, "Trodovyi kollektiv i intensifikatsiia proizvodstva," *Voprosy ekonomiki,* 1988, no. 1, p. 24. The authors point out that capital expenditure per unit of extracted raw material has gone up from one unit fifteen years ago to four today.

17. Ibid., p. 332.

18. *Voprosy ekonomiki,* 1986, no. 2, pp. 20–21.

19. Ibid., p. 155. The return per ruble invested has gone down to 69 in 1986, using an index of 1970 = 100, i.e., there has been an overall decline of 31 percent, but on a steady annual basis.

20. Ibid., p. 155

21. Ibid.

22. *Voprosy ekonomiki,* 1987, no 3, p. 51.

23. *Ekonomicheskaia gazeta,* 1986, no. 9.

24. H.H. Ticktin, "Towards a Political Economy of the USSR," *Critique* 1 (1973); "The Contradictions of Soviet Society and Professor Bettelheim," *Critique* 6 (1976); "The Afghan War and the Crisis in the USSR," *Critique* 12; and "The Ambiguities of Ernest Mandel," *Critique* 12.

25. Stepan Pachikov, "Computing in the Cold," *Personal Computer* (London) 1989,

THE PRESENT ECONOMIC CRISIS   153

no. 10, p. 170. This account of the Soviet computer industry, smuggled out of the USSR, makes hilarious reading and is an excellent introduction to the failure of Soviet industry. The second-hand price of an ordinary PC in the USSR is many times the cost of a car. The author attributes the failure of the computer industry to ideology and the long lead times taken to make decisions by the numerous layers of the industrial apparatus: "Throughout the economy, it takes so much decision making, coordination and adjustment to implement a new product that it becomes obsolete before it gets onto the production line" (p. 171).

26. *Narodnoe khoziaistvo SSSR za 70 let*, p. 431; *Narodnoe khoziaistvo SSSR v 1988* (Moscow: Finansy i statistiki, 1989), p. 77; Goskomstat SSSR, *Trud v SSSR* (Moscow: Finansy i statistiki, 1988), p. 189.

27. *Narodnoe khoziaistvo SSSR za 70 let*, p. 431. The later statistical volumes do not provide details of the pay of the engineering and technical workers (ITR), here called the intelligentsia.

28. N. Rimar, "Novye usloviia—novye trebovaniia," *Sotsialisticheskii trud*, 1987, no. 10, p. 61. The common overfulfillment of plans by workers, which Rimar discusses, follows on the tightening-up procedure of the late 1950s. In other words, control cannot be exercised from the center over the workers.

29. Between 1970 and 1980 the amount of alcohol sold went up by close to 33 percent per capita (*Narodnoe khoziaistvo SSSR v 1988*, p. 115). Thereafter, the campaigns to reduce production meant that the amount sold was under half that of 1980. Illegal production is another matter.

30. I am indebted for this insight to Mr. P. O'Donnell of the Department of Psychology, Glasgow University.

31. "Raikom i Gospriemka" (*Pravda*, 26 November 1987, p. 2) makes it clear that quality fell before Gorbachev. After writing that defective goods were not held back and culprits punished, as previously in the particular plant, it says that as a result "quality began to fall. Defective goods were put to the account of the plant" (and hence by implication not laid at the door of any individual or group of individuals). There is some evidence in the statistics of surveys done of articles of light industry (*Narodnoe khoziaistvo SSSR za 70 let*, p. 196).

32. *Pravda*, 28 January 1990; and *Financial Times*, 9 April 1990, p. 4, which summarizes the Soviet reports for the first quarter of 1990.

33. See Gordon, "Sotsial'naia politika," and the press conference cited in note 10, above.

34. See A. Matosich and B. Matosich in *Soviet Economy*, vol. 4, no. 2 (1988), pp. 144–76.

35. The radical reform economist V. Seliunin calculated that the real relation of producer goods to consumer goods was of the order of 40 percent to 60 percent of the total goods produced, as opposed to official figures nearer to 25 percent and 75 percent. He simply took account of the arbitrary prices and taxes involved and produced an adjustment. The effect, as he points out, is to give the USSR a savings rate of 40 percent of production, which is very high compared to the West. The Soviet economy is far ahead of any other country in the production of metal, fuel, machine tools, tractors etc. He concludes that "the economy is working more and more for itself and not for man." The crucial point here is the implicit acceptance of the view that it is the economy that operates in this way and not the directions of the elite. The economy malfunctions. To ram his point home, the author points to the large amount of unused equipment; 45 percent of workplaces in engineering have no one to work them, and one-quarter in industry as a whole. See Seliunin's article in *Sotsialisticheskaia industriia*, 5 January 1988, p. 2.

36. M. Sonin, "Problemy raspredeleniia i ispolzovaniia trudovykh resursov," *Sotsialisticheskii trud*, March 1977, p. 94ff.

9

Perestroika and the Disintegration of the USSR

The Policy of Reorganization

Over the period from 1985 to 1990 Gorbachev changed his policy quite rapidly. His first program was one of responsibility of bureaucrats for the success of their fiefdoms, tough discipline over labor, the brigade system, concessions to the intelligentsia in material terms, and gestures toward workplace democracy. It was the Andropov policy of facing three ways: discipline and organizational measures responding to the classical forms of control produced by the organizers of the society; stress on economic accountability for the intelligentsia and its section of the elite; and cosmetic references to democracy for the workers.[1] In economic terms he stood for stricter plan performance, with hints of the market, which he quite clearly had in mind. By 1987 this had failed. He had gone through a series of organizational measures that had an immediate impact, but such measures have success for a limited time only. New men in old positions, experienced people in new positions, and the shake-up produced by shuffling some and dismissing others always compel the system to operate in a fresher manner for a limited time. Soon, however, the contradiction of the system shows itself in a new form.

There is obviously a limit to how many times the organizers can reorganize themselves. If the regime is left only with the alternative of reorganization and still more reorganization, it has little life left in it. The post-Stalin period was characterized first by Khrushchev's reorganizations and then by the revenge of the apparatus, which refused to accept any more reorganization. Khrushchev attempted to deal with economic problems by constant reorganization of institutions. It worked in the sense that personnel were redeployed and so previous forms of conservative preventive action were removed. In other words the ministerial autarky was broken, so giving rein to alternative methods of raising production, at first based on regions. Soon regional autarky developed, and that had to be broken.

The elite was not impressed by this reorganization of their lives, and preferred, under Brezhnev, to try market concessions, which flopped when they realized that they would have problems with the workers on their hands. Thereafter they tried to use market-type reforms without any market. Such were the various employment experiments around Shchekino and the use of other plan indicators supposedly based on money returns of some sort. Every reform had a limited effect that tailed off in a short time. The real question is whether this kind of regular change, really amounting to a shake-up of established relations between people or institutions, can still be pursued. Is there a kind of law of a falling rate of output per change? Logically, we would expect this to be the case.

The success of such reforms depends on the same four aspects earlier analyzed. The supply of extra labor to utilize has dried up. Worse, the fluidity of labor is much diminished. Hence, reforms have more and more to concentrate on the means whereby they can either free labor or replace labor. The labor shortage and specificity of labor can only become more acute over time, as the economy demands more spare parts and more completed construction projects.

Gorbachev, and his academic predecessor, Sonin, have insisted on the need to increase the output of technologically sophisticated machine tools and the products of those tools, in order to create the possibility of replacement of labor. The problem with this policy is that it initially requires more skilled labor and semiskilled labor, not less. In order to free labor, the Soviet economy has to employ more labor. Since it is self-evident that the very act of investment in machine tools will lead back to the same problems of poor quality, the organizational solution to the manpower shortage does not exist. Logically, indeed, it led to a still greater manpower shortage. Thus, the technological solution to the economy, associated with the slogan *uskorenie,* or acceleration, failed in the first Gorbachev period. Its failure meant that reorganization of the structures standing over labor could have little effect on the growing power of labor itself.

The Brezhnev period was one of exceptional elite stability. Gorbachev, by contrast, embarked on wholesale dismissals of ministers, the closing down of entire ministries, the merging of ministries, and the devolution of tasks down to enterprises.[2] The simple effect of removing the old corrupt bureaucrats and replacing them with new, dynamic corrupt bureaucrats undoubtedly stirred people up and compelled management to find ways of forcing workers to work better, but this could only last a short time. Workers and managers became increasingly tired of exhortations and threats. Gorbachev could not imprison the large numbers incarcerated under Stalin in order to increase production; he was compelled simply to rant along about "making life harsh for those who do not work."[3]

Thus, the effect of replacing bureaucrats and campaigning for harder work together with replacement of labor did have a temporary effect, an effect more temporary than before.

It was not surprising, then, that Gorbachev's first official policy made little sense, even if his speeches showed him hitting at real targets. His 11 June 1985 speech on the economy did indeed show that he knew the most important features of the Soviet political economy. He stressed the nature of the Soviet product—its poor quality, its wastefulness, and the impossibility of completing projects in any predictable period. In this respect he went beyond his dead leader, who preferred to single out aspects of the same problems. His first official agenda, then, was to hit hard at those in positions of immediate responsibility and force the workers to work. In fact his policy, as he put it himself, was one of compelling everyone to work harder.[4]

The first instruments were dismissal for those in the elite and the use of direct force over the workers, combined with the drive to the brigade system. Gorbachev's speech to the Twenty-seventh Party Congress in 1986 marked a transition from organizational measures toward the market. He was for hard work, new laws to clamp down on shirkers, bribe-takers, and hooligans, and still more laws to raise the quality of production. He was for dealing with bureaucrats who do not perform as required but prefer a quiet life. On the other hand, he was in favor of more enterprise independence, incomes related to performance of the enterprise, presumably profits, flexible prices, and contracts made with wholesale organizations, possible bankruptcy, independent sale of goods above plan levels, greater regional economic independence, and individual supply of services, i.e., private enterprise. Of course, the two sides, repression and the market, fit together if run together. In fact, it looked more incoherent than a plan to introduce the market with repression.

The five-hour exercise appeared more as a brilliant political performance in which every appearance was provided of hard-hitting criticisms with the solution being economic reforms. The problem was that it was only the appearance of change. Gorbachev conceded to the intelligentsia still more by the salary rises, which he specifically mentioned, stressing in more than one place the crucial role of science in raising productivity.

The Pseudo-market Reforms

By 1987 the move to the market became clearer, with the adoption of the Law on the State Enterprise in June at a Central Committee plenum. The law itself was muddled but its intention was clear. It involved moving over to a situation of self-financing, that is, enterprises financing themselves out of profits. This required that prices be changed to reflect costs and that there be some form of independent exchange between plants. Therefore, wholesale trade was to be freed and prices of goods in this sector were to be similarly freed. What exactly this could have meant is not clear since it has never been properly applied, although it has been officially law from 1 January 1988, except to a limited degree in 1989. To the extent that the law could be applied, it seemed to mean that profits would become an indicator rather than the essential drive and form of production. As long as prices were controlled and relations between enterprises were administratively maintained, profits remained secondary.

From this point on, the struggle in the elite was over the speed of introduction of the market and the consequent political attitudes to the working class. Prices would have to be raised and then freed for profits to be meaningful, unemployment introduced to control wages, workers dismissed on a large scale to raise productivity, and competition introduced to permit direct relations between enterprises to be meaningful. Firms would then have to be allowed to go bankrupt. The credit system would have to apply the brakes to firms considered inefficient. Yet none of these measures could really be introduced. The failure of the 1989 experiment, when some prices and enterprise investment were freed and limited direct contact with enterprises was also allowed, was a disaster. The result was inflation running to an official 13 percent, which some reckoned to be at 18 percent. Goods disappeared from the shops, and there were also greater supply difficulties for firms. The problem is theoretically obvious.

Profit as an indicator is no better or worse than volume as an indicator, but when profits can be linked to prices and wages, then monopoly power is bound to show itself. When prices are only partially freed, and by and large do not reflect costs, then between the pent-up demand for goods and the lack of competition, the only way prices could go was up. At the same time, it became less profitable to produce goods whose prices were controlled or were less than possible alternatives. Inevitably, shortages developed.

Profit as an indicator is not even a precursor of the market, since the latter must operate spontaneously with competing enterprises and have no outside determination of inputs, prices, or investment decisions. Profits under such a dispensation, as is now nominally the case, provide the criterion by which to judge the enterprise director, who then has an interest in achieving high profits. As a result, he will reduce the cost of inputs as well as the cost of investment, attempt to fire workers, intensify their labor, and ensure that quality control is maintained or raised.[5] There is a triple-edged problem with such a scenario. First, it will then pay the factory director to obtain the lowest-cost inputs regardless of quality or suitability, or if quality control is strict, he will compromise. After all, quality control can check on reliability but not suitability. Second, his interest in investment will be checked even further and investment will in practice plummet. Third, the workers are not likely to accept that they have to work better or harder even for more pay as long as money is not money. If quality control is not maintained, which is more likely, then the goods could become even more shoddy if that were possible. Since the shortage is absolute, whatever is produced will be sold unless there is an alternative source, such as imports, or the goods wholly malfunction. On the other hand, the stress on profitability will indeed mean that more attention will be paid to money. Fines will then mean something, as they do not at the present time.[6]

Since the enterprise funds will go in part to increased bonuses, it might be thought that some workers would be interested in improved functioning of the enterprise. In fact, surveys of enterprise directors showed that the new rules made little difference.[7] Workers can have little interest, although some workers, foremen, specialists, etc. (that is, relatively more skilled workers, in control of other workers), might indeed be somewhat stimulated. Nonetheless, as long as control over the parameters comes from above, success or failure will be arbitrary and dependent on the usual management skills of getting around the system, rather than on ability to produce a high-quality and needed product at low cost. That these are not merely predictions but a description of the actual situation is shown by the articles describing the enterprises on the new scheme.[8] Everyone is pessimistic of the success of the reforms so far introduced, but they then go on to argue for the introduction of the market as the only real solution.

The regime reached the correct conclusion that only the introduction of the market as a system in one fell swoop would make any sense. By the end of 1989 it had become crystal clear that market socialism was not possible. A labor market and a capital market would have to be introduced. This required a change in the laws on property. On the other hand, the abandonment of the middle way could only mean that all the measures mentioned above would have to be deployed to attack the position of the workers. Up to this point the regime had failed.

The various concrete measures to introduce the market produced a polarization in Soviet society that was entirely predictable but nonetheless unexpected by both Gorbachev and the Sovietologists. On the one side stood workers who would not accept price rises, unemployment, harsher and harder work, while on the other stood the intelligentsia and the Soviet liberals who wanted the market. Stalinoids such as Ligachev made a clear attempt to appeal to workers. We turn therefore to the concrete forms of market reform in the USSR.

The Market, Prices, and Social Relations

The immediate social effect of the market is to raise the salaries of the executive-engineering personnel; and a shrewd political operator would make the shift with maximum effect in order to get the intelligentsia on his side. This would involve dropping the old policy of playing off workers against the intelligentsia in favor of the new policy of developing an alliance of skilled, upwardly mobile labor aristocrats with the intelligentsia and elite. In a nonagricultural labor force of some 115 million persons, there are some 17 million with higher education, and the absorption of some 10 percent of ordinary workers in the above category would bring those in this alliance to some 30 million, or around 30 percent of the work force. In addition, the technicians or lower-level intelligentsia of some 20 million could be partially or wholly delivered to this group of privileged workers. In effect, up to 40 percent of the work force could be won over to market-type reforms. That is a reasonable political strategy for the Soviet elite and that, as I have argued elsewhere, is the only real meaning to be attached to Zaslavskaia's Novosibirsk Report.[9]

The views of the Novosibirsk academics—Aganbegian, the former official economic adviser to Gorbachev, and his protégée Zaslavskaia—are basically no different from Gorbachev's view. Aganbegian's speeches as at the Twenty-seventh Party Congress, where he proposed the most consistent and radical ideas on the introduction of the market, have also incorporated the need today to maintain control over the working class.

In his book *Inside Perestroika,* Aganbegian tackles the problem squarely. "Our backwardness in productivity, in efficiency, in quality of output," he says, ". . . is caused to a great extent by faults in the organization and payment of labor."[10] He then rules out unemployment and plumps for a system of brigades or teams who are rewarded according to their input. They would be self-managing. He calls for an end to alienation by incorporating the worker at a most primitive level. Although he is very careful when talking of unemployment and bankruptcy, and he criticizes Shmelev for his demand for unemployment, he nonetheless does talk of redeployment of some 1.5 million workers per year as well as of closing down plants that are uneconomical.[11] He calls for the abolition of subsidies on food, so announcing that workers cannot be controlled without reintroducing authentic money. No worker will work harder unless his wage will buy goods. If the cheap staples are abolished and workers are paid more so that they might at least retain a similar standard of living, money has some meaning. He also provides a detailed account of the nature of bankruptcy and the consequent redeployment of workers.[12]

By June 1987 the decision was made to follow Aganbegian's advice and indeed that of the many Western economists who urged the same view, on the Pavlovian principle that subsidies are always bad, profits good. Hence, Gorbachev spent some time reiterating the point that price increases were not too bad a thing at Murmansk in October 1987.[13] Since food is the main item in the budget of all persons not in the elite, it is hard to see either how the price rises can be introduced or how they could be done without massive political cost or possibly unrest. Yet without a rise in prices to reflect costs, there can be no move to the market.

By 1990 the question of price increases had become the central political issue of the regime. In February it canceled the prices introduced at the beginning of the year in the face of strike threats from the official trade-union organization. Yet without price rises there could be no question of the introduction of money and so of an incentive system to make workers work.

The regime consistently backtracked on price rises. Shmelev, the extreme marketeer of the USSR, had already proposed a different strategy to raise prices by 1988. He suggested that the budget become the focus of reform. By balancing the budget the regime would remove subsidies, particularly for food, and also compel enterprises to become self-financing or accept lower subsidies. The effect would be the same in that prices would rise. In truth, by 1989 a new campaign started on the impossibility of running a budget deficit. Since money was not money in the USSR, few persons were taken in by what was, after all, a traditional Stalinist campaign. The campaign failed in its objective to get workers to accept price rises. Instead, the emission of money rose by 56 percent, to 18 billion rubles, and wages rose by an official 9.6 percent.[14] Prices rose still more, officially by 13 percent and unofficially by higher figures. The result was massive shortages of goods throughout the country. Rationing was introduced on a number of items ranging from meat to soap. The amounts produced did not go down overall, but the increase in wages, the greater availability of rubles in the economy, and hoarding engendered by threats of change caused an effective breakdown in the distribution system.

By 1990 the question of money had become central in the minds of the reformers. Their program now consisted of the reintroduction of private property, a balanced budget, prices to reflect costs, and so the ultimate reintroduction of the USSR into the world market, which was linked with the convertibility of the ruble. Underlying it all was the need to change the nature of control of the working class. By 1989 many had given up. Zaslavskaia announced that it was hopeless because the workers would not work.[15] Aganbegian ceased to be the official economic adviser to Gorbachev. The choice became clearer; either a sharp move to the market, made if necessary by brutal repression, or continued concessions of a political kind. The Soviet elite hoped that it could draw out its period of rule by limited forms of democratization. Workers would then have to take the next step of directly taking power or suffer the consequences.

Since no working-class party existed or was allowed to form, the elite could reckon on muddling through for a limited time. In that period, they could, they hoped, force through the reintroduction of money.

The Ruble, Real Money, and a Genuine Market

What is money, if it does not exist in the USSR? Soviet economist Oleg Bogomolov made precisely this point, that the USSR does not have money, at a press conference held by *Voprosy ekonomiki*.[16] Money is the universal equivalent. Its precondition, therefore, is that it be a measure of value. If there is no value in the USSR, then there can be no exchange of equivalents and so no universal equivalent. There can only be value if labor power itself has value, or in other words, if it is bought and sold. Yet again Bogomolov made the correct point that labor power in the USSR is semiforced labor. The ruble, as a result, does not have the ability to buy goods at their value. Instead, prices are arbitrary. In turn, the arbitrariness of the prices means that rationing, queuing, corruption, contacts, and the special shops of the elite play a bigger role in the acquisition of goods than does the ruble. In other words, the ruble is a defective medium of circulation. When it comes to accumulation, then the lack of private property and competition in the presence of scarcity has meant that barter and direction have played a crucial role in the movement of goods between plants.

It is useful to ask what the introduction of real money would mean. It would require the introduction of private property, and so individually competing firms, the sale of labor power, and hence a reserve army of labor. Put differently, the condition for the existence of money is the formation of a capital market as well as a labor market.

A capital market needs bankruptcies and a stock exchange, while a labor market requires unemployment, price increases to bring the quantity of money into a real relation with goods, and inequality to encourage harder work and establish control by the manager, who may do little work but whose function is to supervise and so squeeze the worker. In this list, the right to hire and fire, and so unemployment, is the crucial change required.

In fact, a reserve army of labor cannot exist on a planned basis but is a result of the capital market, which must necessarily then come into existence. The Soviet economists have long bitten the bullet, but the discussions have now gone beyond vague references. They now speak of the need to go step by step with dismissals inside the enterprise, then within a group of enterprises, and so ultimately to the creation of a reserve army of labor. More than a hint was provided in the above-cited article on 7 January 1986, and indeed other articles have also been quite explicit.

Although he wants bankruptcy and hence control through dismissal, Aganbegian has made it quite clear that neither unemployment nor a capital market will be tolerated.[17] Whether this is a genuine viewpoint or a tactful expression of an elite attitude is not clear. In any case, there is certainly pressure on the elite to express such an attitude. At the very least, the Stalinoids in the Central Committee, such as Ligachev, would take up the cudgels on this issue in order to gain support in the society. Social democrats are also reluctant to take the road to unemployment.

In that case, however, the change will be only nominal for there will be no change over labor and no difference to enterprises, since they can never go bankrupt. The Hungarians have long since learned from their "actually existing" failure that a market needs capital and labor markets or it is no market. Where, then, is the regime going?

Not surprisingly, the Soviet elite introduced laws on property that effectively reintroduced private property in all important respects. In an interview with Quentin Peel of the *Financial Times,* the new economic adviser to Gorbachev made it quite clear that privatization and the stock exchange were the aims of the economic reforms.[18] We have argued here that this was the only logical outcome of the economic reforms. Abalkin, then deputy prime minister in charge of economic reforms, had already nailed his colors to the mast.[19] Caught by the increasing refusal of the workers to accept worse conditions of employment and their ability to wield a veto, the only alternative was to remove the veto by introducing a capital market and so a labor market.

This was an all-or-nothing strategy.

Social Solutions

In spite of all the cries about the conservative enemies within, the removal of much of the old guard from office did not change Gorbachev's problem one iota. To introduce new technology and change the nature of the Soviet product, Gorbachev had to tackle the social relationship within the plant itself, and this could not be done by fiat.

As we have seen, the elite have used reorganization as a crucial method of securing growth. Under Stalin this took the form of campaigns against the middle bureaucrats, the purges themselves, and the forcible redirection of labor. Under Khrushchev, the process was confined to ministerial and party organization. Under Brezhnev, the return to a period of quietude was in itself a major change, since the so-called period of stagnation was the only period in which the elite enjoyed relative stability. Ironically, that gave a jolt to the system, which wore off by the early 1970s.

Gorbachev replaced personnel and changed the structure of administration. When this failed he turned to a new form of organization. He introduced an electoral system that changed the balance of power within the elite toward the managers and the intelligentsia as opposed to the party apparatus. The Congress of People's Deputies has a Communist party majority, with a liberal opposition. There is no left whatsoever. The republican elections have had the same effect, with the important difference that liberals and nationalists or separatists have obtained majorities.

The effect of the introduction of the limited forms of democracy in the USSR has been to displace old members of the bureaucratic apparatus and replace them with members of the intelligentsia. The level of education and understanding has definitely been raised, but the logic of this shift to the higher intelligentsia involves a movement away from organization itself. Either the regime switches toward the market or it extends democracy to the shop floor. These stark alternatives have resulted in a splintering of the elite and the intelligentsia into the so-called conservatives, who want minimal change, the liberals who want to go over to the free market, the social democrats who want a welfare state, and an incipient left associated with the workers themselves.

There has been an important shift in opinion in the USSR among some members of the intelligentsia, and not just toward Gorbachev and the market. The effect of the world depression and the growth of an alternative left has made its mark, not in producing a Marxist left of a classical kind, but in shifting sections toward what might be called Eurocommunism, if it had still existed.[20] Its failure and the evident failure of social democracy have not yet penetrated a country always a decade behind events. The market remains a goal for these people, a market combined with workers' control. In a sense this is a return to the social democracy of Khrushchev, who spoke of socialist profit as opposed to capitalist profit, a sentence repeated indeed by Aganbegian. But in the new context of mass unemployment in the West and a permanent and open crisis in the USSR, the demand for the market will not last among those not prepared to compromise with the Soviet reforming elite.

At the beginning of the 1970s the Institute of Sociology was purged of its radical elements, but the sociologists were little more than classical liberals. In the early 1980s researchers in the elite Institute of World Economy and International Relations suffered repression. This time their crimes were tied to an attempt to understand the world in more socialist terms. The emergence of the Socialist party, the development of the anarcho-syndicalists, and Marxist groups are also evidence of the emergence of a left, to the left of social democracy.

The intelligentsia had moved sharply to the right after Khrushchev, with Sakharov and Solzhenitsyn exemplifying this change. Sakharov indeed came out in support of Pinochet. By the end of the 1980s, however, social democracy was the new slogan. At the other end of the spectrum sections of the elite who were by now on the right and far right supported the untrammeled operation of the market. Paradoxically, at the very time when social democracy had lost any program and was only able to implement austerity with a human face in countries like Spain, France, and Italy, and when Swedish Social Democracy had proposed draconian laws to control strikes and pay, sections of the intelligentsia proclaimed themselves to be social democrats. The reform sections of the communist parties throughout Eastern Europe took this line and the Democratic Platform group inside the CPSU was of the same tendency.

In the context of the USSR, social democracy represents a belief that the system can be changed into a welfare-state capitalism with a substantial public sector. The personnel in the apparatus will either transfer to jobs in management or retrain, while the intelligentsia will either enter the ruling class or be better off. Hence the social democrats oppose shop floor organization. In the first instance this has been directed at the party apparatus, but they fear genuine workers' organizations even more. Hence the applause at the Congress of People's Deputies for the ending of elections for the post of enterprise manager.

Gorbachev, therefore, has a coalition of social democrats, the party apparatus, and liberals against the left. On the other hand, he has a more limited version of the same coalition for the extension of parliamentary electoral forms. Under these political conditions, the elite as personified by Gorbachev must move to the market and against further democratization. The more it procrastinates, the more persistent becomes the demand for the extension of democracy to the shop floor. The miners' strikes and indeed most of the major strikes of 1989–90 posed the question of workers' committees and control over management.

Given the monopoly of understanding the system that Gorbachev possesses, he above all is aware of the limitations on the ruling elite. He has to provide hope to a population with a perennial food shortage, with consumer goods looking more and more dated. This he has done by talking cleanly about the problems instead of lying about them. The change he has thus provided is that of a discussion about change. That itself worked for a period of time. By 1990 the two solutions of going to the market or extending democracy to the point of abolishing the elite had become quite clear. Gorbachev chose, of course, to preserve the elite by forcing through the market. This was attempted by converting the presidency into an independent source of power, and through a campaign that emphasized the failure of the half-hearted reforms. The population was told that the system had failed and worsening food shortages could only get still worse. The new executive president, with dictatorial powers, but with support from an elected parliamentary body could then force through the market.

The elite solution for the crisis, which began with the coming to power of the secret police with an agenda of introducing the market, disclosed itself as the introduction of the market with an iron fist. Time and again Soviet representatives from different sides of the political spectrum emphasized this point. The system stressed that the crisis demanded firm measures.

The intelligentsia were then forced to support the regime because it introduced nonparty constitutional reforms to implement the market. The workers, who were inherently opposed to the reforms, were increasingly bamboozled by the cries of either no food or reforms, so the elite gambled on the workers' neutrality.

The liberals announced the impossibility of gradualism and so posed the question of the full introduction of the market or return to the previous system. While private property in agriculture could succeed, there was no obvious way of successfully privatizing industry. Hence the logic of the system was toward conciliating the peasantry and developing a prosperous capitalist agriculture in specific regions where it was possible.

By 1990 there were 4.5 million persons working for private enterprise or for the so-called cooperatives. Their prices were twice those of the comparable state shops and their wages also twice as high. Animosity against them was intense.[21] Since their services were performed for the elite, while their supplies had to come from the common pool, it is not surprising that the miners wanted them limited or abolished. Laws limiting their operation were introduced in September 1989 but they continued to expand. The liberal reformers strongly defended this capitalist sector, which was given a fillip with the passing of laws permitting private property in March 1990.

All attempts to introduce price increases met resistance, but the elite kept trying. By 1990 all bodies associated with workers, official and unofficial, opposed them. The elite tried numerous outflanking measures but failed to achieve their object. The entire logic of the reform, therefore, was to a gradual introduction of private enterprise, which could succeed to the degree that private agriculture was successful. In turn, private enterprise in the services and other limited aspects could expand. At the same time joint ventures might make a contribution to the Soviet economy. Such a limited program of private agriculture, cooperatives, and joint ventures stood a chance of delaying the disintegration of the system.

The Redirection of Foreign Policy

Soviet foreign policy has been determined by the interaction of the internal development of the USSR with a hostile but supportive world. The essence of Stalinist foreign policy was the attempt to establish a form of support for its internal policy on an international plane. For this purpose it required foreign communist parties for two reasons. On the one hand, they acted as pressure groups on their local ruling classes in the interests of the USSR, while on the other hand they also prevented the emergence of a genuine left-wing force that might have threatened the USSR. The communist parties then acted as bargaining counters for the USSR itself.

The natural drive of the Stalinist elite was toward the transformation of the world in its own image in order to prevent destabilization of the USSR. On the other hand, it was always too weak to accomplish this mission, so that it preferred to come to an arrangement with the West in the form known as the Cold War. It established buffer states around itself that prevented the population of the USSR having contact with non-Stalinist countries. At the same time, the Western threat ensured that there was a residual nationalism that could be mobilized over the decades. Indeed, there were even those who could accept Stalinism as the lesser evil. The Cold War, as Michael Cox has pointed out, was a system.[22]

It is obviously true that the Cold War emerged without any forethought, but, paradoxically, it served the interests of both sides. That has now become crystal clear is that Western leaders from Thatcher leftward are calling on political movements in Eastern Europe to proceed cautiously. Both the division of Europe and the control over the numerous small countries of Eastern Europe were in the interests of both the United States and the USSR. That the Cold War served the interests of Germany is more open to question, of course. Above all, however, the Cold War ensured that no anti-Stalinist left could emerge with any degree of credibility. There were two camps, that of the left and that of democracy; groups that argued for a genuine socialism that was both democratic and Marxist were regarded as insignificant beside the might of the communist parties and the USSR.

The remarkable changes of the last quarter of 1989 have meant that the USSR is no longer seen as the enemy of the West. There is every reason to believe that the removal of the communist parties from their former positions in Bulgaria, Romania, East Germany, and Czechoslovakia was at the very least coordinated with Moscow. In effect, the liberal faction in the USSR has ensured that the regimes around it can no longer support its own internal opposition. It would now be considerably more difficult to remove the dominant factions in the CPSU. Moreover, the costs of the Eastern European countries had reached a point where it was increasingly counterproductive for the USSR to continue bailing them out. It was no coincidence that the USSR very quickly demanded that Comecon change its exchange mechanism from one based on rubles to one based on hard currency. In that way the USSR would no longer have to supply cheap raw materials to Eastern Europe in return for low-quality industrial goods.

The ring of buffer states that isolated the Soviet population from outside influence was essential to maintain the atomization of Soviet society. The positive political results had to be balanced, however, against the economic costs of maintaining control over Eastern Europe. The subsidization of Eastern Europe was considerable, even though the East European countries tended to see the USSR as an exploiter. Its subsidies were both direct aid and the provision of raw materials at relatively low prices in relation to the goods supplied in return. In addition, the cost of maintaining troops to keep control of these countries was not negligible either. Furthermore, Soviet withdrawal has led to a direct weakening of military pressure on the USSR, facilitating a cut in the military budget.

The Soviet elite will now have a number of countries around it that will have to fend for themselves, and that will in all probability have a working class with a declining standard of living. Given the assistance of the USSR, these regimes will inevitably adopt an Austrian or Finnish type of approach of avoiding anything that might provoke the USSR. Indeed, the local elites have thus far not changed at all and it is very likely that the ruling group will be little more than a modified form of the old elite incorporating some of the intelligentsia. The introduction of private property will change the basis of the elite, though not necessarily the elite itself. Under these conditions the Soviet elite has little to fear. It is true, on the other hand, that sections of the Soviet elite which have been most associated with control will find themselves threatened. After all, the secret police, the less competent party officials, and various corrupt state officials cannot but be worried at the exposures in Romania and East Germany. Nonetheless, the bulk of the Soviet elite, the heads of enterprises, etc., will have everything to gain from a move to the market. They will establish a greater degree of independence at the very least, and become very rich at best.

Put differently, the Soviet elite would like to take the same path as Poland or Hungary, but it does not have the same options. Nonetheless, these new regimes will tend to be its natural allies after the initial period of euphoria in Eastern Europe has worn off. Even if there will be no common market, there will probably be a free-trade area, dominated jointly by Germany and the USSR.

The crucial question, however, is the nature of working-class reaction to the move to the market. It is inconceivable that the workers would not take ever stronger action against those who are causing a decline in their living standards. The Jeffrey Sachs plan for Poland envisaged a 20 percent drop in living standards, substantial unemployment, and greater efficiency in the factories. Against this has to be balanced the aid from the West. Even if more consumer goods are available over time, the workers will find their position considerably changed in relation to management. They are bound to fight the imposition of managerial control of a market type. The only question is whether it will take a longer or shorter time to show itself. For the USSR this will pose a grave problem. The elite will find that Soviet workers respond to the actions of their fellow workers in Eastern Europe. In that case, the Soviet elite will have to clamp down internally.

From the Soviet point of view a united Germany is acceptable as long as it is a neutral or neutralized Germany. It has the advantage that Germany would counterbalance the United States and help to stabilize Eastern Europe. It could also assist the USSR itself. Germany is preferable to the United States because the Germans maintain a social democratic society, which has all the instabilities of a declining capitalism. In other words, it has a powerful working class, which will be even more powerful when united. The German ruling class understands the mode of rule under such conditions and is not fetishized by private property or finance capital. The United States, on the other hand, has a geopolitical disadvantage, which is now also industrial. Its industry, though still powerful on a world scale, is less suited to trade with the USSR. The mode of rule in the United States, with its "segmented" working class and massive immigration, is very different from that in Western Europe. Above all, the mode of extraction of surplus value used by finance capital, as practiced in the United States and the United Kingdom, is one that would militate against investment in the USSR. This is because it demands quick returns and so does not permit investment that provides profits only over a long time span.

The USSR is, therefore, driven to Japan and Germany, as well as to the lesser members of the Common Market outside of the United Kingdom.

The deal struck with the United States has included Soviet withdrawal from around the world. Once the contiguous areas of Afghanistan and Eastern Europe are settled, the retreat from Africa, Asia, and South America is only a matter of time. The Brezhnev policy of supporting guerrilla and terrorist groups has been abandoned. This pseudomilitancy, reminiscent of the third period of the Comintern, has involved supporting guerrilla movements and strikes against various governments even where the situation was hopeless. Nonetheless, they have achieved their object in demonstrating that they can cause the withdrawal of certain countries from the world market and weaken bourgeois governments. This is their chief bargaining counter. The South African Communist Party has been instructed to do a deal with the government. The communist parties in South America can come to terms with Christian democracy, as in Chile. The way is then left open to the United States to install democratic regimes, which could go for industrial expansion. While the structure of shifting the communist parties to a position close to Christian democracy has been in place since 1985, the actual process is not dependent on the USSR or the communist parties alone. It would be dangerous, for instance, for the African National Congress to do a deal with the government, if the workers were to be so incensed that they turned to a more militant party. It is, therefore, a complicated process in which the USSR is not without its cards.

If the USSR moves to the market and private property, the program of its external agents or allies, the communist parties, is not at all clear. Today their policies are effectively to the right of social democracy. At one time, their *raison d'état* lay in their defense of the USSR. They put pressure on the local governments to give concessions to the USSR. They also prevented the emergence of a radical anti-Stalinist left, which on occasion has had the possibility of taking power. Accordingly, if the Stalinist parties vanish, a vacuum opens up on the left that will be dangerous to both the USSR and the existing order in the West. It might, therefore, be thought that it would be in the interests of the USSR to maintain the existence of communist parties, though in a new form. The Soviet elite has not yet developed a view on this question. It is more than likely that they will not be able to control events and the communist parties will become right-wing social democratic parties, while many of their members will leave disillusioned. A vacuum must open up on the left, which over time will indeed be filled.

The USSR has two cards in its hand. One is the opening up of the USSR to the world market, and the second is its pullback from the rest of the world. The West's response has been threefold. In the first place, it has adopted a posture of support for the retreat by damping down any anti-Soviet movements and endorsing the integrity of the USSR. In the second place, it reduced its military pressure, albeit very grudgingly, seeing that the military apparatus serves quite other functions as well. In the third place, it has been providing a limited amount of aid, mainly to Eastern Europe. There are, of course, implicit promises of much more to come.

The problem from the viewpoint of the USSR is that it needs much more support. It would need hundreds of billions of dollars to change to the market in any successful way. That is not forthcoming and is unlikely to be forthcoming, given the decline of the United States and indeed the instability of world capitalism. As argued above, finance capital wants quick returns and the more industrial countries like Japan and Germany can only provide a limited amount of funds. Of course, if capitalism continues the boom of the 1980s through the 1990s, then the USSR might obtain the necessary funds. That is most unlikely, however. It is true the Soviet foreign debt has risen very considerably under Gorbachev, to over 50 billion dollars, but that is a trifle compared to what is needed.

Of course, the USSR can also observe the problems of the world capitalist economy and use them in its own interest. This has been done in two ways. On the one hand, they have played off the Europeans, particularly Germany, against the United States, while on the other, they are aware of the enormous need of the Western economies for a sphere for the investment of their surplus funds. The decline of the United States has meant that the USSR has alternative economic partners who can play independent roles, and the current weakness of the international capitalist system means that an otherwise very weak USSR can continue to be a superpower.

The United States, in its turn, cannot be certain of the outcome of the present political process in the USSR. It is itself too weak to influence the course of events, beyond a limited support for Gorbachev. As a result it has adopted a cautious posture. A resurgent United States would have taken all the advice from Galbraith to Kissinger and gone for a Marshall Plan for Eastern Europe, but a declining United States cannot do this. Consequently, it is locked into an increasingly outmoded though benevolent Cold War posture. It cannot reduce arms expenditure substantially both for internal economic reasons and because it has to police its own empire. On the other hand, the ostensible reason for its arms expenditure has been removed. The end of the Cold War could easily be an economic disaster.

Two superpowers, each declining in its own way, are therefore locked in a posture that can only accelerate their own decline.

It has to be added that the reduction of arms expenditure in the USSR will not have the expected effect on consumer goods, given the enormous levels of waste existing in the USSR, although, of course, it will have a limited and once-for-all effect.

The Disintegration of the USSR

That the USSR is disintegrating now seems obvious. Republics are demanding independence, and authority appears to have broken down. Commands are no longer obeyed in the same way as before. There is an apparently worsening shortage of goods at the same time that the amount of "money" in circulation is increasing. There are three obvious indicators of disintegration: the national, the political, and the economic. Factions have become institutionalized, and ministries and their subdivisions have increasing power. That ministries would operate on an autarkic basis is well known and has always been a fact of Soviet life, in the same way as enterprises also behaved as if they were atomized units that had to maximize their own individual control over their supplies, labor, etc. The difference is that today such atomized behavior is more counterproductive than ever at the same time that it is more difficult than ever to control from the center.

In other words, the center cannot easily supply the needs of the enterprises, so the individual unit is increasingly compelled to find its own way around the rules. Again, this was always the tendency but the tendency is rapidly becoming the rule. There is a movement from "organized chaos" or organization, rather than planned production, to a decay of that organization itself. The unit's reaction to "planning" was to find a method of bargaining with its superior bodies, which then imposed a series of instructions in order to get some kind of result. Today that is increasingly difficult for the superior bodies to do. Hence, the administration has had to be increasingly tiered, but each tier, as with the trusts, acquires its own need for independence. The bargaining system, which has always been the nature of the system itself, has itself degenerated. Whereas before there was a complex structure of bargaining, lateral bargaining has become more usual. The nature of the reforms in 1989 led to enterprises using rubles to bargain for their supplies. The result was that the number of rubles in circulation grew, as did the power of the individual suppliers. This meant, in turn, that the lateral bargaining procedure increased in importance compared with the power of the center. In Soviet parlance, the Mafia became more important.

This drive to independence is inherent in the system; but under the conditions outlined above, where labor is short, where production failures are magnified by supply failures because of the tighter integration, the position of the director of the unit becomes intolerable. His logic is to do deals where he can and cannot. From organized dealing, accepted and approved by the center even if not acknowledged, the enterprise has to move to unorganized dealing to achieve its goals. At first this was limited and amounted to barter or the return of favors, but its extensive employment cannot continue in such a primitive form. It is inevitable that the use of market-type forms expand. It is almost as if the period of the absorption of the absolute surplus has had to be succeeded by the market or its real negation, socialism. Since the market cannot be introduced directly, surrogate forms have come into existence, whether in the form of the second economy or as alternative incentive systems. Neither constitutes the market, much as bourgeois economists would like to assimilate them, but the trend is toward a buildup of relative independence with increasing reliance on forms that simulate a market. Ultimately, the market will burst through in spite of the forces holding it back, but it will be in an explosive form.

The trend to disintegration is obvious to the Soviet elite who keep trying to reintegrate the system, through forms of recentralization, and hence the paradoxical Gorbachev statement that there would have to be more effective central planning as well as more devolution.[23] The problem is that the centrifugal tendencies can only grow in reaction to the extreme control exercised by the center, precisely because the center is forced to increase its control over the system to avoid the periphery increasing its own anarchic power. In turn, the individual unit is compelled to find ways of improving its own environment simply in order to maintain its own in existence. Over time, therefore, an increase in tension must build up within the system between the center and national groups, the center and regions, the center and its economic units, to a point where it cannot be contained because the problems are insurmountable.

There are, thus, three aspects to the process of disintegration: (1) the growth of political or sociopolitical factions; (2) the growth of the independence of economic units; and (3) the increasing independence of the social groups in the society. The first two have been discussed already. The last has been touched on. It refers to the increasing degree of power falling to the inferior groups in the society and their refusal to cooperate, in however unconscious a manner. This refers primarily to the workers, but it has been evident among the intelligentsia and it is thus not surprising that the elite are making conciliatory noises toward the intelligentsia. The concessions in terms of wages and status have already been noted. Thus, the social groups are falling apart, the political factions have established themselves, and the economy is dissolving.

These are only symptoms of the first stage of a crisis, defined as the situation where the opposite poles within a contradiction become conflictual and antagonistic rather than interpenetrative. In the case of the USSR, this situation has existed ever since the 1920s, with planning and the market opposing one another, leading to the elimination of the market and in fact of genuine planning, but with the underlying conflict remaining in a new form—that of an organizational system and apparatus opposing the operations of the individual unit. Indeed, the organizational forms of the USSR are precisely designed to hold back the disintegration and so crisis of the system. The problem is that these forms have exhausted themselves for the three reasons given: the end of the extraction of the absolute surplus, the specificity of labor and its close integration within a socialized division of labor, and the consequent increasing power of the workers. The power of organization rests on the ability to direct labor, so that once that is gone or is limited, the power itself gradually weakens.

If Gorbachev fails, which is the most likely outcome, the price in terms of instability, not to speak of his own political (and possibly more than political) demise, will be far greater than that of his predecessors. Failure is not to be understood as no movement at all, but rather as attempts to get to the market with market-type apparatuses in place that cannot proceed far enough to achieve the desired result. What the Soviet elite need is a viable capitalist economy, capable of at least holding its own in relation to the United States. Anything less will mean that they lose their own positions in society and the workers will start to shift rapidly to the left.

The intelligentsia are getting impatient, not understanding the devious game that has to be played to maintain stability, particularly as the Twenty-seventh Party Congress, the Nineteenth Party Conference, and the new Supreme Soviet have brought no solutions to the table. The Yeltsin affair, the ambiguity over the national question, the tightening up of the laws over assembly and on crimes against the state, and the evident threat from the workers displayed at the time of the miners' strike of July 1989 and the oil workers' threats of 1990 have not made them any happier. At the moment the continuing relative freedom makes them grateful but very apprehensive, continuously expecting the scene to shift back to pre-Gorbachev times.[24]

What might happen some years hence, when fundamentals are seen to be unaltered and problems continue to mount, is of the greatest importance and interest to all who support the democratic rule of the majority and so of the workers in that society. What is now certain is that if Gorbachev fails in his economic program, he will have to find political and organizational solutions of a kind not dissimilar from his first leader, Khrushchev, under conditions where the potential power of the workers is far greater than it has ever been and where a left is emerging from a half-century of total repression.

The Inevitable Failure of the Market Solution

The turn to the market has shifted from using surrogate market forms to the introduction of market aspects and finally to capitalism. I have argued that the Soviet elite would always have preferred the market but it could not install it. Two things have changed over time. First has been the formation of the elite itself as a social group that needed stability and a viable means of self-reproduction. With the growth of the elite has come the vast growth of the intelligentsia, who have seen their fate in the same way, with the difference that they could see no reason for the elite to retain their privileges; they too wished to share them. The logic of change was necessarily toward the market.

The problem, however, remained that the introduction of the law of value, or the market, was only possible if the workers could be made to consent. Whereas the East German workers could readily move over to the market because they were both promised a higher standard of living and could always have a higher standard of living simply by crossing to West Germany, the Soviet workers have had no alternative. Thus, the decline in wages, the rise in unemployment, and the harsher work regime that all followed the introduction of the market repelled workers.

The politics of the Gorbachev years have therefore become a politics of openness for the intelligentsia and deception for the workers. The workers were promised a higher standard of living and democratic forms, but got neither. As a result, the regime has maneuvered to find a way around the working class. The stalemate that has remained has necessarily led to a more rapid decline in the credibility of the elite than if no reform had been attempted. The Stalinoids ally themselves with Russian nationalism and anti-Semitism to oppose the market. They hope thereby to obtain support from the workers in Russia, but in fact they are based on the controlling part of the elite and the lumpen-intelligentsia. The latter are the section of the intelligentsia who find their promotion upward blocked for whatever reason which they identify with the Jews or with some anti-Russian force.

On the other hand, the liberals believe that, given time, the market will create its own supporters. Not having time, however, they either give up hope or argue for an authoritarian way to introduce the market. They forget that the system had no competitor as an authoritarian regime and in the period 1986–89, before the Congress of People's Deputies existed, the regime was unable even to raise prices. On the one side stands the demand for capitalism while on the other the workers demand socialism in a quiet empirical manner. They angrily reject privilege and demand egalitarianism.

There is no third way.

If history has taught the world anything, it has taught mankind that Stalinism and social democracy do not work. Both, in their own ways, are compromises with capitalism.

Why the Market Solution Cannot Work

Apart from the politics, the reasons why the market solution cannot work are part of the epoch itself. It is not just that capitalism has unemployment, a wide range of incomes, waste on a massive scale, a tendency to arms production, and a constant threat of crisis, but that in its nature the transition period is one of capitalist decline.

The word decline immediately conjures up the picture of decrepitude and death, and capitalist decline is then taken to mean the breakdown of capitalism. A dialectical approach, however, is very different. The decline of capitalism involves the decline of its fundamental law and social relation; it is therefore the decline of the law of value itself. All entities come into being, mature, and decay. The law of value must also do the same.

The rise of a needs-based sector, nationalization, government economic interference via interest rates, subsidies, taxation, etc., and control over prices and production by large firms has meant that the law of value, or the market, is greatly limited in operation. Put differently, the idea that there could be an economy today based on competition, free flow of resources, and a free market in labor and capital is a reactionary utopia. It is not a question of whether it is desirable, but of whether it could exist. The very difficulties that face Eastern Europe are a good indication of the difficulties facing such a solution. It will therefore be useful to deal with the reasons for the decline of the market.

In the first place, the socialization of production provides an indication of the reason for the development of the aspects mentioned above. The progress of the division of labor and so technique has meant an increasingly tighter integration of production. Then, too, this process also implies a higher organic composition of capital, or, in non-Marxist terms, a higher capital–labor ratio. In turn, this implies that production schedules have to be planned over time and can indeed take a very long time. Amortization may take decades. Construction can take many years.

When Marx spoke of the contradiction between the internal planning of the factory and the anarchy of the market, he could not foresee how far it would go. At a certain point the "planning" of the factory had to become part of the system as a whole. If the factory has invested its resources over a long period of time to produce a particular product, it wants some guarantee that its products will be sold at a level sufficient to repay the original costs plus profits. Links are then constructed between firms, which must exist over long periods of time. The government then necessarily becomes enmeshed in the economy.

Any modern government must ensure social stability, and that today requires growth and high levels of employment, negating the existence of the reserve army of labor. This, in turn, has required economic development, partly driven by concessions to labor, in education, health, and transport.

The result is that modern capitalist economies are managed by their governments and have extensive public sectors. The private sector is seldom competitive except among small shopkeepers and the like. Some sectors, such as the so-called utilities, are called natural monopolies. Other sectors, such as automobile manufacture, aerospace, and computing, tend to have one or two dominant firms per country. In some cases there is only one firm that is largely dominant over the world, such as IBM.

If there is little competition and overwhelming government interference, the role of the individual capitalist has been limited. Marx, of course, spoke of the introduction of the joint stock company as indicating the unnecessary role of the capitalist. The manager, however, is not otiose. The rise of bureaucracy has become a fact of modern capitalism. Large firms and government apparatuses require rules to govern their staffs since they do not have any market controls. These imposed rules are surrogates for the market itself. They have promotion procedures, bonuses, market-type differentials, and so forth, that mimic the market but are not of the market itself.

This description of a declining capitalism has consequences for the USSR.

First, the disciplining of the work force through the reintroduction of a reserve army of labor is highly questionable. European countries do not have a classic reserve army of labor. This refers to the period of capitalism when some 10–20 percent of the population may have been unemployed, but another 40 percent would go in and out of that reserve army while much of the rest always had reason to believe that they might fall into that condition. At the same time there was no social security to protect the unemployed. Clearly, such a form might exist in underdeveloped countries, but the developed countries could not risk the instability that would follow such a form of control. Soviet workers, however, are accustomed to full employment and control over the work process and hence would need a massive shock to relinquish their defensive position. In other words, a reserve army of labor would be essential to establish a labor market. Thus, the Soviet regime is faced with the need to take a step back from modern Christian democracy. This is simply impossible in the modern epoch. If Soviet workers would object to unemployment at any level, they would object even more to the emergence of a form of labor market that is far more disadvantageous than that in Western Europe.

Second, competition cannot simply be introduced. Even if a capital market is assumed, the so-called natural monopolies would continue. The utilities, transport, housing, health, and education would either be in a monopoly sector or in the state sector. Manufacturing could not be made competitive either, except on an international scale. The automobile, aircraft, shipbuilding, computer, electronics, and extractive industries are all examples of industries where cartels exist in the West, or else there are very few firms in any one country. The point, again, is that the USSR needs genuine free competition to establish quality control, control over prices, and control over the direct producers. But a monopoly or a cartel will simply keep the system going as it now stands. The USSR needs not just competition but a raging competition to reestablish capitalism with all its controls over the worker. The present system effectively eliminates these controls and hence they have to be broken, not timidly bent.

The market on this showing cannot be introduced except by returning to the nineteenth century. In other words, it cannot be done. Of course, if a possible Hungarian solution were introduced, it could be done. The economy could be opened up to world capital and much of industry would go to the wall. Then, with massive unemployment and the use of foreign capital, industry could be rebuilt, though on a much smaller basis. This is not a realistic solution for the USSR.

The Market Socialism Argument

The argument for "market socialism" has fallen into some disrepute in Eastern Europe since the failure of attempts to combine elements of the market with those regimes. Nonetheless, it is still being advanced by groups and individuals within the USSR, notably by Aganbegian, in his books, and by groups associated with the Socialist party.[25] The views of Professor Alec Nove, author of *The Economics of Feasible Socialism*,[26] have been published in a number of Soviet journals, including *Kommunist* and *EKO*.

The model is straightforward. Investment and the infrastructure, in general, would be planned by the center. Health and education would continue to be nonmarket parts of the economy. So-called natural monopolies would remain with the state. For the rest there would be an operative market. The market here really means two things: it means private property and so private enterprise, and also the use of profit/loss accounting for state enterprises.

In one model, services and consumer goods would be in a market situation. Accordingly, they would set their own prices and conclude their own contracts. They would be based on profit and loss. The other firms would have prices set by the center, which would also allocate investments to those firms. Within those limits they would also be based on profit and loss. These latter prices could be allowed to vary within certain limits. In turn, these firms might or might not be allowed to select the firms with whom they trade.

Other models would permit complete flexibility of prices and trading partners, but exert control through taxation and subsidies, while at the "socialist" extreme there would be only a limited choice of prices and contracts.

The crucial variables at the level of the enterprise are the control over prices, the freedom to conclude contracts with partners, and autonomy or lack of autonomy over investment decision making. So-called market socialism gives some power over these variables to the state. Therein lies the problem. Can such a hybrid function successfully? A moment's thought will show that all three variables are closely interconnected. If the enterprise cannot raise its prices, its profits are impaired, and hence so is its control over investment. In turn, this will impair its technological level and ability to compete with other enterprises. Then, either the "planners" must direct other firms to buy from it, or else it must be allowed to wither away. In practice interference can be more fine-tuned, but it will always have negative side-effects that have to be dealt with by new measures taken by the state. This kind of constant plumbing of a leaky mechanism has its limits.

The absolute condition for the operation of the market is competition. Such has been the repeated statement of members of the Gorbachev government. Unless firms can choose among suppliers and customers, enterprises are compelled to buy and sell on a fixed, long-term basis. There is then no stimulus to raise quality, improve technique, or increase profits, unless commanded by the "planners." Competition, in the sense of a large number of competing firms making approximately the same product, hardly exists in any developed country for any important product. We have already argued above that such industries as automobile manufacture, electronics and computers, aerospace, transport, the manufacture of consumer durables, and even major retailing are dominated by a few firms. Even if we assume that the competition of a few firms is still competition, particularly if the market is part of the world market, and we further assume that all other conditions are favorable (so excluding the USSR), we still have the problems of limited competition.

When limited competition is added to the hybrid nature of the market, the result is somewhat dubious. For instance, the individual firm producing washing machines may find that it has a limited and specific market, agreed with its competitors. Prices will be agreed. Its suppliers may also provide goods at similar prices. Improvement in technique will proceed at a leisurely pace, if at all. A socialist government would tax profits at a level consistent with its goals, but the remaining profits would have no obvious internal outlet. It would therefore have to expand production in another sphere.

If there were no capital market or labor market, the state would have to approve of such expenditure as conforming to its stated goals. It would not permit investment in areas of potential profitability that harmed the environment, or were injurious to the population, such as cigarette production, or subjected the worker to mental or physical injury, such as certain kinds of labor process equipment and certain kinds of labor process. Cement production would not be permitted without extensive protection for workers' lungs and skin, and many forms of chemical production might be completely banned or permitted only under very strict conditions. The point, however, is that in the first place, a whole bureaucratic apparatus has to be in place, in order to approve investment applications, while in the second place, the obstacles are so numerous that it would pay the firm simply to distribute its profits.

Worse still, the necessary conflict between the state sector and the private sector would have no resolution other than the elimination of one or the other. If health and education are based on needs, as they would have to be, and housing, transport, and the utilities at least partly based on need rather than on effective demand, then much of the modern economy is removed from the private sector and even from the market. As already argued, this would mean a conflict with the market sector. The needs-based sectors would tend to expand without limit, so squeezing the private sector, which would only expand where it was profitable and permissible. On the other hand, if so-called market socialism were only cosmetic, then the expansion driven by human needs would be limited by the market, and the needs-based sectors would shrivel to the point where the services would be extended on the basis of ability to pay.

The ultimate limit of "market socialism" is given by the discontent of the population and the actions of the working class. Since "market socialism" cannot permit unemployment, the power of the workers, in the absence of a police state, can only grow. Either the system will permit workers' control and self-managing enterprises with democratic government, subject to real control from below, or it will not. If managers are given the right to manage, then the workers will turn against the system as soon as their standard of living reaches a level where they feel secure or whenever they despair of that happening. The ultimate demand of workers is a question not just of standard of living but of control over their own lives to the point where they are performing creative labor as part of a democratically controlled collectivity. In fact, however, the very hybrid nature of the system would make workers' self-management a mockery. Either the market rules and there is managerial control or the market is removed. There is, as we have insisted, no third way.

The two crucial questions remain the nature of the capital market and the nature of the labor market. If there is no capital market, then firms cannot go bankrupt or be bought and sold, and consequently there is little competition. Inefficiency in the use of capital goods remains unpunished. Inevitably, under these conditions, the state banks are compelled to bail out the inefficient firms. Money, since it is supplied on demand, ceases to be money. If there is no labor market, then workers can work as they now do and establish control over the labor process, and, if strong enough, even over the product itself. If the banks are privatized or given strict money quotas and are themselves based on profits, they might not lend money, but then the state would be faced with the problem of firms unable to operate because they lacked the money to purchase their inputs. It would have either to declare the firms bankrupt and sell their assets or to subsidize them. If the firms went bankrupt, then their assets would have to be sold. Logically, this would lead to a labor market and a capital market or the continued absence of money and so the continuance of the Stalinist system.

If there is a labor market, then workers are entitled to ask whether they are any better off under so-called market socialism than under capitalism. After all, they remain subject to the domination of the machine in production, they remain abstract laborers and hence are alienated. They remain the objects of production rather than the subjects, whatever their standard of living. Indeed, there may be a strong argument that they would be better off without the controls of market socialism. After all, the only benefits they actually get are a limited number of free goods and services like health and education. Why have a lower growth rate and fewer goods in return? The crucial point here is that under this view of market socialism, the bureaucratic elite remains in charge of the administration and so of the surplus product. Such an exploitative system will inevitably be rent by a struggle between workers and the elite. It therefore has no future.

When one turns back to the capital market argument, we have to ask whether anything is left of "market socialism." If there is a market in investment goods, there will have to be a stock exchange. This then raises the whole question of property. The problem is that the sale of whole factories or sections of enterprises is difficult to accomplish except on a joint-stock basis. Shares and bonds simply have to exist in order to have an efficient capital market. Accordingly, without a change in property relations there can be no capital market. This, of course, as we have noted, is the conclusion reached by the liberal advisers to Gorbachev.[27]

The real question is never spelled out by Nove, Kagarlitsky, or the others. Can an exploitative society with limits on the nature of exploitation ever exist? The fundamental question is the nature of the ruling group. Nove stands by the view that an elite must always exist. Hence, exploitation of the worker is a necessary evil. He motivates the argument that an elite must always exist in two ways. On the one hand, he argues that a ruling group has always existed and hence we may assume it will continue so. On the other hand, he also asserts that all attempts to abolish a ruling class have been abortive. Human nature, it would appear, requires to be controlled from above. Otherwise people do not work and the law of the jungle returns. This is a return to Michels's iron law of oligarchy. Having established that an elite will always exist, he proceeds to find ways in which society can be made more bearable.

There is no reason to accept the view that an elite will always exist. The alternative is a thorough democratization of the society at all levels. This would involve the election of managers and of all persons who are in charge of others. Nove's riposte is that specialization makes this impossible, either because the select few will necessarily be elected or because an election would eliminate the specialists. The assumption that managers have some special knowledge must be called in question. Specialist knowledge, insofar as it genuinely exists, can be delegated to separate advisory departments. The manager's real job is to make crucial decisions, which would be better taken by all those affected, either directly or indirectly. Nove's reply would then be that only a very small factory could function on that basis, for, according to him, there has to be an authority.

It is, of course, true that regular decision making cannot be assumed by thousands or even hundreds. That is not the question, however. If a manager is elected, he will be careful to act in accordance with the desires of his constituents, particularly if he can be recalled at any time by a general meeting. It is obviously not necessary to have constant meetings if there are elections. Nor need there be an election every few weeks. An annual election is enough.

The point is that an appointed manager is answerable to his superiors only, if they exist. As a result, the manager or the capitalist has an income far greater than that of ordinary workers and interests diametrically opposed to theirs. The manager wants to extract the maximum surplus product with least cost. The worker needs the highest possible wage with the best possible working conditions. The income and position of the manager depend on his performance as manager. This conflict has no resolution. In the market situation the superior force held by the manager compels workers to perform until such time as they can strike, leave the job, or simply revolt against the system. "Market socialism" simply retains the conflict and so the fundamental contradiction of modern society. There is only one alternative: to democratize at the level of the factory.

The second argument adduced by Nove against the abolition of the market is that there is a necessary antagonism of interests between different producers. Factory A will oppose Factory B, skilled workers will fight unskilled workers, and so on. That such antagonisms exist in the USSR and the West is undoubted. If they are projected forward to all eternity, then socialism could not exist as originally formulated. A market is necessary to integrate these opposing interests. It would be impossible, for instance, to imagine that an individual unit of production could do anything other than maximize its own interests as opposed to those of everyone else. Of course, if that were the case, then planning would be impossible.

There is no reason to assume that either competition or antagonism between sections of workers is part of human nature. If one argues that it is a natural part of a competitive system, then it is an open question whether it would exist if such a system were abolished. If a planned society were to come into existence, in which the planning involved all members of the society, then it is hard to see why the antagonisms would not be resolved. In other words, while it might be in the interests of a particular part of the economy to act in a way inimical to the whole, that could only be true for a particular period of time, since the economy as a whole would be damaged. Then the part of the economy that was against the individual interest would find itself worse off than might otherwise have been the case, even if it is better off than other sections. Again, even if one section appeared to be favored over another, it would not necessarily mean very much if incomes were broadly similar. The real question is whether the abolition of class interest could not usher in a period when the interests of the individual and the whole were broadly similar. If over a medium term this were true, individuals would not want to fight over trifles since they would all gain over time.

In a Stalinist society and under capitalism the interest of the individual worker and that of the capitalist and manager are antagonistic. Whatever the rhetoric, there is a conflict between workers' pay and the conditions under which he works, on the one hand, and profits and the interests of the factory director on the other. It is not necessary to be a Marxist to accept this proposition. Once this conflict is eliminated, it becomes necessary for the different parts of the factory or enterprise to work to the advantage of the whole. It is in the interest of the worker to transform himself into an individual performing socially creative labor over which has he has a large measure of individual control, even if it is in part exercised through the society.

That is only possible under two conditions. First, socialism can only come into being on a world scale. Second, socialism assumes a high level of production and ultimately relative abundance. These are the original conditions put forward by the Marxist thinkers of the nineteenth and early twentieth centuries. While it is difficult to dispute the correctness of the above conditions today, with the fall of Stalinism and its doctrine of socialism in one country, the modern Communist party answer is that they are utopian. The discussion, therefore, becomes one of the nature of socialism itself and whether the working class is indeed the universal class.

Notes

1. See H.H. Ticktin, "Andropov: Disintegration and Discipline," *Critique* 16, p. 111ff.
2. Anders Åslund, *Gorbachev's Struggle for Economic Reform* (Ithaca, NY: Cornell University Press, 1989), pp. 113-20; *The Soviet Reform Process, 1985-1988* provides a detailed description of organizational changes to 1988.
3. *Pravda*, 22 February 1985.
4. Central Committee Meeting, 23 April 1985. He delivered a speech that had considerable force in exposing the economic problems but only produced this mouse of a solution. Since that date he has repeated the same injunction in practically every speech he has made, and he has made many speeches. From the June 1987 Plenum of the Central Committee he adopted a more paternalistic tone toward workers, congratulating them for responding to his injunctions, but once the miners' strikes began, his speeches took on a more fearful tone in relation to workers.
5. *Pravda,* 8 January 1988, has an article on p. 2 describing the workings of a successfully reformed enterprise ("Ne bylo ni grosha, da vdrug million"). It is interesting also on the question of obtaining supplies in time, in that it says that the enterprise provided funds for the supplying plant. Some detail is provided of how quality control operates: it appears to be a special division of the plant, with a director with fairly wide powers of inquiry. However, the weakness is revealed when the article points out that his authority was raised by being put on the party committee.
6. See *Pravda,* 8 January 1988, p. 2, for a description of the difference in attitude to fines. In *Izvestiia,* 12 November 1987, p. 2 ("Chego khochu, chego boius', na chego nadeius' . . ."), stress is placed on finance in a similar way. The meaning boils down to the increased power over management through use of finance, and the use of finance to control subordinates.
7. In "Sovetskaia ekonomika na perelome," *Kommunist,* 1987, no. 12, pp. 33-42, Professor E.G. Iasin points out that self-financing is not working for those plants actually on the new rules. In fact, it turns out that after six months there is no change in the efficiency of the enterprises. The trouble is that the enterprises still have to accept the indicators from above and the interference of the state economic organizations. To prove this point, a survey conducted of enterprise managers under the new scheme showed that

whereas 60 percent of those questioned approved of the new rules in 1985 only 36 percent did so in 1987 and over half of the latter argued that the rights of enterprises had not increased.

8. See the articles cited above in *Pravda*, 8 January 1988, and *Kommunist*, 1987, no. 12.

9. [T. Zaslavskaia], "The Novosibirsk Report," *Survey*, Spring 1984, pp. 88-107 (discussed in *Critique* 16).

10. Abel Aganbegyan, *Inside Perestroika: The Future of the Soviet Economy* (New York: Harper and Row, 1989), p. 61.

11. Ibid., pp. 58-72.

12. Interview with Abel Aganbegian, *Izvestiia*, 25 August 1987, p. 2 ("Otstupat' nekuda"). In an interview reported in the London *Guardian* of 26 January 1987, Aganbegian also discussed the implementation of the market, with the necessary caveats on unemployment. Thence he made the absurd distinction between capitalist profit and socialist profit.

13. *Pravda*, 1 October 1987.

14. Official Plan Results, *Ekonomika i zhizn'*, 6 February 1990, p. 15.

15. Quoted by Abalkin in an interview given to *Ogonek*, 1989, no. 41 (7–14 October), p. 2 ("Ne delit' a zarabatyvat' ").

16. See *Voprosy ekonomiki*, 1990, no. 9, pp. 3–12, for the transcript of a press conference given by Popov, Bogomolov, Lisichkin, Abalkin and Tikhonov, 16 June 1989 ("Deputaty-Ekonomisty o radikal'noi ekonomicheskoi reforme"). Bogomolov's remarks are on p. 4.

17. Aganbegian makes this point in *Inside Perestroika*, pp. 166–67, as well as in the *Guardian* interview.

18. *Financial Times*, 19 February 1990.

19. Abalkin, "Ne delit' a zarabatyvat'," p. 2.

20. This is the trend outlined by Boris Kagarlitsky in "The Intelligentsia and the Changes," *New Left Review* 164.

21. *Pravda*, 28 January 1990.

22. Mick Cox, "The Cold War and Stalinism in the Age of Capitalist Decline," *Critique* 17, p. 19.

23. *Pravda*, 11 April 1985.

24. See the articles by Kagarlitsky in *New Left Review* 164 and 169.

25. *Draft Program of the Socialist Party* (unpublished), pp. 19–25. The program was presumably written in large part by its major spokesman, Boris Kagarlitsky.

26. Alec Nove, *The Economics of Feasible Socialism* (London: Allen and Unwin, 1983). Some have preferred to interpret Nove's subject as feasible capitalism.

27. See the interview with N. Petrakov, then newly appointed economic adviser to Gorbachev, in the *Financial Times*, 19 February 1990. Petrakov speaks of only 30 percent of the economy being controlled by the state.

10

Where Are We Going? The Nature of the Transitional Epoch

This book has argued that the USSR is bound within a conflict that has no solution. The antagonism between the organizational drive of the elite and the individual interest of the unit and the worker can no longer be mediated. It is no longer possible to extend the number of labor hours absorbed by the economy, and the absolute surplus product, in Marxist terms, can no longer be expanded.

The conflict described can be regarded as deriving from the original conflict, which first surfaced in the twenties, between plan and market, although it is transmuted. At that time, the peasantry, much of trade, and small industry were private. The nationalized organizations operated within a market environment but under the control of the government. It was in fact the first experience in the world of such a conflict. The world historical context is crucial, since some such aspect of this conflict came later to be part of the economy of every country. We have argued above that the two cannot coexist with any degree of efficiency and hence one or the other has to decline. This, of course, was the traditional argument of the left opposition of the 1920s.[1] The problem was that the conflict continued in an acute form over years and seemed to stretch into the distant future. The left argument was posited in terms of a classical transition period to socialism. The conditions for such a transition were absent. There was no world revolution, the USSR was cut off from the world division of labor, and the USSR was itself a very underdeveloped country. Under these conditions, the conflictual relations could not continue without some mediated resolution. The only possible result was that the elements of planning and those of the market would so intertwine and interpenetrate each other as to form a new entity.[2] Clearly, this is what happened.

The USSR has neither plan nor market. That much is now the accepted wisdom within dominant academic circles in the USSR. *Planning* may be defined as the conscious regulation of the economy and society by the associated producers themselves, and the *market* as the sphere of action of the law of value. In non-Marxist terms, planning requires knowledge, consistency, and a means of implementation of the directives. All of these are absent in the USSR. The market needs competition, the sale of labor power, and a capital market. All of these also are absent in the USSR. It needs money and commodities, both of which the USSR states that it needs to introduce.

What does the USSR have then? The Soviet elite used the organizational aspects of planning, which it adapted for its own needs, to impose a hierarchical form on the economy in imitation and in lieu of the market. History had compelled them to act in this manner. It was impossible in 1929 to return to capitalism; had the elite simply denationalized, they would have been displaced by the former owners. The very backwardness of Russia required the elite to hold on to the forms of nationalization if they were to survive against the peasantry and the backward technical and social forms of the old Russian empire. Then, too, the social base of the elite was in the towns, and the workers would not have supported a return to capitalism, particularly with the ideas of the left opposition still current. Hence, the choice for the elite was an ignominious surrender to the West or a pragmatic leap into the unknown. They preserved their position and privileges, but only by maintaining the form of nationalization.

This new entity then constituted an unstable system of its own, without a fundamental law able to drive and integrate it. It is riven by an inherent conflict of forms deriving from the market and forms that are antimarket. On the one hand, the elite must organize the system to prevent it falling apart, while on the other, it cannot determine its own development.

It was argued above that the contradiction lay within the product itself, in its defective use value. Actual use value stands opposed to potential use value. The two are united as long as the elite can control and administer the necessary labor to overcome the contradiction. However, once labor no longer can perform that function, the elite have lost their historic role. The defective product stands directly opposed to the intended product in an absolute contradiction. Put differently, and in less Marxist language, the system can no longer function once the supply of labor becomes static. There is no new form of mediation. The removal of the commodity form and so the market strips bare the social relations. It is the precise nature of the transitional period that its contradictions are themselves part of transitional forms. The form is necessarily a temporary form.

Logically, the system demanded either plan or market. If the system were planned, however, the means by which the elite derive the surplus product from the workers would be abolished, because planning demands the trust, involvement, and consent of the direct producers. The alternative was to go for a more and more centralized organized form, which ultimately would be controlled by one man. That did indeed happen, and forcible collectivization, the purges, and labor camps are all part of this process.

It can be seen that once the left opposition and their program of world revolution for a genuinely planned society was defeated, the die was cast. First the market was tried under Bukharin's aegis. This was clearly the preferred solution of the bureaucratic apparatus. From this viewpoint, Bukharin appears as the originator of Stalinism. He invented Stalin's doctrines, most particularly that of the possibility of building socialism in one country, and it is not surprising that the present regime in the USSR is Bukharinist. The problem was that it did not work. The logic of the concessions to the peasants was further concessions on land ownership or possession and to private industry. That threatened the control of the urban apparatus.

Various authors have argued that there was no "kulak" threat at that time.[3] It was certainly true that the "rich" peasant of the period was poor by historical or international standards. That was beside the point, however, because the real question was how the bureaucratic apparatus could continue to exist, under conditions where the whole drive was toward a capital market. The apparatus reacted against this solution because, as we have argued above, it could not preserve itself.

History is an intertwining of the necessary and the accidental. During the crucial period of 1917–29, world capitalism was sufficiently vigorous to mount a very effective economic blockade, but not sufficiently strong to extend a helping hand to the new elite in the USSR. The 1922 Genoa Conference demonstrated to the USSR not just that the capitalist powers wanted recompense for the canceled debts, but that they simply did not have the money to assist the USSR. The Kissinger doctrine of the early 1970s was instrumental in breaking up the Warsaw Pact and tying the Soviet elite to the West. Had it been applied in the period after Lenin's death, the USSR could have evolved into a capitalist power. That it did not happen was not just a function of the nearsightedness of the capitalist statesmen; it was also because the British empire was in decline and the United States not yet ready to assume the burdens of a world empire it inherited after the war. Once the 1929 depression took hold, the Soviet elite could not go over to capitalism.

Because the alternative that the Soviet bureaucratic apparatus embraced was not really a viable alternative at all, it could only proceed from crisis to crisis, from one pole of its conflictual laws to the other, from total organization to forms of decentralization. It cannot repeat the Stalin period and hence it must find forms of decentralization, even if it does so in fits and starts. History has now shown the elite that limited decentralization does not work and hence it must go over to the market itself.

At this point in history (1990), world capitalism has been sufficiently strong to provide some aid for the Eastern bloc to integrate it into the world market, but not sufficient to ensure success. If U.S. capitalism were as vibrant as it became after the Second World War, it might have been able to provide a Marshall Plan for the USSR, but it is in decline and cannot assist the Soviet elite. Worse still, the very decline of Stalinism now threatens individual capitalist powers and capitalism itself.

WHERE ARE WE GOING? 185

We live in a world where the old order is dying, where capitalism is in decline, and the world is in a transition to a new mode of production that has not yet been born. In this epoch three sets of laws are operating: the laws of capitalism itself, the laws of a declining capitalism, and the laws of transition. This book has really been concerned with the last. The fundamental law of the transition period is that of the growing conflict between incipient and often distorted forms of planning and the market. The bourgeoisie puts its every effort into maintaining the market and slowing down the inevitable progress of the embryonic planning forms. In this they have been assisted by social democracy, and hence Keynesianism, in its attempt to reconcile the two. It is a hopeless task.

The real effect of trying to retain the value forms is one of enhancing the role of the state in supporting the market. In the United States, arms production, which is effectively a state-controlled industry, plays an enormous role in maintaining capitalism. Banks are bailed out and so effectively nationalized on a bigger and bigger scale. In the United Kingdom the Thatcher government was dedicated to the free market, but it intervened far more in the life of the economy and society than any peacetime government. It is true that its intervention was in part through the use of exchange rates and interest rates, but it also did its best to enforce a wage policy. It conducted a war against the unions and smashed the miners' strike of 1984–85. Its success was illusory, for it wiped out sections of industry and allowed the infrastructure and needs-based sectors to decay. That is the way to barbarism, not progress. The succeeding government has inevitably to rejuvenate the decaying sectors. The lesson of the monetarist failures is that only the destruction of capitalism itself can slow the inevitable progress of the embryonic planning form.

In this period of transition, accident can play a greater role than in ordinary periods of the development of a social formation. Likewise, the role of the subjective is enhanced during a period of transition toward a society where the consciousness of the ordinary population must play a determining role, rather than the invisible hand of the market. At a simple level, it is obvious that where the economy is organized, directed, or controlled, the subjective understanding and acts of governments become far more important than in economies where atomized private firms rule. More theoretically, as the law of value and so the market declines, so subjective control becomes more important. A struggle has ensued between the ruling class and the population for influence over the central control of society.

We would argue, therefore, that the victory of the Stalinist bureaucratic apparatus represented a counterrevolution in the USSR that had a world historic role in determining the whole nature of the transitional epoch. Stalinism, a subjective doctrine, was implanted in the USSR and affected every country. It thereby became an objective fact that had to be countered both objectively and subjectively. Indeed, the objective and subjective are now so closely intertwined that it is difficult to separate them. Precisely for that reason, it has become easy for those who support the old order to argue that the USSR is itself an awful warning as to what would happen if socialism struck any country. To the extent that this has been believed, socialism itself becomes impossible. Even if few workers actually opposed the concept of socialism, many would now see it as a utopia. As a result, other doctrines that have the advantage of a long historical role necessarily become more important. The oppressed and alienated clutch therefore at religion and nationalism. Strange combinations have come into existence from Liberation Theology to the combination of nationalism and religion found in Khomeinism.

The defeat of the revolution in the West has led to its defeat in the East, but the form of that defeat has been so colossal that it has destroyed millions of people and given rise to ever more grotesque forms of change, from Pol Pot's Cambodia to Ethiopia and Angola. Just as the evolution of man went through a series of byways that could not evolve further, so too the transitional period away from capitalism has seen a number of noncapitalist alternatives. An analogy can be made with Neanderthal man, which could not evolve into man. While the analogy is correct in that the USSR has no future, the dynamic is absent.

There are three potential components of these regimes. There are the organizational and punitive forms, the market, and various forms of workers' incorporation. They may be combined in different ways leading to different forms. Exactly what form has come into existence has depended on contingent circumstances, relating to the history of the particular country and the overthrow of the previous regime.

While it might appear as if these entities, including the USSR, are the results of failed experiments or of moves to socialism, in fact they represent the victory of capitalism in preventing a move to socialism. The repression universal in these regimes is particularly reserved for those on the left; they are invariably wiped out first. In the USSR, Trotsky remains the ever-haunting ghost. In this sense, the Stalinist regimes have performed an inestimable service for the bourgeoisie, about which many have commented. They have destroyed the left internally and externally and thereby prolonged the transitional epoch. The enormous destruction wrought by these regimes must in the end be laid at the door of capitalism. It has been done by regimes that are not capitalist, and hence they have had a license to wreak a vengeance on the working class far worse than any capitalist class could have permitted.

The disintegration of the USSR can only bring this chapter in the transitional epoch to an end. Unfortunately, the struggle in the USSR itself will be protracted. There is, of course, no guarantee that there will not be further deviations on the road to the society that corresponds to the needs of humanity, which is socialism. Nonetheless, the alternatives are limited and there is reason for optimism that the millions who have died in the struggle for a better society will not have done so in vain.

Notes

1. Evgeny Preobrazhensky, *The New Economics* (Cambridge: Cambridge University Press, 1965). Trotsky's speech at the Twelfth Party Conference on the scissors crisis described NEP as follows: "NEP is our recognition of a legal order for the arena of struggle between us and private capital." Earlier, he made it clear that the market was essential for all countries undergoing a transition to socialism. At the same time he made it clear that it was the use of "methods and institutions of the capitalist system" that would be phased out as quickly as the new socialist methods of planning, centralization, and accounting could be introduced. See *Dvenadtsatyi S"ezd RKP/b. Stenografischeskii otchet*, pp. 310, 313.

2. I have made this case in more detail in two articles: H.H. Ticktin, "Trotsky and the Social Forces Leading to Bureaucracy," in *Pensiero e Azione Politica di Lev Trockij* (Florence: Leo Olschki Editore, 1982), vol. 2, pp. 451–67; and "Trotsky's Political-Economic Analysis of the USSR" (unpublished manuscript).

3. See, for instance, Moshe Lewin, *Russian Peasants and Soviet Power* (London: Allen and Unwin, 1968).

Index

Abalkin, Leonid, 49, 161
Afghanistan, 167
Aganbegian, Abel, 49, 105, 106, 109, 130, 159, 160, 162
Alcoholism, 99, 101, 144
Amnesty International 42
Andreeva, Nina, 51
Andropov, Yuri, 41, 49, 50, 98, 128, 154
Anti-Semitism, 9, 17, 18, 23, 51, 54, 74, 76, 132, 172
Arendt, Hannah, 20
Armenian earthquake, 11
Atomization, 12–13, 16, 24–46
   contradictions of, 45–46
   dependence and, 34–36
   of elite, 49
   institutional forms of, 39–45
   modern society and, 28–29
   in Nazi Germany, 25–26
   new theory of, 27–32
   social groups and, 36–39
   of workers, 38, 86–87, 92–117

Baran, Paul, 10
Bauer, Tamas, 127
Behemoth (Franz Neumann), 25–26
Belkin, V.D., 109
Beria, Lavrenty, 49
Black market, 133
Bogomolov, Oleg, 84, 133, 160
Braverman, Harry, 142
Brezhnev, Leonid, 5, 41, 43, 46, 49, 55, 56, 77, 85, 101, 116, 117, 128, 130, 149, 155, 162
Brigade system, 106–107, 156
Brzezinski, Zbigniew, 24–25, 31
Budget, 3, 159

Bukharin, Nikolai, 23, 76–77, 79, 131, 184
Bureaucracy, 14, 36, 62, 96, 137, 151, 185–86

Carlo, Antonio, 117
Capitalism, 11, 12, 30, 33–34, 63, 97, 102, 121, 124, 134–35, 168, 172, 173–75, 184, 185
Chebrikov, V., 59
Censorship, 39, 42, 52, 75
Chernenko, Konstantin, 130
Chernobyl, 136
China, 125
Christian democracy, 167, 174
Class, 14, 26, 60–62, 86
Cold War, 165, 169
Comecon (Council for Mutual Economic Assistance), 165
Common Market, 167
Communist Party of the Soviet Union, 6, 7, 19, 32, 51, 56, 163
   Central Committee of, 8, 50, 53, 89, 101, 104, 108–109, 156
   conflicts in, 57–58
   Nineteenth Conference of, 46, 51, 171
   Politburo of, 50, 58, 130
   Seventeenth Congress of, 39
   Twenty-fifth Congress of, 128
   Twenty-seventh Congress of, 88, 140, 156, 171
Communist parties, 167
Congress of People's Deputies, 42, 46, 50, 51, 53, 91, 162, 163, 172
Consumer goods, 3, 19, 92, 93, 94, 121, 122–23, 127, 139, 147–49, 166
Contradiction, 13
Cooperatives, 4, 89, 104, 111, 163

189

Corruption, 46, 63–64, 155
Council of Ministers of the USSR, 100
Cox, Michael, 165

Daniel, Yuli, 41
Decentralization, 108–109
Defective production, 136
Democratic Platform, 163
Democracy, 99, 103, 121, 162, 178
Dependence, 34–35, 75, 78
Disintegration, 14
Dzarasov, S., 100

Eastern Europe, 7, 110, 126, 151, 163, 168, 173
Economic accountability, 48, 95, 175
Economic growth, 122, 124–26, 138, 140
Economic Problems of Socialism (Joseph Stalin), 23, 151
Economics of Feasible Socialism (Alec Nove), 175
Elections, 24, 51–52, 57, 90–91
Elite, 37, 48–68, 124, 158, 166–67
 as a class, 60–63
 factions of, 49, 50, 52, 54–55
 functional divisions of, 55–57
 legality and, 78–80
 social characteristics of, 64–67
Equality, 17, 46, 104, 172
Export sector, 95, 110

First Five-year Plan, 131
Foreign investment, 110
Foreign policy, 165–69
Friedman, Milton, 88
Friedrich, Carl J., 24–25, 31

Germany, 165–68, 172: *see also* National Socialism
Genoa Conference, 184
Glasnost', 24, 37, 103
Goebbels, Joseph, 32
Gorbachev, Mikhail S., 4, 5, 10, 14, 21–23, 37, 39, 46, 50, 53–55, 57–57, 64, 79, 85, 88–89, 90, 92, 95, 109, 116, 125, 128, 130, 147–48, 154, 169–72, 176
Gordon, Leonid, 84, 104, 130
Grishin, V., 50, 56
Gromyko, Andrei, 57

Gulag Archipelago (Aleksandr Solzhenitsyn), 42
Gvishiani, Germen, 49, 63

Hitler, Adolf, 9, 23, 25, 33
Hungary, 111, 166

Ideology, 16–22
 levels of, 18–19
 as means of social control, 16
Individualization, 29, 45
Industrialization, 123, 132, 145
Inequality, 17, 161
Inflation, 126
Inside Perestroika (Abel Aganbegian), 159
Institute of Sociology, 163
Institute of World Economy and International Relations, 163
Intelligentsia, 37, 60, 61, 68, 73–76, 96, 158, 170
Interest-group theory, 6, 9
Internal passport, 43, 83

Japan, 167–68
Joint ventures, 110

Kagarlitsky, Boris, 178
Kantorovich, Leonid, 49
KGB. *See* secret police.
Khrushchev, Nikita, 7, 36–37, 40, 41, 46, 48, 68, 85, 116, 120, 127, 128, 142, 154, 162, 171
Khrushchev, Sergei, 36
Kirov, Sergei, 39
Kissinger doctrine, 184
Kosygin, Aleksei, 49
Kriuchkov, Vladimir, 40
Kulaks, 184
Kunaev, D., 56

Labor camps, 40
Labor process, 12, 83–86, 137
Labor shortage, 87
Law on the State Enterprise, 100, 108, 156
Laws of the Soviet system, 118–19, 121, 150, 185
Lederer, Emil, 26
Left Opposition, 182
Lenin, Vladimir, 18, 19, 22, 38, 76, 77, 85, 90, 184
Leveling, 17

INDEX   191

Leys, Robert, 33
Liberals, 51, 53, 54, 74, 164
Liberation theology, 186
Ligachev, Egor, 17, 22, 46, 53–55, 56, 161

Makhaisky, 75
Marchenko, A., 76
Marcuse, Herbert, 20
Market, 8, 9

Market socialism, 158, 175–80
Marshall Plan, 169, 184
Marx, Karl, 134, 174
Marxism, 17, 19, 20–22, 28, 54, 180
Marxism-Leninism, 17, 18, 20–22
Matthews, Mervyn, 64
Mikoyan, Anastas, 37
Military industry, 11, 95, 166
Molotov, Viacheslav, 56, 77
Money, 3–4, 34–36, 84, 109, 147, 159–61, 169

National Socialism (Nazi Germany), 9, 25–26, 30–34, 40
Nationalism, 23, 33, 50–52, 74, 75, 172, 186
Neumann, Franz, 25
New Economic Policy (NEP), 123, 131
Nomenklatura, 60, 65
Nove, Alec, 175, 178–79
Novosibirsk Report (Tat′iana Zaslavskaia), 107, 158
Nyers, Reszö, 111

Okudzhava, Bulat, 40
Orwell, George, 16

Pamiat, 23, 51, 57
Pasternak, Boris, 41
Pavlov, Valentin S., 107–108
Peel, Quentin, 59, 161
Pervushin, 141
Peukert, Detlev J.K., 33–34
Pipes, Richard, 8
Planning, 61, 86, 99, 118–19, 121, 133–34, 179, 182–83
Poland, 107, 166
Popov, Gavriil, 4, 53
Prices, 4, 107–108, 157, 159
Privilege, 63, 67, 90, 94, 95, 104, 172

Producer goods, 3, 19, 123, 131, 147–49
Przeworski, Adam, 19
Purges, 55–57, 62, 150

Quality control, 98

Rakovsky, Christian, 131
Rationing, 107
Reagan, Ronald, 8, 121
Rehabilitations, 76–78
Republics, 169
Right, 51, 52
Romanov, Grigorii, 50, 56
Rule of law, 78–80
Rumiantsev, A. M., 90

Sachs, Jeffrey, 166
Sakharov, Andrei, 76, 163
Secret police, 13, 30, 32, 52, 52, 55, 58–60, 76
  under Brezhnev, 41, 43
  under Gorbachev, 42–43
  under Khrushchev, 40
  under Stalin, 39–40
Shelepin, A., 56
Semichastnyi, 40–42
Shchekino elperiment, 155
Shcherbakov, 103, 105
Shevardnadze, Eduard, 50
Shmelev, Nikolai, 53, 88, 159
Short Course (Joseph Stalin), 19
Siniavsky, Andrei, 41
Social democracy, 163, 167, 172
Socialism in one country, 23, 55
Socialist realism, 19
Social mobility, 65, 97, 158
Social patriots, 50, 55
Social structure, 9, 170
Solzhenitsyn, Aleksandr, 19, 42–43, 163
Sonin, M., 128, 155
Sorokin, 149
Stakhanovism, 101
Stalin, Joseph, 19, 25, 37, 39, 49, 54, 56, 59, 68, 76, 77, 101, 131, 150
Stalinism, 5, 14, 22, 23, 25, 51, 77, 172, 180
State Commission on Prices, 107
State Committee on Labor, 102, 103
Strikes, 4, 111, 133, 163, 171
  miners' strikes, 4, 87, 89, 91, 92, 94
  right to strike, 44

Surplus product, 10, 48, 88, 118, 120, 145, 146, 182, 183
Sweezy, Paul, 10
Szelenyi, Ivan, 75

Technocrats, 48
Technology, 85, 116, 138, 142–47
Totalitarian Dictatorship and Democracy (Friedrich and Brzezinski), 24–25
Totalitarian theory, 6, 9, 24–27, 32
Thatcher, Margaret, 121, 165, 185
Think tanks, 49
Torkanovskii, E., 89
Trotsky, Lev, 9, 32, 51, 60, 61, 76–77, 186
Twelfth Five-year Plan, 3, 128

Unemployment, 4, 105–106
Union of Russian Writers, 23
Uzbekistan, 41, 63

Vaksberg, Arkady, 78–79
Vyshinsky, Andrei, 78

Wages, 105, 137, 144, 170–71
Warsaw Pact, 184
Waste, 10–11, 13, 117, 173
Workers, 4, 12, 31, 55, 76, 83–111, 144, 149–51, 166
  atomization of, 38, 86–87
  as collectivity, 38, 87
  consumer goods and, 92
  control of, 83–86
  divisions of, 93–97
  perestroika and, 88–92
  prejudice against, 74
  secret police and, 44
  self-management and, 89–90, 99–100, 177

Yeltsin, Boris, 40, 42, 52–55, 57, 58, 90, 94, 171

Zaikov, Lev, 52
Zaslavskaia, Tat'iana, 49, 102, 107, 158–60

About the Author

Hillel Ticktin, educated at Cape Town, Kiev, and Moscow universities, has been lecturer at the Institute of Soviet and East European Studies, University of Glasgow, since 1965, and visiting professor in the Department of History, University of California, Los Angeles. Ticktin is the founding editor of *Critique: A Journal of Soviet Studies and Socialist Theory,* which began publication in 1973.